KLAVDIYA ANTIPINA
ETHNOGRAPHER OF THE KYRGYZ

KLAVDIYA ANTIPINA
ETHNOGRAPHER OF THE KYRGYZ

Bibira Akmoldoeva and John Sommer

Spring Hill Press
McKinleyville, California

Klavdiya Antipina
Ethnographer of the Kyrgyz

by
Bibira Akmoldoeva and John Sommer

© John L. Sommer 2002

All rights reserved
No part of the contents of this book may be reproduced or transmitted in any form or by any means, electronic or mechanical, including photocopying, recording or by information storage and retrieval system without written permission from the authors.

Library of Congress Catalog Card Number: 2002103630
ISBN: 1-890539-02-3

Design: Rita Ter Sarkissoff, Spring Hill Press, McKinleyville, California
Printed in Korea

For information about permission to reproduce selections from this book, contact:
    John L. Sommer
    4575 Odell Court
    Fremont, CA 94536

To the Memory of
"Misha"

CONTENTS

DEDICATION v

LIST OF ILLUSTRATIONS viii

PREFACE xiii

FOREWORD xiv

ACKNOWLEDGMENTS xvi

INTRODUCTION xvii

PART ONE: BIOGRAPHICAL
    Introduction 2
    Narrative 3
    Sidebars:
      1. *The Film "Fate"*
         Introduction 14
         Sound Track 16
      2. *Letters ("Misha")*
         Introduction 20
         January 3, 1937 (8 pages) 20
         January 18, 1937 (postcard) 28
      3. *Newspaper Articles*
         Introduction 30
         Slovo Kyrgyzstana 8/1/92 30
         Vechernyi Bishkek 5/11/94 35
         Kyrgyzstan Chronicle 5/24/94 35
      4. *Stalin* 36
      5. *Christ The Savior Cathedral, Moscow* 40
      6. *Ata Beyit and Chinghiz Aitmatov* 44

PART TWO: INTERVIEWS
    Introduction 49
    Interviews:
      1. *Kushbek Usenbaev (deceased)* 52
      2. *Bibina Omurzakovna Orusbayeva* 56
      3. *Svetlana Dunovskaya* 64
      4. *Roza Otunbayeva* 68
      5. *Dinara Chochunbaeva* 72
      6. *Toktosunova Gulchahra* 76

PART TWO: INTERVIEWS (CONT'D)
- 7. *Akylai Sharshenalieva*   82
- 8. *Rysbubu Abdieva*   86
- 9. *Stella Mateeva*   90
- 10. *Kalipa Asanakunova*   92
- 11. *Bolotbek Karakeev*   94
- 12. *Temirbek Musakeev*   96
- 13. *Kathleen Kuehnast*   104
- 14. *Bibira Akmoldoeva*   110

PART THREE: PHOTO ARCHIVES
Introduction   118
Selections   119

PART FOUR: WRITINGS
Introduction   160
Selections:
- 1. *Osobennosti Materialnoi Kultury I Prikladnogo Iskusstva Iuzhnykh Kirgizov*
  - Introduction   163
  - Pile Weaving   189
- 2. *Narodnoe Dekorativno-Prikladnoe Iskusstvo Kirghizov*
  - Pile Weaving   210

AFTERWORD   257

GLOSSARY   258

BIBLIOGRAPHY   266

FOR FURTHER READING   267

ILLUSTRATIONS

MAPS

MAP		
1	Map of Central Moscow, 1980s	41
2	The Kyrgyz Republic	253
3	The Kyrgyz Republic, showing the Oblasts (regions)	254
4	Fergana Valley Region	255
5	Routes of Klavdiya Antipina's 1955, 1956, 1958 ethnographic field work	256

PHOTOGRAPHS

FIGURE		
1.1	Klavdiya Antipina with three siblings, c. 1907-8	3
1.2	Family portrait, c. 1910-11	4
1.3	Ivan Akimovich, Klavdiya Antipina's father, c. 1910	4
1.4	Klavdiya Antipina with brother and sister about time of move to Moscow, c. 1922	5
1.5	Mikhail ("Misha") Rabinovich, Klavdiya Antipina's schoolmate and husband, 1926-7	5
1.6	Klavdiya Antipina with "Misha" and friends, c. 1926	5
1.7	Klavdiya Antipina and "Misha", c. 1930	5
1.8	"Misha", Lev (Leo), and Klavdiya Antipina, c. 1934	6
1.9	Klavdiya Antipina and Leo, c. 1937	6
1.10	Klavdiya Antipina and Leo at time of exile, 1937	7
1.11	Klavdiya Antipina, Bishkek, c. 1940	7
1.12	Klavdiya Antipina, Bishkek, c. 1950-51	7
1.13	Klavdiya Antipina during ethnographic field work, Kyrgyzstan, 1955-60	8
1.14	Klavdiya Antipina in the field, Kyrgyzstan, 1955-60	10
1.15	Klavdiya Antipina at the time of her 85th birthday, Bishkek, 1989	11
1.16	Klavdiya Antipina at home, seated at her desk, Bishkek, 3 September 1992	12
1.17	Klavdiya Antipina at ninety, speaking to a traveling Textile Museum group, 1994	12
1.18	Dedication of the memorial at Klavdiya Antipina's grave, Bishkek, May 2000	13
1.19	Klavdiya Antipina in a still from the film, *Fate,* 1988	14
1.20	Klavdiya Antipina with companion in a still from the film, *Fate,* 1988	15
1.21–1.28	Letter XVIII from Mikhail Rabinovich ("Misha") to Klavdiya Antipina, 3 Jan 1937	24
1.29–1.30	Postcard from Mikhail Rabinovich to Klavdiya Antipina, 23 Feb 1937	28
1.31	The Cathedral of Christ the Savior, Moscow, 19th century	40
1.32	Demolition of the Cathedral of Christ the Savior, 1931	42
1.33	Demolition of the Cathedral of Christ the Savior, 1931	42

1.34	Site of the demolished Cathedral of Christ the Savior, official rally, 1932	42
1.35	The Palace of Soviets, artist's conception of the unbuilt structure	43
1.36	Moscow Swimming Pool, built on demolished Cathedral of Christ the Savior site	43
1.37	Re-built Cathedral of Christ the Savior, consecrated in August 2000	43
2.1	Professor Kushbek Usenbaev (deceased), Bishkek, June 1997	52
2.2	Professor Bibina Omurzakovna Orusbayeva, Bishkek, June 1997	56
2.3	Svetlana Dunovskaya, Bishkek, June 1997	64
2.4	Ambassador Roza Otunbayeva, London, June 2001	68
2.5	Dinara Chochunbaeva, Bishkek, September 2000	72
2.6	Toktosunova Gulchahra, Bishkek, June 1997	76
2.7	Akylai Sharshenalieva, Bishkek, June 1997	82
2.8	Rysbubu Abdieva, Bishkek, September 2000	86
2.9	Stella Mateeva, Bishkek, June 1997	90
2.10	Kalipa Asanakunova, Bishkek, June 1997	92
2.11	Bolotbek Karakeev holding the first drawing, Bishkek, June 1997	94
2.12	Bolotbek Karakeev's first drawing	95
2.13	Temirbek Musakeev, Bishkek, June 1997	96
2.14	Traditional Kyrgyz man's costume, artwork by Temirbek Musakeev	100
2.15	Traditional Kyrgyz man's costume, artwork by Temirbek Musakeev	101
2.16	Traditional Kyrgyz woman's costume, artwork by Temirbek Musakeev	102
2.17	Kathleen Kuehnast, Alexandria, Virginia, 2001	104
2.18	Bibira Akmoldoeva, Bishkek, September 2000	110
3.1	KA 1564: Tian Shan	119
3.2	KA 0725	119
3.3	KA 1372	119
3.4	KA 0682: Suzak Area, Collective Farms Karl Marx	120
3.5	KA 0751: 1969	120
3.6	KA 0805: Toktogul area, 1967	121
3.7	KA 3796: Toktogul area, 1967	121
3.8	KA 2354: Kulanai Village, Tian Shan	121
3.9	KA 0757: Batken Area, Collective Farms Andreeva, Barzun Village	122
3.10	KA 0770: Kyzyl Uran, 1966	122
3.11	KA 0888: Molotov Area, Collective Farms Voroshilov	123
3.12	KA 0797: Toktogul Area, 1967	124
3.13	KA 9778: 45 4-1-5	124
3.14	KA 3337: Suzak Area, Collective Farms Karl Marx	125
3.15	KA 1495: Archa Village, Tian Shan	125
3.16	KA 0870: Egat, Daki, Amanchik, Omurakhan, Saken, Abla, and Aitvai. Toktogul, 1966	126
3.17	KA 3886	127
3.18	KA 0884	128

3.19	KA 0883: Choi-Kra, 1969	128
3.20	KA 0686: Frontier Village, 1954	129
3.21	KA 0845	130
3.22	KA 0820	130
3.23	KA 0826	131
3.24	KA 0833: Djangadjolskii Area, Collective Farms Jdanov, 1963	131
3.25	KA 0734: 1954, Atbashi District	132
3.26	KA 0735: 1954, Atbashi District	133
3.27	KA 0839	134
3.28	KA 0904: Molotov Area, Karakul Village, Collective Farm Voroshilov	134
3.29	KA 0902: Toktogul Area, Collective Farms Karl Marx	134
3.30	KA 0847: 1954, Leninopol District	135
3.31	KA 2708A: Emgen, 1963	135
3.32	KA 2798: Emgen, 1963	136
3.33	KA 2710: Emgen, 1963	136
3.34	KA 2711B: Emgen, 1963	136
3.35	KA 2714: Emgen, 1963	136
3.36	KA 2716: Emgen, 1963	136
3.37	KA 2717: Emgen, 1963	137
3.38	KA 2722B: Emgen, 1963	137
3.39	KA 2724A: Emgen, 1963	137
3.40	KA 2725B: Emgen, 1963	137
3.41	Antipina Archives, photograph by S. M. Dudin, early 20th century	138
3.42	KA 0927: Pile Carpet, Batken Area, Collective Farms Malenkov, Karabulak Village	138
3.43	KA 0428: Bazaar, Kyzyl-Kia City (Noukat), 1969	139
3.44	KA 3210	139
3.45	KA 0930	140
3.46	KA 0929: Carpet, Kurshabad Area, Collective Farms, Kyzyl, October, Kara-Suzak Village	141
3.47	KA 0640: Djangidjolskii Area, Byimom Village, 1969	142
3.48	KA 0920	142
3.49	KA 0177: Suzak Area, Collective Farms Karl Marx	143
3.50	KA 1769: Weaver Baibushan Bailieva (date of birth: 1942), Osh Region, Soviet Area, Kok-Art Village, 1977	144
3.51	KA 2835	145
3.52	KA 1360: No. 28 Chon-Alay District, Village of Chak, Jailoo Kom Kaiyn	146
3.53	KA 1538: Detail of interior of yurt, Lylyak Area. Collective Farm: Tralina, Togua, Julak Village	146
3.54	KA 0663: Uzgen Area, Kara-Kuldjuk Village, 1969	147
3.55	KA 0749: 1969	147
3.56	KA 0003: 1962 Kyrt; the master *chiy* maker, *chyrmakchy*, seated on a mosaic felt, *shyrdak*, wrapping dyed, but unspun, wool onto an individual dried chiy grass stem.	148

3.57	KA 0001: A plain reed screen (*ak chiy*) being woven on an outdoor weaving frame.	149
3.58	KA 0045: Batkenskii Region, May First Collective Farm. *Ashkana*. Interior view of yurt with close-up view of *ashkana chiy* (space divider reed screen) in use.	150
3.59	KA 0025: A 34/68, Suusamyr; a kanat chiy surrounding the lattice wall (*kerege*) of the yurt.	151
3.60	KA2675: Gulchinskii Area, Toguz Bulak, Socialism Village, 1956	152
3.61	KA 0806: The Kuibyshev Area, 1963	153
3.62	KA 1568: Frontier Village, Tian Shan	154
3.63	KA 1574	155
3.64	KA 3082: No. 56 Kurshab District, Village of Kara Taryk, the Karl Marx Collective Farm	156
3.65	KA 2643: Kalanak Village, Tian Shan, 1968	157
4.1	Preparation for weaving a large rug, 1903, Fergana Valley	175
4.2	Pile woven *chavadan*, Naukat region	175
4.3	Pile woven *chavadan*, Frunzen region	176
4.4	Pile woven *bashtyk*, Alay region	176
4.5	Pile woven suspended shelf (*ayak koychuk*), Soviet region	177
4.6	Rug loom, Batken region	178
4.7	Detail of pile woven rug showing *Orus Kochot* design, Osh region	179
4.8	Pile woven rug. The field design is divided longitudinally, Frunzen region	180
4.9	Pile woven rug with *kytay shak* and *mashaty* designs, Frunzen region	180
4.10	Pile woven rug, cruciform ornaments in field, Naukat region	181
4.11	Pile woven rug, arranged tile design, Batken region	181
4.12	Pile woven suspended shelf (*ayak koychuk*) with *mashaty* design	182
4.13	Two "tent bands" (*tegirich*) sewn together, Frunzen region	183
4.14	Designs in rug fields	184
4.15	Designs in fields of pile weavings	185
4.16	Rug border designs	186
4.17	Pile woven bag with *chaydosh* design	187
4.18	Flat woven Palas (*arabi kilem*), Batken region	188
4.19	Small pile carpet, *ayak kaochu*. Osh region, Uzgen district, Ulgulu village, State Museum of Ethnography. Inventory #6371-8	228
4.20	Pile woven door rug for yurt, *eshik tysh*. Osh region, Batken district, Raut village, 1958	229
4.21	Floor carpet. Pile woven tent bands (*tegirich*) stitched together. Osh region, Frunze district, Okhna village, 1955	230
4.22	Kumush Ormonova, a carpet weaver, demonstrates her work. Jalalabad region, Ala-Bukinskii district, Telman Collective Farm.	231
4.23	Rug loom, Batken district	232
4.24	Variations of Rhombic pattern with branches	233
4.25	Examples of ornamental motifs for central field	234
4.26	Examples of ornamental motifs for central field	235
4.27	Examples of ornamental motifs for carpet borders	236
4.28	Examples of ornamental motifs for carpet borders	237

4.29	Overall carpet designs	238
4.30	Overall carpet designs	239
4.31	Pile carpet woven in workshop at the State Artist Association of the Kyrgyz SSR., designed by M.A. Abdullaeva, Frunze 1960	240
4.32	Pile carpet woven in workshop at the State Artist Association of the Kyrgyz SSR, designed by D. Umetova, Frunze 1962	241
4.33	Pile woven *bashtyk*, crafted in early 20th century by female weaver of the Kydyrsh tribe	242
4.34	Pile woven *kilem*, crafted in 1908 by female weavers of the Noigut tribe.	243
4.35	Pile woven *kilem*, crafted in 1936, lead weaver Adzhar Moldokeeva (Adigin)	244
4.36	Pile woven *kilem,* crafted in 1934; lead weaver Gulbu Bataeva (Mongoldor)	245
4.37	Pile woven *kilem*, crafted in 1934; lead weaver Tadzhi Karimova (Kypchak)	246
4.38	Pile woven *kilem*, crafted in early 20th century; lead weaver Zuleikhan Koshoeva (Naiman)	247
4.39	A tent band for a wedding yurt, *tegirich*, crafted in early 20th century, Jalalabad region	248
4.40	Pile woven *chavadan*, crafted in early 20th century, Osh region	249
4.41	Pile woven *chavadan*, crafted in 1936; lead weaver Adzhar Moldokeeva (Adigan)	250
4.42	A pile woven *japsar* rug, crafted in early 20th century by a weaver from Basyz tribe	251
4.43	A pile woven tent band for a yurt (*tegirich*), crafted in 1915 by Topchu Baimurzaeva	252

PREFACE

To one of us (Bibira Akmoldoeva) she had been a mentor, a teacher, and an academic colleague. To the other of us (John Sommer) she had been only a name on a page. Klavdiya Ivanovna Antipina was someone I should meet, Bibira Akmoldoeva (co-author and my hostess in Bishkek) had urged. She arranged it and, together, Bibira Akmoldoeva and I visited Klavdiya Antipina. That was in 1992.

Klavdiya Antipina spoke in Russian. Bibira Akmoldoeva interpreted. Quickly I realized Bibira had been right. Klavdiya Antipina was special. Not only was she friendly and hospitable, she was knowledgeable, resourceful, and erudite. She was generous. At age eighty-eight, she was evidently delighted to discuss her work with me, a stranger from the other side of the earth. No longer was she just a name on a page in a footnote in a book. She was real. She was important.

The more I learned *from* her and the more I learned *about* her, the greater became my admiration and respect.

From speaking with Klavdiya Antipina, and with others, I came to realize something Bibira Akmoldoeva already knew—that Klavdiya Antipina had nearly single-handedly preserved ethnographic information about the unique traditional Kyrgyz culture, and that she had accomplished this despite formidable personal barriers.

We recognize that today in The Kyrgyz Republic, Klavdiya Antipina and her work are not well known. And, perhaps because she had worked during the Soviet era, she is quite unknown in the West. However, Klavdiya Antipina is the towering figure of Central Asian ethnography.

Bibira Akmoldoeva and I have combined our efforts to create this book. We hope that it can begin to change this lack of awareness of an important scholar, Klavdiana Ivanovna Antipina, and of her contributions.

— John Sommer, for the co-authors

FOREWORD

Clavdia Ivanovna Antipina's book *Kyrgyz Ornament* has not been published to this day to the great disappointment of many of her followers. Still full of energy and enthusiasm, amending and polishing her writings, she reluctantly finished the book. Artist T. Musakeev completed the exquisite drawings of the costumes for the manuscript with greatest care and authenticity. I held this work (the finished maquette, the "mock-up") in my hands at the time. During the Soviet times it was difficult to publish an art book in the republic because the required publishing standards were lacking and there never were enough financial resources.

It has been five years that Clavdia Ivanovna is no longer with us, yet her book has not seen light. We owe her the debt of publishing her book to this day. In fact, I believe the whole nation is indebted to this great ethnographer of the Kyrgyz people and should pay homage to her memory.

Since the 50s Clavdia Ivanovna travelled by horse across the south of the country, visited hundreds of houses, yurts, settlements, met common folk, and made a myriad of priceless photographs of the lifestyle, clothing, interiors, and carpet patterns. She collected and systematised a wealth of factual material.

Her personality always attracted craftsmen and talented youth. She was the kind guardian angel and teacher, unifier, and inspirer of many generations of traditional craftsmen, artists, and researchers. She personally knew village craftsmen, kept close contact with them, and invariably succeeded in reaching the most well kept secrets of their work. I recall one summer evening at the end of 1980s in my house, when Clavdia Ivanovna and Anara-apa from Samarkandek, then in Batken region, were discussing and arguing about the nature and sources of the *kurak* pattern. Clavdia Ivanovna well understood the fragile nature of folk art. With death of each craftsman a rich world of colours, imagination, and fantasy vanishes. In effect, with the death of each craftsman, a gallery, a museum is gone forever.

Particularly fluid is the art of nomads. Urbanisation and social changes of the XX century substantially transformed our ethnographic make up. The Kyrgyz of the XXI century are fascinated, when examining the *elecheks* of Alay women in Antipina's archives, by the look and shape of the head-dresses and clothes of our ancestors. We are also fascinated by the great effort, energy, and wisdom of Clavdia Ivanovna who tiresesslly collected this information and documented the drawings of the Kyrgyz national dress, men, women and children, rich and poor, old and young, festive and casual alike.

The extent to which she loved the Kyrgyz people is suggested by the passionate pursuit of her life-long interest—ethnographic research of the Kyrgyz for the support and preservation of this cultural heritage. I can still remember her words: "How much I still want to continue living, working, writing, collecting, and creating…"

A significant contribution belongs to John Sommer who is doing a lot to acquaint the Western reader with the work of Antipina. The wealth of colours and ideas of the still unknown

Kyrgyz applied art are being made known to the wider audience including anthropologists and art specialists in John Sommer's books, The Kyrgyz and Their Reed Screens and in this book, Klavdiya Antipina, Ethnographer of The Kyrgyz. Other contributions have been made by the late George O'Bannon who edited and published The Kyrgyz Carpet I by C. Antipina and The Kyrgyz Carpet II by L. Bereseneva—two volumes, in English.

Much effort and time have been invested into this book, the result of collaboration between John Sommer and Buybuyra Akmoldoeva. From the words and memories of Clavdia Ivanovna's friends and colleagues, they have written about the long and fruitful life of the person who accomplished a significant and important task for the history, science, and life of the Kyrgyz people. As a wife of a political exile during Stalin's repression years, she was not only able to survive in a foreign country with a little son on her hands and in the climate of political censorship, but she was able to establish herself as a respectable scientist. She researched and wrote some valuable works on the ethnography of the people that sheltered her. To the last day Clavdia Ivanovna remained a humble worker, and a person of strong inner culture and high moral principles.

Unfortunately the works of Antipina are little known even in Kyrgyzstan. Since our independence we are facing a great challenge of searching and establishing our nation's identity while building a democratic society and overcoming much economic hardship. With the purpose of understanding ourselves and opening our unique culture and lifestyle to the world we have started a journey into our past, our history, culture, and folk art.

Senator Daniel Patrick Moynihan had once said, "The central *conservative* truth is that it is culture, not politics, that determines the success of society. The central *liberal* truth is that politics can change a culture and save it from itself."

Today, the Kyrgyz, as the ancient nation and the young state, are on independent paths. Our challenge is to understand how culture impacts economic and political development and to best utilize our heritage and cultural capacities to speed up the process of political, economic, and social growth for the well-being of people.

How much we miss Clavdia Ivanovna. These days we badly need people like her.

—Roza Otunbayeva, Ambassador
The Embassy of The Kyrgyz Republic
London, UK
2001

ACKNOWLEDGMENTS

Donna Sommer, who fed, kept on schedule, and tolerated an often grumpy, pre-occupied spouse. She also tolerated a paper-strewn house and the expenditure of considerable amounts of time and fortune during the preparation of this book.

Roza Otunbayeva, ambassador of The Kyrgyz Republic to the United Kingdom, who wrote the Foreword. She had known Klavdiya Antipina well and had been extraordinarily helpful during the last years of her life. We thank Ambassador Otunbayeva for her willingness to share her insights about Klavdiya Antipina, and for her help and encouragement of this project.

All those persons interviewed. Their insights and reminiscences about Klavdiya Antipina, their willingness to be interviewed, their courtesy, and their hospitality are much appreciated. Those interviewed:

- Professor Kushbek Usenbaev (Deceased)
- Professor Bibina Omurzakovna Orusbayeva
- Svetlana Dunovskaya
- Ambassador Roza Otunbayeva
- Dinara Chochunbaeva
- Toktosunova Gulchahra
- Akylai Sharshenalieva
- Rysbubu Abdieva
- Stella Mateeva
- Kalipa Asanakunova
- Bolotbek Karakeev
- Temirbek Musakeev
- Kathleen Kuehnast
- Bibira Akmoldoeva

Shailoo Akmoldoeva, Professor of Philosophy, The Kyrgyz National University and The American University in Kyrgyzstan, for her considerable helpfulness and her good humor.

Heather Taylor, the inspiration for this book's writing.

Kasymov Ravil, the retired history teacher and curator in the museum at Ata Beyit. We thank him for his helpfulness and for sharing his knowledge.

Keneshkan Ysmanova, the director of the Issyk-Kul museum in the village of Cholpon-Ata for her kind reception and enthusiasm for this project.

Rita Ter Sarkissoff, designer of this book, for her pleasant optimism and helpfulness in bringing order to the materials presented to her.

Leo Antipin, Klavdiya Antipina's son, now a specialist in chemistry and a teacher in Moscow, his memory and knowledge, and for his support and encouragement from the start.

Natalie Cherry (Hayward), **Nathan Hodge** (New Haven), **Ovadan K. Omanova** (Tucson), **Sharon Weinberger** (New Haven), and **Boris Wolfson** (Berkeley), who translated the Russian with skill and subtlety.

Shailoo, Aibek, Janibek, and Kenjeke for the many ways in which they made life comfortable for the authors in Bishkek.

Many others of good will who have helped in variety of ways and circumstances.

INTRODUCTION

The Kyrgyz

Kyrgyz traditional culture had been that of central Asian pastoralists—yurt-dwelling, nomadic herdsmen, migrating seasonally with their animals. In the early twentieth century, however, the Soviet government put an end to this traditional way of life and gave the old tribal name to The Kirghiz Soviet Social Republic. Bordered on the north by The Kazak SSR, on the west by The Uzbek SSR, on the south by The Tajik SSR, and on the east by China, "Kirghizia" was located at the remote periphery of the Soviet Union. Since 1991, however, this central Asian country, known as "Kyrgyzstan" (see map) has been a member of the Commonwealth of Independent States (CIS) and the official name is now "The Kyrgyz Republic."

In this book, we have tried to use the names of places as they were used at the time under consideration. Thus, "The Kirghiz Soviet Socialist Republic," "Kirghizia," "Kyrgyzstan", and "The Kyrgyz Republic" are generally synonymous terms. Some place names have greatly changed, however. Thus, "Przewalski" at the east end of Lake Issyk-Kul is now again "Karakol", and "Frunze", capital of The Kirghiz SSR, is now "Bishkek", The Kyrgyz Republic.

In the West, many do not know of The Kyrgyz Republic. North and South America are commonly seen in the center of world maps. Often it is not realized that the Eurasian land mass, which includes *all* of Europe and *all* of Asia, encompasses fourteen time zones and extends more than halfway around the earth. But the maps cut that land mass into two pieces, separate those pieces, and place them at opposite sides, with the "Far East" at the *left* margin. Such maps can be misleading. Central Asia can be "lost".

Reference to *The Steppes of Central Asia* is just as likely to bring to the western mind the music of Alexander Borodin as it is a bio-geographic environment of tall grass. The vast grasslands of central Asia, the "steppes", are indeed akin to North America's "Great Plains", to South America's "Pampas", and to Africa's "Savannas". The Kyrgyz people know these grasslands as well as they know the snow-covered mountains of the Tien-Shan range. And there is no exaggeration in stating that, environmentally, The Kyrgyz Republic has much in common with Switzerland.

The Baibichye of Kyrgyz Ethnography

Klavdiya Antipina was known as the "*Mother* of Kyrgyz Ethnography" and sometimes as the "*Babushka* of Kyrgyz Ethnography." However, as suggested by Professor of Philology, Bibina Omuzakovna Orusbayeva, a better term would be the Kyrgyz word transliterated as "Baibichye" [Bye-**BEECH**-Yeh]. A *baibichye* is a respected older woman. This word once was the term for the first wife of a wealthy herdsman. In the modern Kyrgyz language, *baibichye* is a word of respect, honor, and esteem.

Why not use *babushka*? (Even Westerners recognize *that* word. In the popular mind a babushka is an elderly woman, a traditional grandmother with a shawl on her head, a big warm heart, much empathy, and little to no education.) The Oxford Russian Dictionary defines *babushka* as "grandmother, granny." For Klavdiya Antipina, the term would *not* be appropriate. She did not at all see herself as a "babushka." We choose, instead, to use the Kyrgyz word *baibichye*, a fitting term. Klavdiya Antipina was "the *Baibichye* of Kyrgyz Ethnography."

The name *Klavdiya* is the Russian equivalent of *Claudia*. Sometimes the name is transliterated from the Russian as *Clavdiya* or *Clavdia*. Sometimes, informally, the "middle name" (*Ivanovna*) is used with the "first name" (*Klavdiya*). Sometimes she is referred to as *Klavdivana* (*Clavdivana*), a more familiar form. Her husband "Misha" used variations of endearment in his letters. Nonetheless, these names refer to the same person, Klavdiya Antipina.

The Outsider

Some years ago, the renowned American historian, Henry Steele Commager, conducted a televised graduate seminar at Amherst College on *The Role of The Outsider*. Professor Commager's prime example of the "outsider" was Alexis de Tocqueville, the young French nobleman who visited the United States in the early nineteenth century and then wrote *Democracy In America* which, more than a century and a half later, is still read by Americans in the United States to learn about themselves. Professor Commager emphasized that it sometimes takes an *outsider* to see the important things. Those aspects of a culture that people take for granted, those aspects that they cannot help but feel should be the way things are to be done—those can be the very aspects identified as distinctive and important by the *outsider*.

> "[Alexis de Tocqueville] was thorough and indefatigable in his search for facts, patient and skillful in their organization, sympathetic and perspicacious in their interpretation, luminous in their presentation. His purpose was lofty, his learning solid, his understanding profound..." (Henry Steele Commager in the Introduction to Alexis de Tocqueville's *Democracy in America*, translated by Henry Reeve, edited with an Introduction by Henry Steele Commager, The World's Classics, Oxford University Press, London 1946. Reprinted 1961.)

Professor Commager could have been writing about Klavdiya Antipina. She was an *outsider* to the Kyrgyz. It was perhaps because she was an *outsider* that she saw those cultural aspects local people took for granted. (One person we interviewed told us, "[Klavdiya Antipina] taught me to see...") As an outsider, Klavdiya Antipina was "thorough and indefatigable in her search for facts, patient and skillful in their organization, sympathetic and perspicacious in their interpretation, luminous in their presentation. Her purpose was lofty, her learning solid, her understanding profound..." Klavdiya Antipina was an *outsider* to the Kyrgyz—an *outsider* in the best sense.

This book is in four parts:

PART I BIOGRAPHICAL

Along with a biographical narrative, relevant related subjects are addressed in sidebars. An example of this is the transcription of the translation of Klavdiya Antipina's filmed monologue of reminiscences, the film Fate. This is rare footage. Klavdiya Antipina did not usually speak about herself. Another sidebar concerns the story of the Cathedral of Christ The Savior (Church of The Redeemer) in Moscow, a subject mentioned with some emphasis in the film. Other sidebars are about her husband's letters following his arrest; Stalin and his terror; Ata Beyit; and the respected Kyrgyz writer, Chinghiz Aitmatov.

Klavdiya Antipina had kept personal mementos and often un-labeled photographs in a small zippered bag in her possession. Even though we speculate as to the exact time and place, we include some of these.

PART II INTERVIEWS

Each of the fourteen persons we interviewed had known Klavdiya Antipina personally. Among those interviewed are an ambassador, several academic colleagues, former students, neighbors, artists, and friends. Through these sometimes surprising reports, we become better acquainted with Klavdiya Antipina and learn things she would never have told us herself.

PART III PHOTOGRAPHS

A few dozen photographs cannot be truly representative of thousands in Klavdiya Antipina's photographic archive. Therefore, we have selected those showing Klavdiya Antipina's *first interest*—people. In these photographs we also glimpse the Kyrgyz landscape and costume, as well as other items of Kyrgyz material culture.

PART IV WRITINGS

The texts of these selections have been translated into English. All the original figures and illustrations accompany them. Although these examples concentrate on one of her special interests, viz., pile weaving, Klavdiya Antipina also wrote on many other subjects.

Ethnography has been defined as "descriptive anthropology." Ethnographers have tended to concentrate on the material culture of a people. Material culture—the structure and furnishings of dwellings, harness and animal trappings, tools and products of hand work, costume and the people—all of these are studied by the ethnographer. The ethnographer is interested not only in what is made and used, but how and why it is made and used. Also the ethnographer is interested in the structures and the meanings of those things. Much of the ethnographic material in this book is, indeed, "descriptive anthropology." Many elements of the traditional pastoralist culture persist, even though modern Kyrgyz life is becoming increasingly urban. Parts of this traditional material culture deserve to be studied and not lost, examined but not forgotten.

In this book, there are outright discrepancies. Events, as related, are decades past. Despite such inconsistencies of detail, general principles remain, and, in our consideration, they are the more important.

In our effort to make this book more readable, many instances of translation, interpretation, and editing have occurred. It our hope that original meanings have not been lost. For any errors, we accept responsibility.

—Bibira Akmoldoeva and John Sommer

Klavdiya Antipina

Part 1: Biographical

Introduction to Part I

Klavdiya Antipina's long life (1904-1996) encompassed the entire time of the Soviet Union, symmetrically filling the twentieth century. It combined an aristocratic childhood; education; marriage; motherhood; exile in 1937; widowhood; and a delayed career as an ethnographer of the Kyrgyz. Remarkably, this educated Moscow "blue blood" descended into poverty thousands of miles from her place of birth, but then rose again to become the respected "mother of Kyrgyz ethnography." This is the story of the much loved and respected Klavdiya Antipina.

In conjunction with the Klavdiya Antipina's biographical narrative, we include a group of sidebars. One is a transcription of a translation of her monologue of reminiscence from the sound track of the short film *Fate*, made for Kyrgyz television. Another is the story of a great Moscow cathedral destroyed by Stalin. Other sidebars include two of her husband's letters written after his arrest and imprisonment, a group of newspaper articles, several writings about Stalin and his terror, an account of the discovery of a secret mass grave near Bishkek, and Chinghiz Aitmatov's comments about his own father's "repression."

Many persons in the West do not fully understand "fear of government", nor can they conceive of the degree of stark terror evoked by the mass arrests, imprisonments, disappearances, and executions. Such terror, however, was a prominent part of Klavdiya Antipina's remarkable life.

— Bibira Akmoldoeva and John Sommer

PART ONE   BIOGRAPHICAL

Possibly no one could write a definitive biography of Klavdiya Antipina. She did not easily or willingly speak of herself. Occasionally over the years she would make brief reference to her past. We can only speculate about the degree of the anxiety, the uncertainty, and the personal terror she experienced at the time of her exile with her young son in 1937, during the time of Stalin.

Details of her earlier life—details that we believe to be factual—are based largely on information from documents, photographs, and letters; from information in interviews with Klavdiya Antipina conducted by others; and from interviews we ourselves have conducted with Klavdiya Antipina's colleagues, friends, students, and acquaintances. Our speculations are either self-evident or we identify them.

In 1989, in commemoration of her 85th birthday, Klavdiya Antipina agreed to be filmed for Kyrgyz television. The result is the film *Fate*, rare footage in which Klavdiya Antipina reminisces about her life. A transcription of the interpreted sound tract from that film is included here as a supplement to this biographical narrative. [SEE THE FILM, *FATE*: 14–19]

Klavdiya Ivanovna Antipina was born 5 May 1904. Her family lived in Morshansk, near Moscow. She was the fourth child (Fig. 1.1, 1.2) in a large family. Her grandfather had been a "person of the church." Her father (Fig. 1.3), who preceded every meal with a prayer, carried a title of nobility, which he lost at the time of the communist revolution. The family lived in a two-story house with a piano on the second floor. We may conclude that the family was prosperous, aristocratic, religious, and disciplined. Klavdiya Antipina was a "blue blood", a member of the gentry.

In 1922, Klavdiya Antipina, eighteen years old, moved to Moscow. (Fig. 1.4)

In Moscow, she entered a Forestry Institute and became interested in dendrology. Her interests widened and she was accepted by the prestigious Moscow State University. There she studied ethnography and became, along with several of her classmates, a respected scholar. She met and married a fellow student, Mikhail ("Misha") Rabinovich (Fig. 1.5), who edited the University's student newspaper. She worked as a proofreader for a publishing house. They lived full and happy lives. (Fig. 1.6, 1.7). In 1932 as son was born (Fig. 1.8, 1.9). Evidence suggests that she and her husband were ardent Marxists and Leninists.

Then Joseph Stalin came to power.

Fig. 1.1 Klavdiya Antipina (second from left) with three siblings. Morshansk, c. 1907–8 (Antipina Archive: KA 2943)

KLAVDIYA ANTIPINA

Fig. 1.2 Family portrait. Klavdiya Antipina is in the white dress to the left of center. Morshansk, c. 1910–11 (Antipina Archive: KA 3900)

Fig. 1.3 Ivan Akimovich, Klavdiya Antipina's father. Morshansk, c. 1910
(Antipina Archive: KA 2B-7)

Without warning, and while she had been with her young son hospitalized at the time for scarlet fever, her husband, "Misha," was arrested, taken away, and imprisoned as "an enemy of the people." *Klavdiya Antipina never saw him again.* [SEE MISHA'S LETTERS: 20–29]

Klavdiya Antipina, too, was labeled "an enemy of the people." Shortly thereafter, and with only twenty-four hours notification, she was deported into exile. Her little son, Lev (Leo), was four years old. (Fig. 1.10) After as long as ten days on a train, Klavdiya Antipina found herself and her son in Frunze (The Kirghiz SSR), a small provincial town in a remote part of the Soviet Union. She knew no one, she did not speak the language, she had no place to live, and her reception was hostile. Some of the locals threw stones at her. They knew her to be "an enemy of the people."

She was required to report to the local office of the NKVD. (Later the NKVD became the KGB). Years later, she was still being required to report periodically, although less often, to the local secret police.

PART ONE   BIOGRAPHICAL

Fig. 1.4 Klavdiya Antipina (left) with a brother and sister at about the time of her move to Moscow.
c. 1922 (Antipina Archive: KA 2950)

Fig. 1.5 Mikhail ("Misha") Rabinovich, Klavdiya Antipina's schoolmate and husband. Moscow, c. 1926–7
(Antipina Archive)

Fig. 1.6 Klavdiya Antipina (right) with "Misha" and friends. Moscow. c. 1926 (Antipina Archive: KA 2942)

Fig. 1.7 Klavdiya Antipina and "Misha". Moscow, c. 1930 (Antipina Archive: KA 3901)

5

KLAVDIYA ANTIPINA

In 1953, fifteen years after Klavdiya Antipina's arrival in Frunze (Bishkek), Joseph Stalin died. Her life began to change. She was no longer required to report to the local office of the NKVD, and she was informed that she was now free to live where she wished in the Soviet Union and to do what she liked. Now, for the first time in her life, it had become possible for her to do the kind of scholarly research for which she had been trained—ethnography. At a point in life when most persons have reached the peak of their careers, Klavdiya Antipina was about to *begin* her career.

At her next birthday she would be fifty years old. She remained in Bishkek, and studied the Kyrgyz people she had come to love and to admire.

In 1937 when she and her young son had arrived in Frunze, they had found shelter in the railway station, in a barn, in haystacks. Survival had

Fig. 1.8 "Misha", Lev (Leo), and Klavdiya Antipina. Moscow, c. 1934 (Antipina Archive)

been the immediate concern. She eventually made the acquaintance of a Russian-speaking family of simple means, who understood her situation and offered a room. The room was "like a storage room." The floor was earthen; Klavdiya Antipina polished it. There was an open interior doorway; Klavdiya Antipina hung up a cloth. She found a job washing laboratory equipment.

Her abilities were recognized. Eventually she was instructing teachers—in their homes—in pedagogical techniques, in curriculum development and in the writing of syllabuses. Later she herself taught the Russian language and Russian literature. (Fig. 1.11, 1.12) When, in 1953, she was "freed," she began scholarly work in earnest and studied the Kyrgyz people ethnographically. For the first time in her life, she felt she was doing what she had been trained to do and what she had long wanted to do. Gradually, the hostility she had met on her arrival in Frunze (Bishkek) gave way to a genuine friendship and respect for her. She had acquainted herself with the people of Kyrgyzstan and their ways. She had "fallen in love" with them and with their material culture.

Fig. 1.9 Klavdiya Antipina and Leo. Moscow, c. 1937 (Antipina Archive)

PART ONE BIOGRAPHICAL

Fig. 1.10 Klavdiya Antipina and Leo at time of exile. Moscow, 1937 (Antipina Archive: KA 2940)

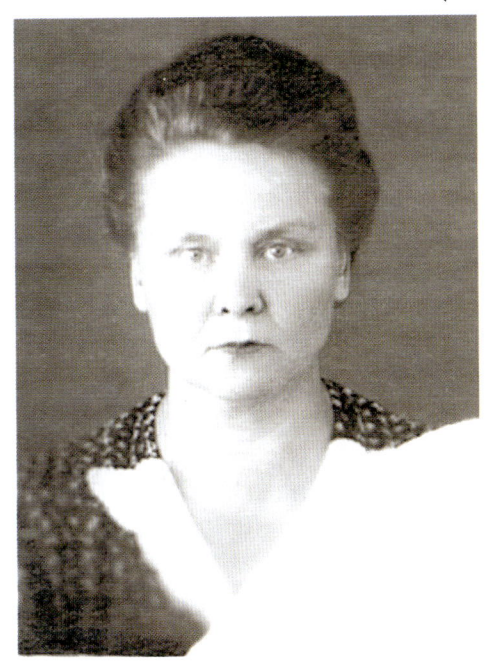

Fig. 1.11 Klavdiya Antipina. Bishkek, c. 1940 (Antipina Archive)

Fig. 1.12 Klavdiya Antipina. Bishkek, c. 1950–1 (Antipina Archive)

KLAVDIYA ANTIPINA

Thus, late in her life she pursued her "calling." (Fig. 1.13, 1.14)

Klavdiya Antipina was an ethnographer. She did field work, she wrote, she published, she taught, she consulted, and she photographed. Her archive of photographs constitute a true ethnographic treasure. She was given the title of "Honored Science Worker", was a "Laureate of The State Prize of Kyrgyzstan", and was a recipient of a Presidential Stipend. She had become a much-loved "respected older woman", a *Baibichye.* (Fig. 1.15)

[SEE NEWSPAPER ARTICLES: 30–35]

During recent decades, Klavdiya Antipina had been working on a book about Kyrgyz Costume. From time to time she worked with artists. For Klavdiya Antipina, who was an exacting and meticulous ethnographer, working with an artist was not always easy. An artist tends to have a particular temperament, tends to add things or to omit details that do not "fit." Such a person cannot always work with one who is meticulous and who stresses accuracy. We interviewed two artists who had worked with Klavdiya Antipina—one successfully and one unsuccessfully. *(See Part II, Interviews, 47.)*

The book on Kyrgyz costume was finished in maquette form, a model. As envisioned, it would bring people to recognize their own past, to recognition of Kyrgyz Design, Kyrgyz Pattern, and Kyrgyz Costume. When published, this would be an important book, a capstone to an illustrious career. *But, it is not published.* In fact, now—in 2001—its very whereabouts is not certain.

That it has *not* been published is cause for considerable concern. It would be a landmark, a monument to the long career of an eminent ethnographer—*Klavdiya Ivanovna Antipina, Ethnographer of The Kyrgyz.*

We fervently hope the book can be located and published.

In 1992, one of us (John Sommer) met Klavdiya

Fig. 1.13 Klavdiya Antipina during ethnographic field work. Kyrgystan, 1955–60
(Antipina Archive: KA 3902)

Antipina for the first time. She was eighty-eight years old. She was friendly, hospitable, knowledgeable and erudite. (Fig. 1.16) In 1994, at age 90, Klavdiya Antipina spoke to a traveling group with vigor and vehemence. (Fig. 1.17).

One of us (John Sommer) had written a book, *The Kyrgyz And Their Reed Screens*, dedicated to Klavdiya Antipina. But, in October 1996 when a copy of the book was to be presented to her personally by the author, she had died the day *before* his arrival in Bishkek. (Fig. 1.18)

Never, according to our informants, would Klavdiya Antipina say anything negative, bad or ill about anyone. If she had nothing good to say about a person, she said nothing. She *never* mentioned the name of Josef Stalin. [SEE STALIN: 36–39]

In the film *Fate,* Klavdiya Antipina equates the "greatness of Moscow" and the "greatness of The Cathedral of Christ The Savior." (She emphasizes this.) She names the streets along which she had passed daily on her way to Moscow State University—passing by the Cathedral of Christ The Savior on her way. She would have been there, indeed she would have seen the site when, in 1931, the cathedral had been dynamited on the orders of Joseph Stalin. We speculate that without saying his name, but by emphasizing the cathedral, in the film *Fate,* she obliquely and indirectly criticizes Joseph Stalin. [SEE CATHEDRAL OF CHRIST THE SAVIOR AND MAP OF CENTRAL MOSCOW: 40–43]

We know that Klavdiya Ivanovna Antipina's husband, Michael (Mikhail) Rabinovich ("Misha"), had been arrested, taken away, and imprisoned. She never saw him again. We speculate that his remains are among those to be found in a mass grave somewhere in the former Soviet Union, perhaps in the vicinity of Moscow.

In his book *Steeltown, USSR: Glasnost, Destalinization and Perestroika In the Provinces,* the Princeton University historian, Stephen Kotkin, describes the events of 1937 and 1938 as they affected the city of Magnitogorsk, where the intelligentsia were removed and eliminated. He states, "The episode remains largely mysterious to this day."

Nor was Kyrgyzstan spared. There is Ata Beyit, the mass grave, now the site of a major Kyrgyz national memorial southeast of Bishkek. There the remains of 137 (or 138) victims were found. Many of the bodies have been identified. Daniel Prior, in his Bishkek Handbook, Inside and Out (Literary Kyrgyzstan 1994), describes the time when, under the peculiar terroristic regime of Stalin, many of the local Kyrgyz intelligentsia were eliminated by unpublicized executions. At Ata Beyit the remains of the father of the distinguished Soviet writer, Chinghiz Aitmatov, were found. [SEE ATA BEYIT & CHINGHIZ AITMATOV: 44–45]

In May 2001 the authors visited Ata Beyit. In the museum was a photograph of Chinghiz Aitmatov with Askar Akiev, president of the Kyrgyz Republic. Together they were shown lifting a box containing the remains of Torekul Aitmatov, Chinghiz Aitmatov's father. The photograph had been made at the re-burial ceremonies for the victims at Ata Beyit. Chinghiz Aitmatov is quoted as having said at the time, "Father, I have looked for you for fifty three years. Now I have found you…"

In another place in the museum there is a photograph of a rather pleased-looking Josef Stalin. Beneath this is a second photograph, this one of bones and a skull—a skull with a holes, bullet holes.

One is reminded of the words of Learned Hand, the respected American judge:

> "…Those who begin coercive elimination of dissent, soon find themselves eliminating dissenters. Compulsory unification of opinion achieves only the unanimity of the graveyard." (1)

Klavdiya Antipina's very best friend in Bishkek had been Sophie Petrovna Choy, who was Korean. Sophie's husband, K. Shorukov, had been a local government official. His body was one of those identified in the mass grave at Ata Beyit. Klavdiya Antipina and Sophie Petrovna had had much in common. Each had lost a husband during the Stalin regime. Each had been labeled an "enemy of the people." They were about the same age. Their sons were of the same age. Klavdiya Antipina would have known at the time that Sophie Petrovna had lost her husband even as she herself earlier had lost her own husband to arrest, imprisonment and eventual death.

Over the years, Klavdiya Antipina seriously considered, but ultimately rejected, living once again in Moscow. She loved the Kyrgyz people, she loved the things they made; and, in Bishkek, she had friends. Despite formidable barriers, Klavdiya Antipina nearly single-handedly preserved ethnographic information about the unique Kyrgyz people of Central Asia. She did this work during the latter half of her life and during the Soviet period. Still largely unknown in the West, Klavdiya Antipina deserves to rise from obscurity to take her place among the world's prominent scholars of Central Asian Ethnography.

Klavdiya Ivanovna Antipina, an aristocratic resident of Moscow, a "blue blood" whose father carried a title of nobility, a gifted student educated as an ethnographer in the finest university in the Soviet Union, had been exiled as "an enemy of the people" to a hostile reception in a remote provincial town where she lived on a dirt floor and looked for a job. She was a thirty three year old mother, unaware that she was becoming a widow. Such experiences would break many persons.

But this remarkable woman, this "outsider," this ethnographer whose career began when she was nearly fifty years old, this optimist who never spoke ill of anyone, rose to become the much loved and the highly respected "mother of Kyrgyz ethnography." Klavdiya Antipina, Ethnographer of the Kyrgyz!

---

(1) As quoted by Theodore B. Schwartz in Perspectives in Biology and Medicine, volume 44, number 3 [Summer 2001]: © The Johns Hopkins University Press 2001, page 434.

Fig. 1.14 Klavdiya Antipina (center) in the field. Kyrgystan, 1955–60 (Antipina Archive)

PART ONE   BIOGRAPHICAL

Photograph by D. Svetlakov

Fig. 1.15 Klavdiya Antipina at the time of her 85th birthday. Bishkek, 1989

KLAVDIYA ANTIPINA

Fig. 1.16 Klavdiya Antipina at home, seated at her desk. Bishkek, 3 September 1992.
Photograph by John Sommer

Fig. 1.17 Klavdiya Antipina at ninety, speaking to a Traveling Textile Museum Group. Bishkek, 1994
Photograph by John Sommer

Fig. 1.18 Dedication of the memorial at Klavdiya Antipina's grave.
Bishkek, May 2000

Pictured (left to right): *Urmat Osmoev, Toktosunova Gulchahra, Bibira Akmoldoeva, Dinara Chochunbaeva, Svetlana Dunovskaya, Medet Tulegenov, Gulnara Kasymalieva, Sapara Mambetova, Francois Colcanap, and Murat Djumaliev*

The film *Fate*
Introduction

In 1988, at the time of Glasnost, and in preparation for public recognition of her 85th birthday, Klavdiya Antipina agreed to the making of a film, Fate, a retrospective of her life and career. It was to be made for Kyrgyz television. The short film is a monologue of reminiscence. Her voice, and only her voice, is heard over the musical background. (The transcription given here is based on translations of the sound tract and notes of Bibira Akmoldoeva, Irisbubu Beybutova, and Boris Wolfson.)

Fig. 1.19 Klavdiya Antipina (still from *Fate*)

Early in the film we see the curtained window of a modest apartment interior. Klavdiya Antipina is seated at her desk (Fig. 1.19) as she reminisces about her life, her "childhood", memories of the greatness of Moscow, of the development of her early interest in dendrology, of the growth of her interest in ethnography, of working as a publishing house proofreader, of her marriage to a fellow student, and of their little son. We see old photographic images of her happy life in Moscow, her family and her friends.

Then, she mentions that in 1937 her husband was arrested, and that she was sent out to Kyrgyzstan—with her young son—to begin a new life. In the film, suddenly she is unable, she says, to recall accurate details of the "difficulties" of her life.

Her husband had been arrested as an "enemy of the people" and imprisoned. Soon thereafter she had been exiled to the outermost edge of the Soviet Union—to The Kirghiz Soviet Socialist Republic—with a four-year-old son. Although she had been highly educated as an ethnographer, now, as an "enemy of the people", she was not allowed to use this training. Instead, she did menial tasks in order to survive. Fifteen years later, on Josef Stalin's death in 1953, she was informed by the secret police (NKVD) that she was no longer an "enemy of the people" and that now she would be allowed to pursue her ethnographic career. At a time in life when most persons have reached a career summit, she was being allowed to begin her career. For the first time in her life, she was able to pursue scholarly ethnography. She would be fifty years old on her next birthday.

Fig. 1.20 Klavdiya Antipina with companion (still, from *Fate*)

In the film, we see her in autumn walking with a companion in a Bishkek park (Fig. 1.20). Then, again, we see her at her desk surrounded by books and papers. We see a work in progress—a book on costume. And we see an artist reviewing illustrations with her. Then we see her in the Museum of History and, once again, we see her walking in the park with a companion. Finally, we see her in a crowd of people as she approaches the entrance to the Museum of History—alone.

She respected the Kyrgyz people and their material culture. During an Ethnographical-Archaeological expedition in the 1950's, she began to study the people of southern Kyrgyzstan. Subsequently, she wrote *Osobennosti Materielnoe Kultury I Prikladnogo Iskusstva Iuzhnykh Kirgizov (Specific Features of the Material Culture and Applied Art of the Southern Kirghiz)*. This scholarly work, published in 1962, served as the dissertation for her Ph. D., a degree eventually granted in Moscow.

By the time of her death, at the age of 92, she had become known as the loved and respected "Mother of Kyrgyz Ethnography." She was an "Honored Science Worker" and a "Laureate of the State Prize of Kyrgyzstan." She was a recipient of a Presidential stipend. She had become a "respected older woman"—a *Baibichye*.

Soundtrack to the film *Fate (Sud'ba)* (1)

Klavdiya Ivanovna Antipina

Starring Candidate of Sciences (History)
Laureate of the State Prize of the Kirghiz SSR
Distinguished Worker of the Arts

Screenplay by S. Kuruchbekov
Directed by L. Turusbekova
Photography by M. Dzhergalbaev
Sound by L. Kaliuzhina
Edited by D. Sadykova
Unit Production Manager E. Rysalieva

Kyrgyzfilm
THE "CHRONICLE" PRODUCTION UNIT, 1988

Certain images vividly remain in one's memory. Now it seems as if it all happened in my childhood, rather than in my youth.

Here is one of these vivid images that have stayed with me for my entire life: It's the grandeur of Moscow (2). The street noise, the roar of the city, and Volkhonka and Mokhovaya Streets where I found the first college to which I applied. My memory has preserved the splendor of the Cathedral of Christ the Savior (3), located on my way to the Forestry College (4). The magnificence of the cathedral cannot help but impress one. I think that everyone who has ever seen it as a child must somehow connect that splendor with the grandeur of Moscow itself. At least that is how it has been preserved in my memory.

There I found the Forestry College, the institution to which I was eligible to apply after completing my schooling, [in] the comprehensive secondary school from which I had graduated in Morshansk (5). I became interested in dendrology. I found the wood texture fascinating. Perhaps the strongest impression was left by the trees. As students we cut down trees, as part of our practicum. There were no machines then. We cut the trees, chopped them, sawed them. The fall of a tree has this… there is this pity for something that is leaving us, something so graceful, so beautiful, so green, so large—departing for some unknown place…

Unfortunately, I would not graduate from the Forestry College (6). Fate decided this for me. I received the position of a copy editor at the Exemplary Printing Plant No. 1 (7). Now I'm happy about that. I learned a great deal. I was trained in a remarkable tradition of book production. I began thinking about something more serious. Then my attention was drawn to the Anthropology Institute at the Biology Department, in the Division of Physical and Mathematical Sciences, of Moscow State

University No. 1 (8). Soon I applied for admission there. This Institute gave me much knowledge.

As part of our ethnographic field trips we studied the Volga region. I gained a great deal from the field work—knowledge of the everyday life of the Mari and of the Mordva. My only regret was that I did not have the opportunity to spend time with the Chuvash (9). I regret this now, because, as I study the Kyrgyz I find many parallels.

After graduating from the University I was invited to join the editorial staff of a scholarly work on the beliefs and religions of various peoples. And so I worked in Moscow and lived in Moscow, and there found my family, which added great joy to my life. The friend, to whose life I had decided to join mine, worked at the printing plant. A son was born to us. I remember how difficult it was to bring him up. But nothing got in the way of our common, shared existence, of our desire to live and to be useful (10).

In 1937 (11) my husband was the managing editor of a newspaper, a major student printed (12) newspaper. He was arrested, and I was sent to Frunze with the child. I came here, and a totally new life began. A totally new life. It's difficult to find a way to describe everything about that life (13).

A prominent scholar, Nikolai Nikolaevich Cheboksarov, who had been a colleague of mine at the University, came to Kirghizia (14) on a field trip devoted to studying the Dungan (15). He was surprised to see that I was not working in my field. He did everything so that… they transferred me to the Academy of Sciences.

And so in the fifties my first field trip within Kirghizia took place, the trip to Issyk-Kul. We wrote a book about the villages of Chichkan and Darkhan, *The Material Culture of the Kyrgyz People* (16). I found a new calling, or rather, found the very thing I yearned for when I was at the University. It seemed to me that I was finally entering into the world of scholarship… that I was finally given an opportunity, despite all of the difficulties I'd had to live through, that I am on the right track, that I'm "in" as far as scholarship goes. I was writing an article, albeit a rather brief one—my section is rather short in the book—but I'm "in." And that meant a great deal.

In terms of human relationships, it may have even become easier for me. Maybe it became easier not to notice certain looks I had been getting which had been tormenting me, some improper looks. The thoughts that had preoccupied me in connection with my move to Frunze began to dissolve. They no longer distressed me. On the contrary, I began to feel that I had found some kind of new home, a new home for myself, a new place for myself in this new life.

The prospects of a museum began to materialize, a brand new museum which would demand an investment of significant effort on my part. A Museum of History demands a great deal of support, needs the attention of a sizable community of supporters. I have never abandoned that museum, to this day.

I simply could not let the beauty, which I had found not only in nature but among the people, pass unnoticed. There is a great deal of that beauty among the people. You can really see it—the beauty of the decoration of the dwelling. The beauty of the decorations, the care devoted to the dwelling, the care devoted to the horse. In the fifties, this was striking. There were no longer many yurts, very few of them, but in the new houses I couldn't help noticing the art. Now we call it applied art, the art born of the people.

The study of that art has led me to believe firmly that it cannot be separated from the material culture itself. Art is inseparable from the object itself and inseparable from the function of the object. It is the Kyrgyz woman who is the true creator of the Kyrgyz pattern and ornament, that complicated representational medium—indeed the principal representational medium—in the whole realm of Kyrgyz folk art. When an object is made the craftsman puts his whole soul into it. The craftsman makes it interesting.

Life has convinced me that we need extensive scholarly literature, extensive data about the life—the everyday life—of the Kyrgyz people. I have accumulated a great deal of thoughts and notes, many of them interesting. I want so badly to spend the rest of my time here, the rest of my days, doing this work. To publish good, interesting books—also about folk art. Right now this kind of generalized historical and ethnographic material is absolutely necessary. The entire meaning of my life right now is in doing as much as possible for my field of [Kyrgyz] ethnography.

Note: The above translation is based on that of Boris Wolfson, Berkeley, California. Notes have been compiled from the comments of Bibira Akmoldoeva, Irisbubu Beybutova, and Boris Wolfson.

Notes

1. The Russian word *sud'ba* corresponds both to the English notion of fate, with the implication that a person has been meant to live in a certain way, and to the more general concept of a narrated life story. In defining this word, the Oxford Russian Dictionary, uses the terms *fate, destiny, fortune,* and *lot*.

2. Klavdiya Antipina lived in the center of Moscow.

3. See Cathedral of Christ the Savior, pg. 40

4. "Lesnoi institut." Most likely the Moscow Forestry College *(Moskovskii lesotekhnicheskii institut)*, founded in 1919.

5. In 1918 the Soviet government scrapped the old educational system and introduced primary and secondary "comprehensive polytechnical schools" for students from 8 to 17 years of age. The curriculum emphasized natural and social sciences in contrast to the previous curriculum, which had included classical languages and religious education. The new curriculum required students to participate in "socially useful labor activities."

6. In the late 1920s the Forestry College was closed and the Agricultural Academy taking over some of the College's functions. The Forestry College was re-opened in 1943 in a different location (a Moscow suburb) and still exists as the "State Forestry University."

7. One of the largest printing plants in Russia, founded in 1876 by the prominent publisher I. E. Sytin, and nationalized in 1919 as the Zhdanov Printing Plant.

8. The university founded by Elizabeth I in 1755 was for the first 160 years of its existence the only university in Moscow. In 1918, however, the Soviet government transformed what had been the Moscow Women's College into Moscow State University No. 2. and the "old" university acquired the words "State" and "No. 1" as part of its title. This is where Klavdiya Antipina studied. In 1930 the second university underwent a three-way split and numbering was no longer necessary.

9. The Chuvash people speak the oldest Turkic language.

10. Many such persons at that time were enthusiastically seeking to contribute something important to the Soviet people and to the Soviet Union.

11. There is time discrepancy here. Rabinovich was already in Ukhta in January 1937, and wrote from there reminiscing about spending January 1, 1936, together with his family. It seems more probable that he was arrested at some point in 1936.

12. "Printed" as distinguished from the so-called "wall newspapers" *[stennye gazety]*—a popular genre of self-made publications in the Soviet period, drawn or written on large pieces of heavyweight paper and posted for all to see.

13. Klavdiya Antipina omits here at least a decade of life, which she claims difficulty in finding a way to describe, implying that she does not remember. This seems doubtful. Perhaps she doesn't want to remember. Perhaps it is too painful. *Is it that she has developed the habit of avoiding the subject, not speaking of it with anyone?*

14. Nicholai Nicolaiovich Cheboksarov had been exiled at about the same time as Klavdiya Antipina.

15. An ethnic group related to the Chinese.

16. The film at this moment shows the cover of the book. Its title is *The Everyday Life of the Collective Farmers in the Kyrgyz Localities of Darkhan and Chichkan.*

Misha's Letters

Introduction

Klavdiya Antipina had preserved several of the communications from her husband following his arrest and imprisonment. Two of these are reproduced here in translation. One, an eight-page letter, is dated 3 January 1937. Another, a postcard written on 18 January 1937, is postmarked more than a month later. Discrepancy occurs. Klavdiya Antipina has indicated that Mikhail Rabinovich's arrest and imprisonment had occurred in 1937. But, correspondence suggests that on the first day of that year, he had already been confined. Was it, instead, 1936? Such details, although important, do not alter the grim sequence of those events more than six decades ago. These communications are some of the last received.

Klavdiya Antipina, herself exiled from Moscow to The Kirghiz SSR in 1937, had felt that her husband's arrest and imprisonment had been a mistake, that the authorities would eventually realize this, and that her husband would return. Years later, and after much false information, she sadly concluded that "Misha" was dead. She would never know with certainly the date or the circumstances.

The postcard (front and back), and the letter, both in their original form, are illustrated.

The notes and translation are by Boris Wolfson of Berkeley, California.

Letter (XVIII 8 PAGES)

XVIII   January 3, 1937

My beloved! My beauty! My life, Kalyushok! (1) Do you remember the production of Bernard Shaw's The Devil's Disciple at Zavedsky's theater? (2) Do you recall the sudden transformation, the rebirth, of the play's two principal characters? Our correspondence reminds me of that transformation. Yes, we've swapped roles. You write to me so often, your letters are so long and so interesting. And what has happened to me? I write rarely and with difficulty; my letters are dull. Yours are full of love, of infinite tenderness. In a recent letter you remarked with regret that a lack of youthful enthusiasm and fantasy prevents you from writing even more tender and loving things. You, my joy, underestimate your talent as a writer! I cannot put your letters down. I read them over and over. And not only for your affection, for your boundless tenderness. I also re-read them for their literary merits. Remember, you said once that you used to write with ease. I claimed then that I did not see any talent for writing in you. I must admit that I was wrong. You show unquestionable literary promise—your writing is effortless and captivating. If you happen to have any free time, you might consider trying your hand at it.

But let me go back to the parallel I was drawing between Shaw's play and our correspondence, our relationship. You have, both in our private life and especially in letters, always reacted with reticence and bashful tenderness to my passion, my ardor. I discerned a few passionate notes in the marvelous expressions of affection which pervade (so uncharacteristically for you) the letters you have been sending to me here at the works. I noticed them and yet did not dare mention this to you. I was afraid of scaring you off, afraid that you would stop writing about it. Truth be told, I also had my doubts. This was just so unlike my little girl—this display of passionate affection. Today, right after the first six letters I received your tenth letter. All of my doubts vanished, dispelled by your frank explanation of the reasons for wanting to work as much as possible.

You have to agree, my darling, that my analogy with The Devil's Disciple is fairly apt. And not only with regard to our correspondence, that is, the display of our feelings for each other, but also with regard to those feelings themselves. Back at the Butyrki (3) I promised myself to be faithful to you, to belong to you alone, as long as we are apart. Remember how you said, at the very beginning of our romance, as we held each other: "I love you forever, until the grave." I objected then: "Love knows no bounds, no term limits." And now how many times since we have been apart has it flashed through my mind: "I love Kalyshok forever." You may find this paradoxical. But this is what I live by. How many times have I visualized my return to you, our subsequent life until old age. True, until now it was not difficult for me to abide by my own decision. Not difficult at all. The passion has vanished. I no longer recognize myself. How much has changed in my relationship with you. Torn away from you, I am now endlessly infatuated with you as a friend. My love is now devoid of passion; it is dominated by veneration, by admiration. This has surely had an effect on my letters. But my "passionlessness" is not the only reason my letters have been so short on affection, the affection which is otherwise so typical of me. I have been writing so infrequently, writing about such tedious matters and with such lack of affection because there has been so little time, and because I've been extremely tired, and because I have not yet become accustomed to my new circumstances.

It was also at Butyrki that I came to a conclusion that much, very much, would now have to change in our life. I had thought, at one point, about asking you to go ahead and make your life without me. Quickly I realized that this was foolish: I could hurt you. And if life should lead you to that, the last thing you will require is my consent or advice. Then I thought: "Kalyushen'ka is demure; she is modest; she loves me. She will allow herself to become intimate with someone else only if a serious feeling arises in her. But whatever happens, I will always adore Kalysuha—my friend, the mother of my Levushok (4), my love." These are the thoughts that went through my head. And under the influence of a bad mood I wrote to you in detail about this, from the train. The very next day, though, I took it all back and begged for your forgiveness. Later I wrote about this in passing. All this came to my mind now as I finished reading your tenth letter (of December 8). And again my reason repeats the same. And what about my passions? They thirst for your undivided love.

My dearest Penelope! Your Odysseus has been roughly torn away from you. True, he is not being tempted by any enchantresses—and even if he were, he would not have succumbed to them. Of this you can be absolutely sure. It is not likely that my Penelope has had to ward off a multitude of suitors besieging her house. She has not had to spend her nights unraveling what she has woven during the day. But she has had to strain her eyes as she toils over proofs night after night. And she has had to fight, stifling her "high potential" with excessive work. How poorly did I know my beloved after all! Or, rather, how much did the conditions of our life prevent me from knowing her.

My love! I did not want to bring all of this up. I carefully tried to avoid giving you the impression that I wanted to bind you to myself, I was afraid even to hint at limiting your freedom. But since all this has come up, let me finish. This might be called egotism or a vestige of a proprietary, retrograde instinct. But I am a one-woman man. In my love I give myself completely. And this is the only way I can imagine love. I also know only too well that even the most accidental, fleeting encounter will leave a crack in my Kalyoshok, will irreparably damage our intimacy, the joy and the purity of our affection, our passion. Once again: I did not want to bring all of this up. Now I don't even know whether I should send these lines along, whether you might discern in them a trace of doubt, whether you might be offended by them. I have decided to send them. Let Kalyushen'ka know about all of my thoughts; I do not want to conceal anything from her. And I hope that you, too, will not rush to improper conclusions and will share all of your experiences with me.

My love! I trust you as I do my very own self. I know that you live by me alone, I know that you will live to see me return. Just like during the happiest days of our love there will be nothing in my life I will ever conceal from you. Absolutely nothing!

The reminiscences of the joyous days of our life together have become particularly intense of late. How much did trivialities, material difficulties overshadow all the beauty, all the joy of our love. And how one values the former happiness now. In the past few days memories have taken complete hold of me. They overcome me chaotically, piece by piece. But how vivid they are! Often entire pictures pass before my eyes. The images of summer scenes are particularly numerous; I've seen many of them from different years. I spent New Year's Eve on duty at the main office of the works. This was my first all-night watch here. And I remembered, in great detail, our marvelous New Year's celebration last year. Your return from the Klyaz'ma. Photographs. Miraculous, rare minutes in our life when you and I were alone together and free from work! I love you, my dearest! I love you! In one of your earliest letters you wrote that you sang for me once. Sing for me! Sing! I want to hear your voice one more time, my dear.

Then I remembered January 1, 1936. The journey to you. Levushka with us. His being late to a New Year's party. What party did he go to this year? Did you have a party for him? I await a detailed description of the day. I kiss my tiny one endlessly. Please tell him that Daddy is with him in his thoughts at all times and that he dreams about the day when he can once again play with his Levushok. You ask for my advice regarding taking Levochka to an ophthalmologist. By all means, do take him. And while you're at it have the dentist take a look at his teeth as well.

And then I remembered skiing downhill with you. The only time! We never had an opportunity to try it again, we never managed to go skating. Try to make up for it now, my joy. By the way, how is your bruised finger doing? Does it ever bother you? There is a skating rink here, but I don't skate because there's no time. On days off I am only free at night and I use the time to go take a shower, go to the movies, relax. I try going for walks before going to bed. Whatever I do I try to spend an hour a day outside.

I get into bed. I remember my charming one. Marvelous honest eyes, delicate warm lips that conceal a sea of affection, the dear, charming nostrils, so irresistibly joyous in moments of laughter. I remember my darling's shoulders, which somehow always seem cold in my memories. The feeling is so real that my hands cannot wait to try to warm them up. This desire has not left me now for several days. I remember every bit of my miraculous one… Take good care of yourself, my joy, dress warmly, wear long underwear. What a pity that my letters take so long to arrive. If they hadn't, you could have bought yourself a pair of overshoes instead of buying me the felt boots which I ended up not needing since they issued me a pair here at the works on January 1. I have not yet received any of your parcels, Kalyushen'ka. They are being held up due to insufficient means of transportation. Perhaps they will arrive soon. Ever since receiving the money, I have been waiting for them very calmly. Thank you for your troubles.

Now I will fall asleep thinking of you. My dearest…

Notes to Letter

1. Kalyushok, Kalyusha, and Kalyushen'ka are all diminutives of Klavdia.

2. Yuri Alekseevich Zavedsky (1894-1977) directed the production of Shaw's The Devil's Disciple (1897) at the Zavedsky Studio Theater in Moscow in 1933.

3. The Butyrsky jail (Butyrskaia tiur'ma) is one of the largest facilities in Moscow. It was colloquially referred to as Butyrka. Rabinovich uses a plural form, Butyrki, by analogy with the name of the main St. Petersburg/Leningrad prison, Kresty (a plural form of the word "krest," cross).

4. Levushok, Levushka and Levochka are all diminutives of Lev (Leo).

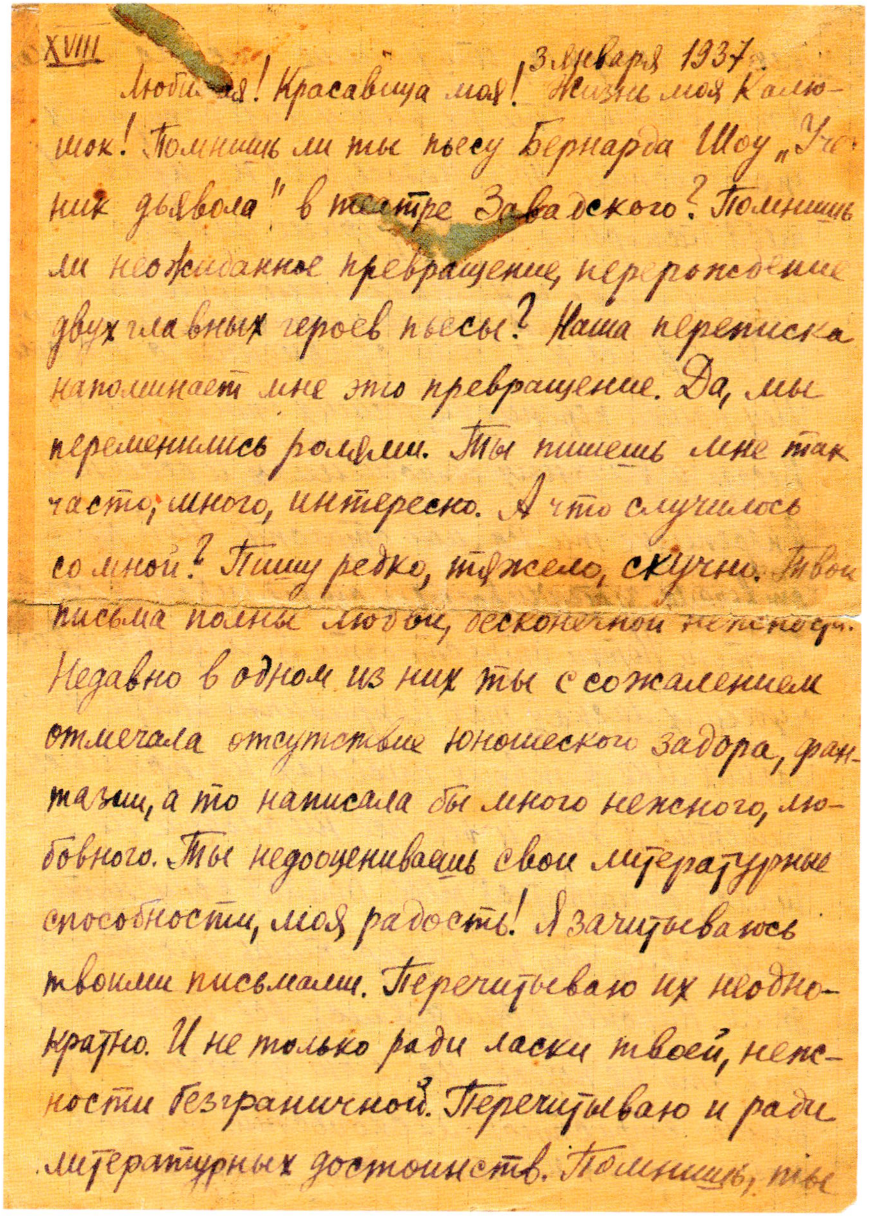

KLAVDIYA ANTIPINA

XVIII   3 января 1937 г.

Люба́я! Красавица моя! Жизнь моя какая-
то! Помнишь ли ты пьесу Бернарда Шоу "У
них добра!" В ноябре. За два дня до...? Помнишь
ли положение превращения героя — положение
двух главных героев в неё? Наша переписка
напоминает мне это превращение. Да, мы
переменились ролями. Ты пишешь так так
часто, много, интересно. А что случилось
со мной? Пишу редко, тускло, скупо. Твои
письма полны того юного, радостного веселья,
недавно в одном из них ты с сожалением
отмечала отсутствие юношеского задора, ранее
так, а ты написала бы мною немного что-
либо. Ты недооцениваешь свои литературные
способности, шлёшь радость! Я загисывалось
твоими письмами. Перечитывало их под-
крадя. И не только ради ласки твоей, нем-
ности безграничной. Перечитывало и ради
литературных достоинств. Помнишь, ты

как-то говорила, что ранее писала легче.
Я же говорил, что ты не пишешь литературных
способностей. Признаюсь, был не прав. У
тебя бесспорно литературные данные —
пишешь легко и убедительно, будь у тебя
свободное время, надо было бы попробовать свои силы
по крупной к своему сравнению с писем
Шоу нашей переписки, наших отношений.
Всегда и в личных отношениях, и особенно
в переписке ты на меня отрогать, мой нежный
ответный. Я перечитывал отложенные в сто-
рону письма. Страшно стыдно я погряз в певых
чудесных листах, так неприятно щедро посы-
лаемых мне в твоих письмах на прошлых.
Заметил я это и всё же ни словом не ре-
шалось обмолвиться тебе. Боялся возмущения
твоей, боялся, что ты прекратишь писать об
этом. Наконец и сомневался всё-таки. Это
так это не похоже на мою девочку — прав-
димую страстной ласковости. Сегодня
после первых писем сразу почуял

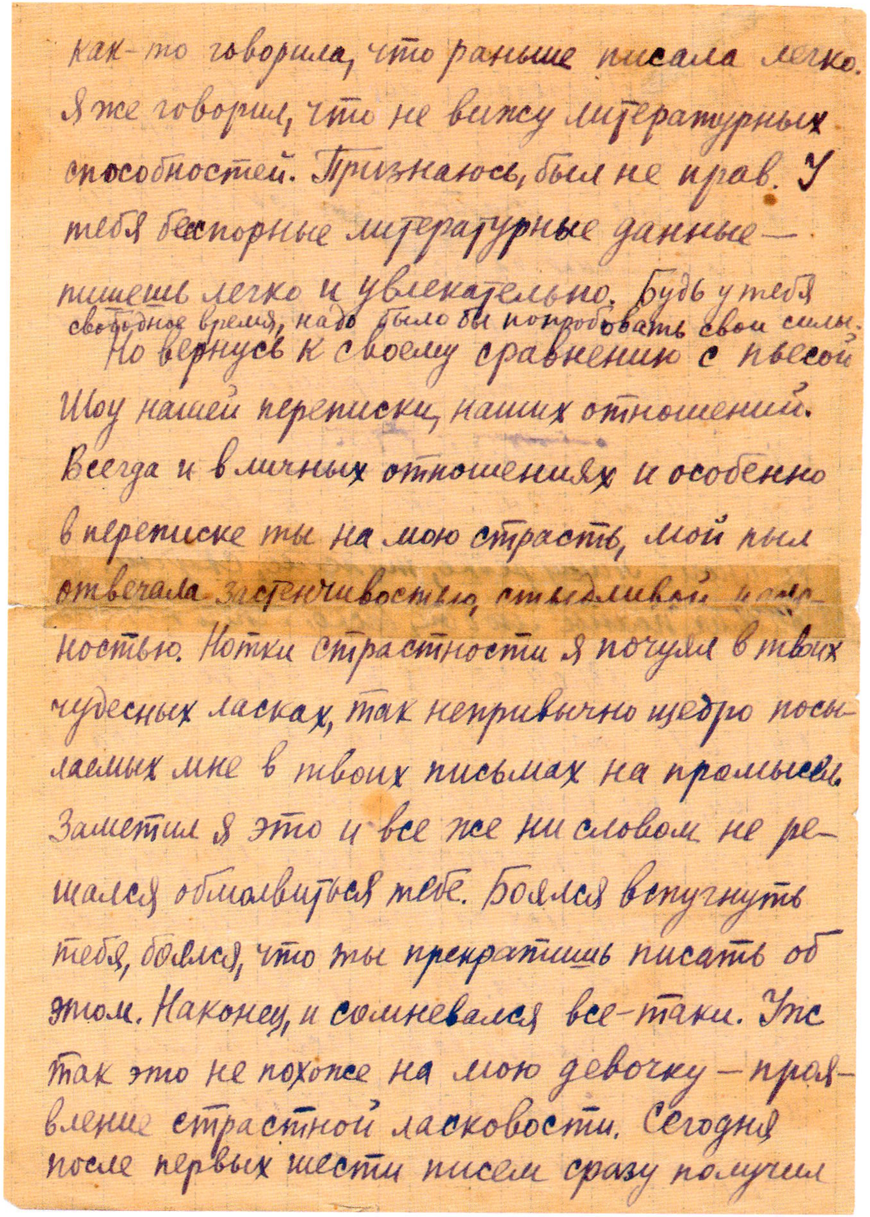

Fig. 1.21 Letter: January 3, 1937 (Letter XVIII, page 1) Mikhail Rabinovich ("Misha") to Klavdiya Antipina

Fig. 1.22 Letter: January 3, 1937 (Letter XVIII, page 2) Mikhail Rabinovich ("Misha") to Klavdiya Antipina

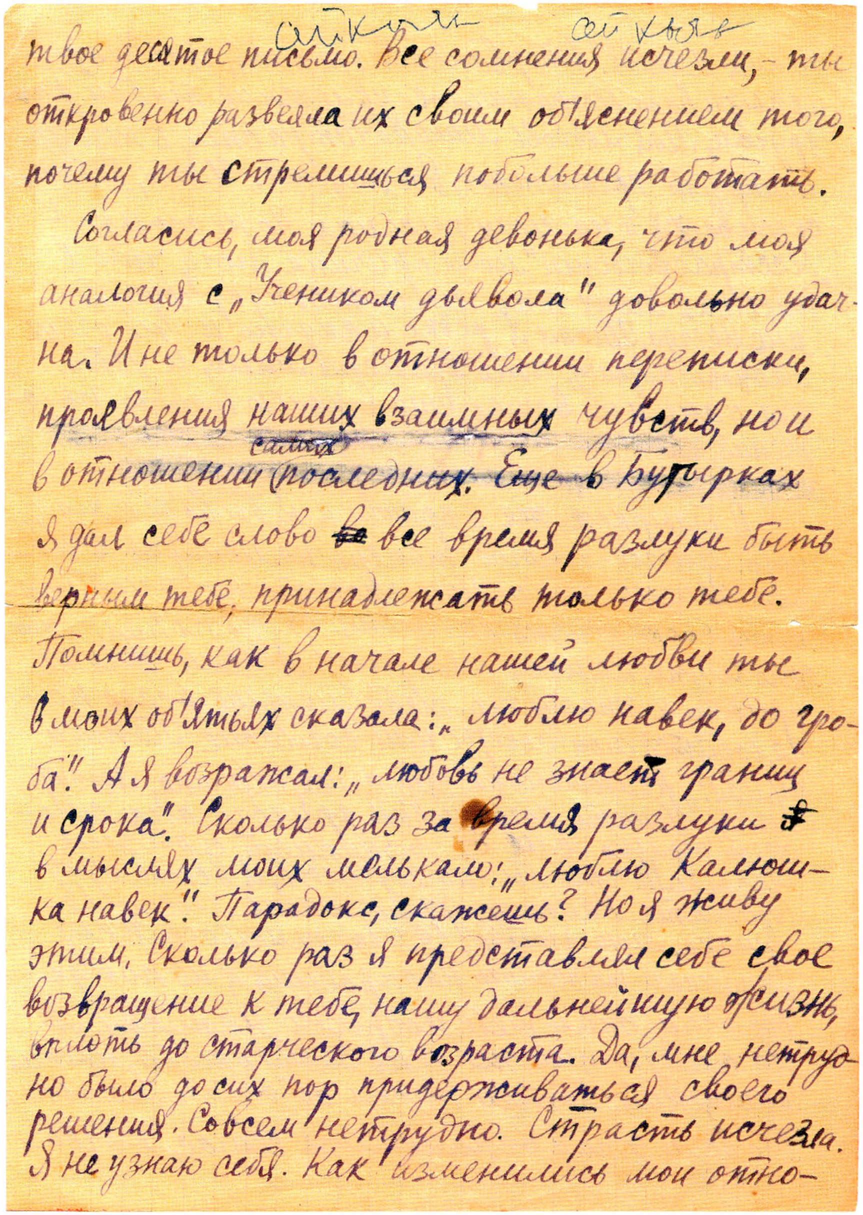

PART ONE   BIOGRAPHICAL

Fig 1.23 Letter: January 3, 1937 (Letter XVIII, page 3)
Mikhail Rabinovich ("Misha") to Klavdiya Antipina

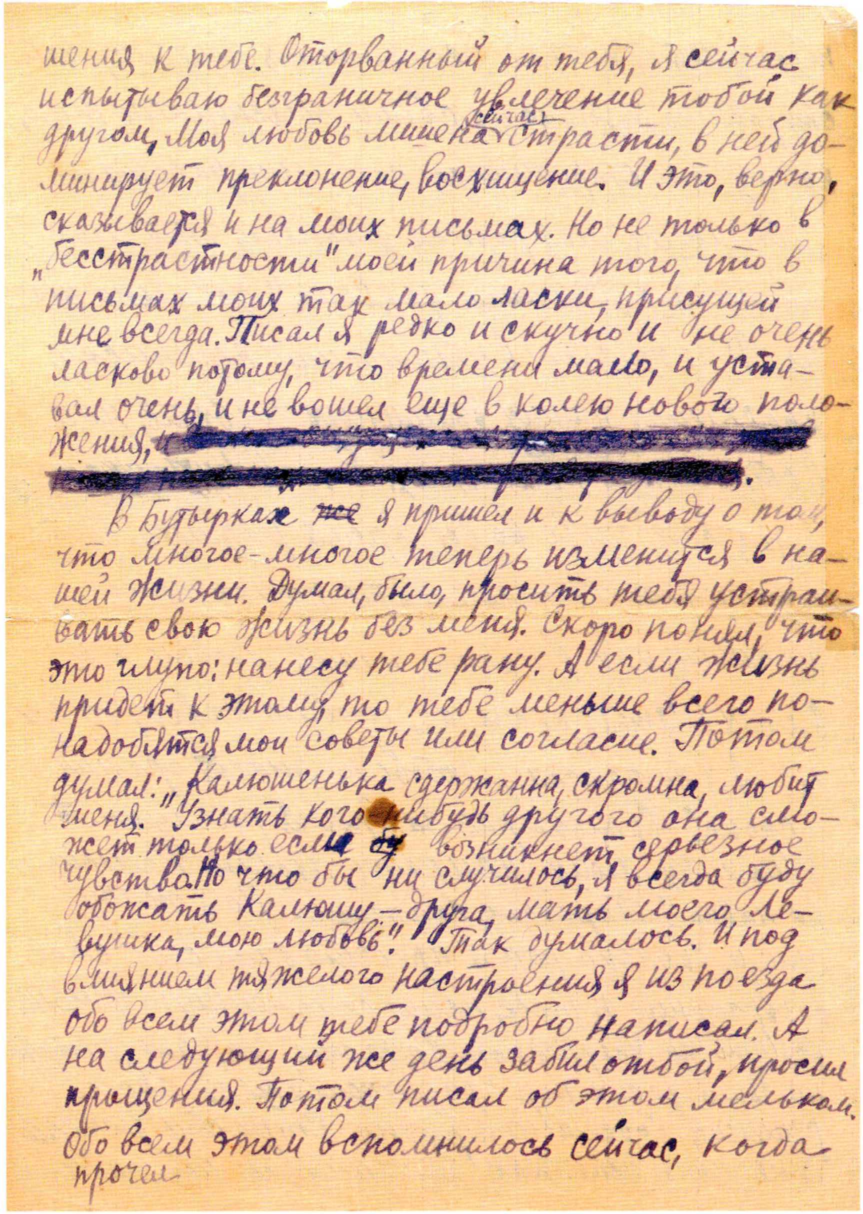

Fig. 1.24 Letter: January 3, 1937 (Letter XVIII, page 4)
Mikhail Rabinovich ("Misha") to Klavdiya Antipina

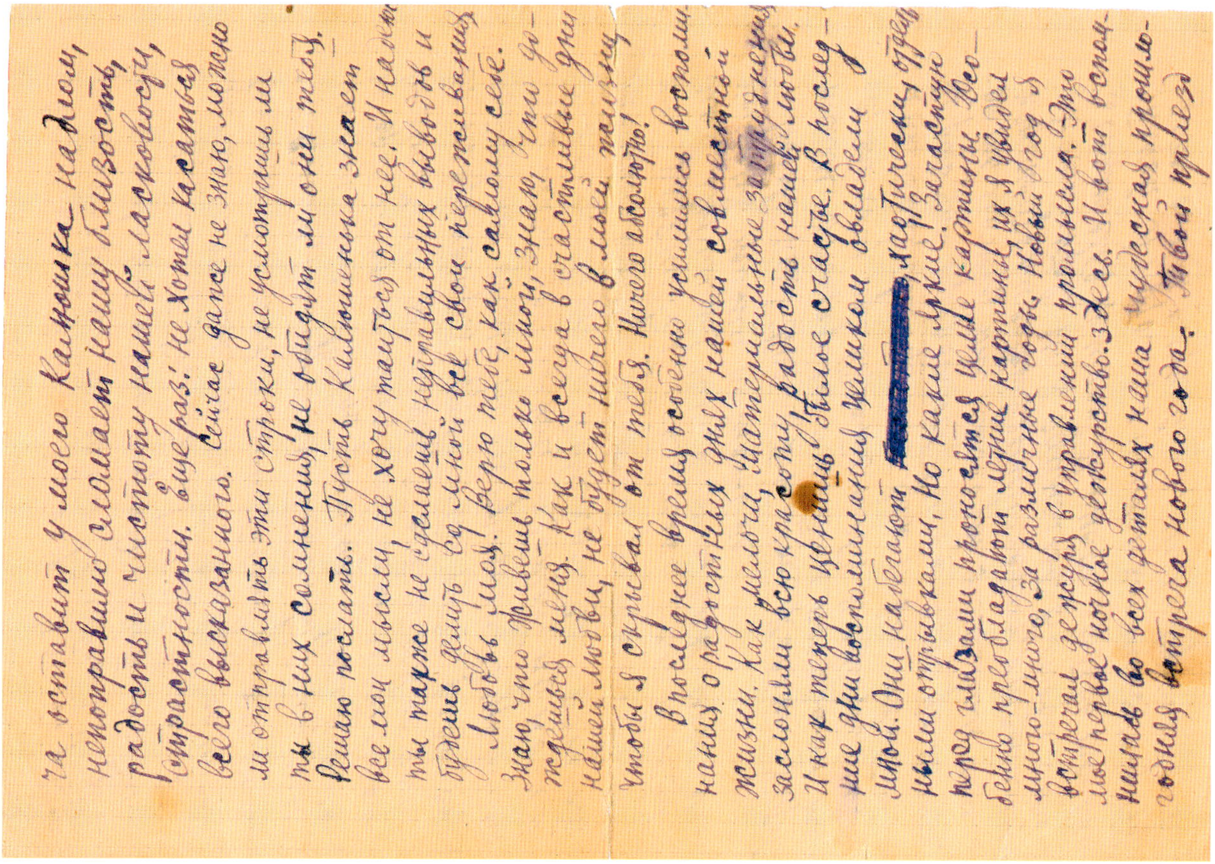

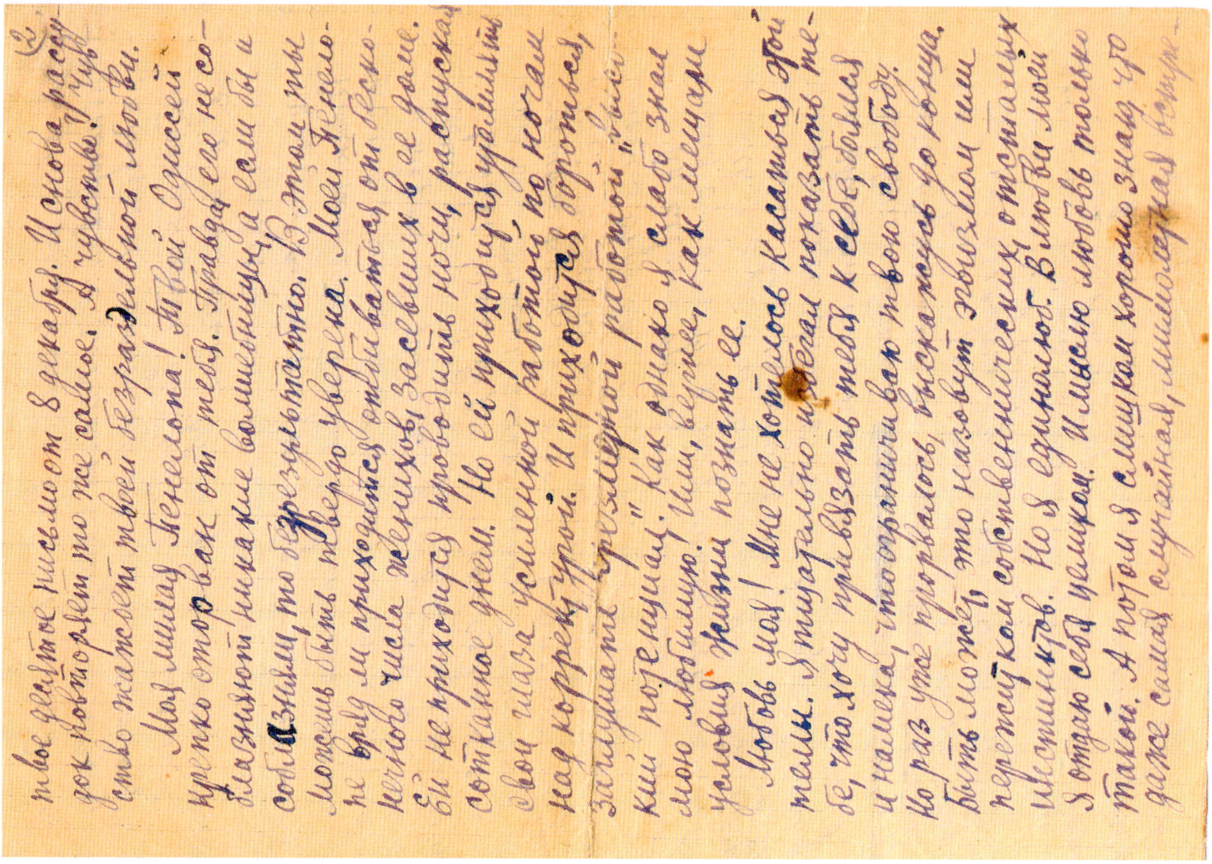

Fig. 1.25 Letter: January 3, 1937 (Letter XVIII, page 5)
Mikhail Rabinovich ("Misha") to Klavdiya Antipina

Fig. 1.26 Letter: January 3, 1937 (Letter XVIII, page 6)
Mikhail Rabinovich ("Misha") to Klavdiya Antipina

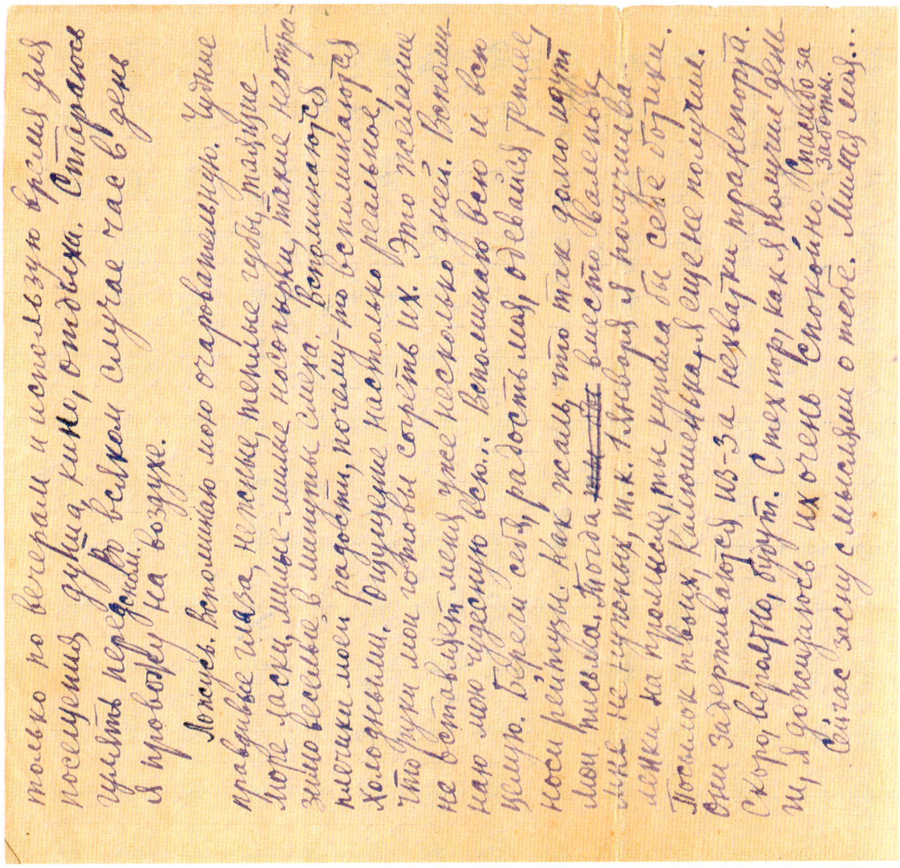

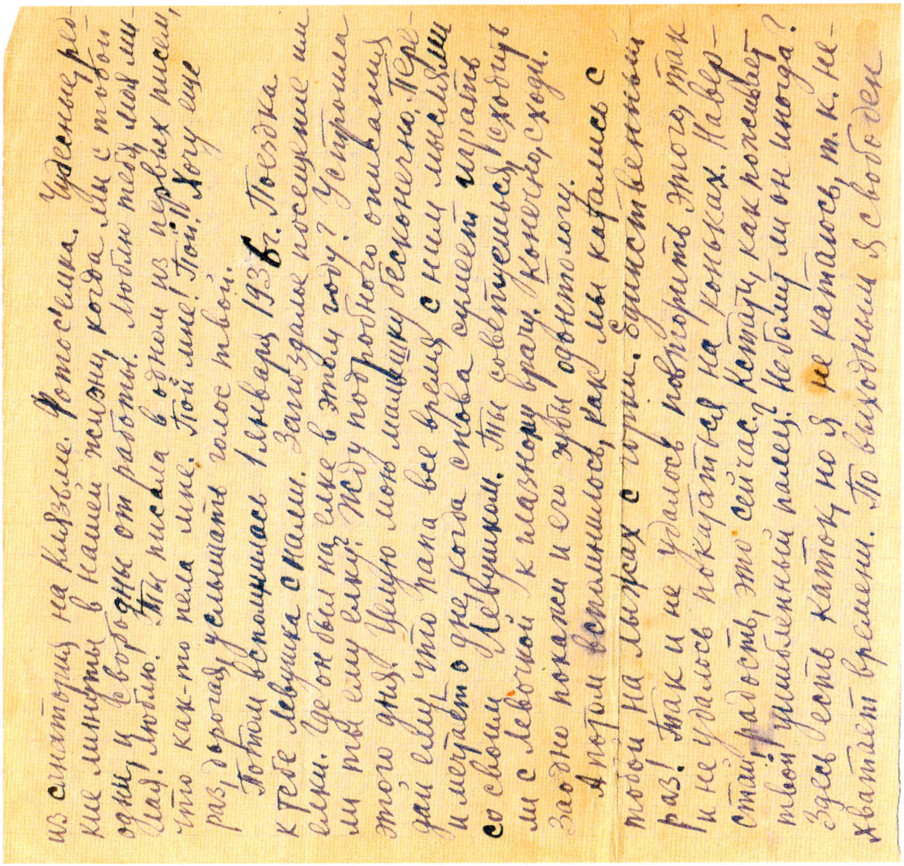

Fig. 1.27 Letter: January 3, 1937 (Letter XVIII, page 7)
Mikhail Rabinovich ("Misha") to Klavdiya Antipina

Fig. 1.28 Letter: January 3, 1937 (Letter XVIII, page 8)
Mikhail Rabinovich ("Misha") to Klavdiya Antipina

KLAVDIYA ANTIPINA

Fig. 1.29

Postcard (Front) Fig. 1.29

Post Office Stamp:
February 23, 1937, 1600 hours, Moscow, Frunze Station

Address (To):
Moscow 69
Khlebnyi per., 19, kv. 3
[19 Bread Lane, Apt. 3]
K. I. Antipina

From:
M. A. Rabinovich
Chibyu, Komi ASSR (1)
Construction Crew, Production Unit 2 (2)

Postcard (Back) Fig 1.30

XXI   January 18, 1937

My dearest!

Last night I received a cable from you. Today I cabled back that I have not yet received the parcels. I expect them to arrive shortly, since after a long delay packages have begun to arrive at the works. (3) On January 14 I received your letter No. 14, dated December 26, and hope to be able to read your letters Nos. 11, 12, and 13 soon. Don't send me any food packages, Kaliushen'ka, until you've received a confirmation from me that the parcels have arrived. I beg you in the future to send me small packages, and at most once a month. In the meantime please send only the items I requested: a steel crown drill bit, which I wrote you about earlier, a slide rule, a cap, envelopes, paper and the other trifles I had asked for. I've been writing you much more frequently in January: on the 1st, 3rd-4th, 7th-8th, 13th-14th. Please confirm receipt. I've recovered. Am feeling good. Am eating better. I'm waiting impatiently for you to have a photo taken of yourself with Levushok and then send me the picture. Countless kisses to you, my own ones. Greetings to all the dear ones.

Misha

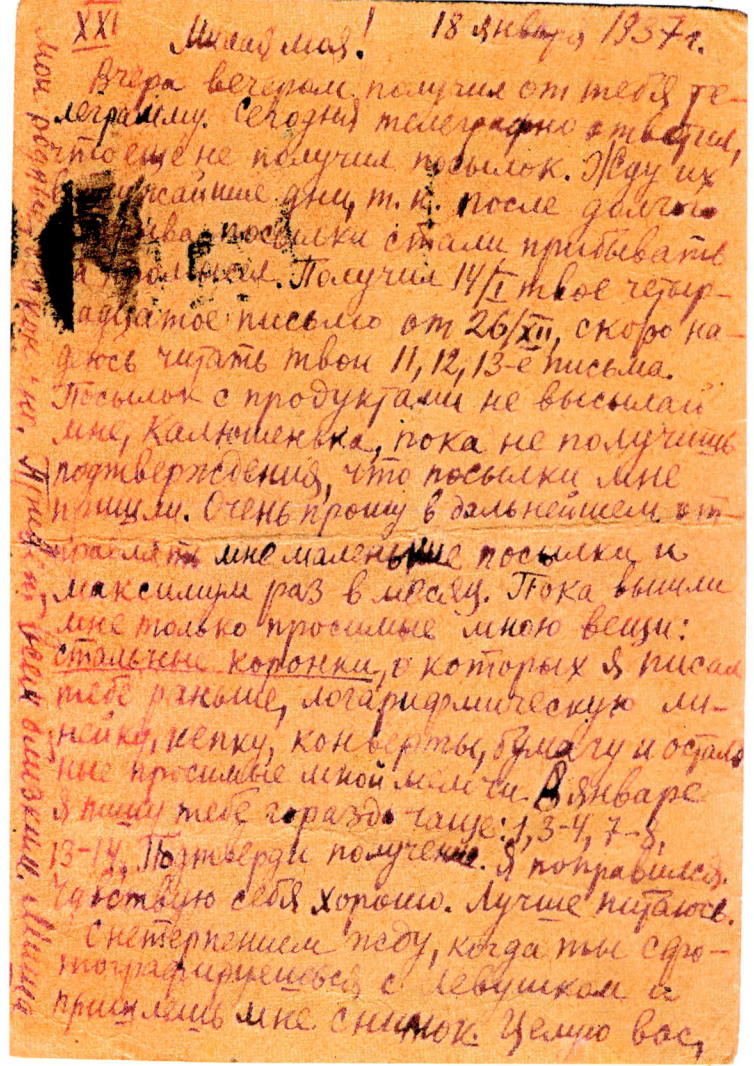

Fig. 1.30

28

Notes to Postcards

1. The settlement of Chibyu was established in August 1929 by the Ukhta Expedition of the OGPU (The Soviet secret police, the forerunner of the NKVD) some 800 miles northeast of Moscow, on the Ukhta and Chibyu Rivers, within the Pechora Basin (a significant oil and natural gas area), in the geographical center of the Komi Republic (then the Komi Autonomous Soviet Socialist Republic). In 1931 Chibyu was granted the status of town; in 1939 it was renamed Ukhta; and in 1943, after it had been linked to the Pechora railway, it became a city. In June 1931 the headquarters of the Ukhta Expedition was transformed into the administration of the Ukhta-Pechora Correctional Labor Camp (Ukhtpechlag) within the GULag system, and in November 1932 the OGPU organized the Ukhta-Pechora Trust (Ukhto-Pecherskii trest OGPU) to supervise all oil and natural gas exploration and production activity in the region. The Trust was authorized to use the prisoners of Ukhtpechlag as a labor force for the projects it sponsored (the camp warden served as the chairman of the trust). For over twenty-five years the administration of the trust and the camp (which was reorganized in May 1938 and again in May 1955) was located in Chibyu/Ukhta. On January 1, 1937, the Ukhtpechlag held 31,035 prisoners. The official 1939 census listed the town of Ukhta as having a population of 3,000 people, and made no mention of the camp's existence. As of January 1, 1998, Ukhta had a population of 131, 400 people and served as one of the main extracting and refining centers for Lukoil, Russia's largest oil company.

2. The Russian term, "stroikolonna" ('construction crew' or 'construction column') refers to the fundamental organizational units—'chain gangs'—in the camps, which suggests that Rabinovich may have been a camp prisoner. If that is the case, the very fact that he was allowed to correspond with his family indicates that he had received a relatively mild sentence. Furthermore, the references he makes later in the postcard to a slide rule and a drilling bit suggest that his position within the camp, and specifically on the construction crew, may have been that of a "specialist," that is, a prisoner who was employed in positions requiring technical knowledge or skill. The "specialists" were sometimes rewarded with additional privileges and often had somewhat more personal freedom than regular prisoners. In the letter of January 3-4, 1937, the reference to going to the skating rink and to the movies may give some idea of the privileges granted to Rabinovich. There is another possibility: that rather than being sentenced and put into a camp he was simply deported or exiled, which meant that he had never been formally charged (deportation was an administrative procedure) and, as such, was free to move about the town in the hours he was not occupied at "the works," i.e., the oil fields. As a deportee, he would be entitled to corresponding with his family. This scenario is somewhat more exceptional: few people were deported (as opposed to receiving a camp sentence) in 1936, and those who were, belonged to well-known class (the "kulaks") or ethnic groups (the Volga Germans). Still, if Rabinovich had been a prominent enough mid-level party functionary, he could have been deported "for error of political judgment"—for instance, in connection with the Zinov'ev-Kamenev Trial of 1936. The other piece of evidence that may support that hypothesis is the "list of martyrs" of the GULag camps in the Komi Republic, published in Syktyvkar in 1998-1999. Rabinovich's name appears nowhere on that extensive list, which may either mean that he was not a camp prisoner or, alternatively, that he was one and died of "natural causes" rather than by being shot. In any case one should be wary of treating any information he provides about his life in Komi as statement of fact; every outgoing piece of mail, whether from a privileged camp prisoner or a deportee, was examined and approved by the NKVD censor, and specific references to the actual state of affairs at "the works" were forbidden.

3. *Cf.* The final paragraph of the January 3-4 letter: "I have not yet received any of your parcels, Kalyushen'ka. They are being held up due to the insufficient means of transportation. Perhaps they will arrive soon. Ever since receiving the money, I have been waiting for them very calmly."

Notes and translation by Boris Wolfson, Berkeley, California

Newspaper Articles
Introduction

Articles about Klavdiya Antipina from three different Bishkek newspapers are reproduced here.

The first article (from Slovo Kyrgyzstana) appeared in 1992 and is the longest. It is based on the reporter's interview of Klavdiya Antipina, who was eighty eight at that time. She spoke rather freely about certain details of her life. (Kyrgyzstan had been independent for nearly a year.) This slightly edited transcript is of a translation by Boris Wolfson.

The second (from Vechernyi Bishkek) and the third (Kyrgyzstan Chronicle, an English language newspaper) appeared in 1994 in celebration of Klavdiya Antipina's 90th birthday. Although the latter is excerpted, the former (translated by Nathan Hodge) is complete.

I.

Slovo Kyrgyzstana, August 1, 1992

An edited transcription of the article translated by Boris Wolfson, Berkeley, California, who also wrote the notes.

The Grandmother (Babushka) of Kyrgyz Ethnography by Ella Taranova

There is something enigmatic about old age; it is so distant, so aloof. It seems that so much has been lost that little remains at the threshold of life. And yet one has a feeling sometimes that old people possess innumerable riches, that they are privy to the kinds of things we will never know anything about.

…She walks, moving her feet with difficulty, as if she were carrying the entire planet on her shoulders. Perhaps the years she has lived through weigh more than the planet. After all, she is Time itself. And there was a time when this stooping old woman did not look old at all.

The Other Life

Kaliya (Klavdiya) Ivanovna Antipina was just a teenage girl when she arrived in Moscow, the "capital of youthful socialism," straight from provincial Morshansk. The Moscow of the 1920s raged and roared. It instilled hope. It demonstrated unlimited possibilities. Kaliya was burning with a desire to grasp the world, to understand herself.

She walked around the city as if in a spell. She stood in front of the Cathedral of Christ the Savior (not yet demolished)—a tiny speck next to such grandeur. It was right there, on Volkhonka Street, that she saw the sign for the Forestry College. ("Lord, what more could I be looking for? You couldn't imagine anything better than that.") She adored nature. Getting in was easy, but staying in was much harder. On all of her papers next to "class origins" stood the unambiguous [word] "gentry." Those who were "workers" or who came from a peasant background did not pay tuition. For her, however, the tuition fee was two hundred rubles. She had to drop out. She found a job at the Exemplary Printing Plant No. 1. The salary was good; she bought a lot of pretty dresses.

She also met her future husband there. Mikhail ("Misha") Rabinovich was from an educated family, a lifelong resident of Moscow. His father was the editor of a major newspaper. Mikhail, the son, began his career as the editor of a university daily. Under her husband's influence, Klavdiya Antipina developed an interest in the human sciences. This time her decision was more deliberate: she enrolled in the Anthropology Institute [of Moscow State University]. She was taught by famous and distinguished ethnographers. Among them was Nikolai Nikolaevich Cheboksarov, an authority on the Dungan (1). He was known by his students simply as Nick Nick. He was the one who, in the future, would see her through a most difficult time. But that time had not yet come. Nothing portended a tragedy.

They lived joyously, vigorously. Her husband's editorial assignments put him in touch with such well-known persons as Radek (2), with Krupskaya (3). Enthusiastically, he related details of these encounters to his wife, Klavdiya Antipina. Their son was now four. He was growing up. When he developed scarlet fever he went into the hospital. While with her son in the hospital, Klavdiya Antipina learned that her husband, Mikhail, had been arrested and taken away. She did not yet know that the year would become an annus horribilis. Nor did she realize that it would be like this, as well, for many other Moscow families. For her, it was to be a crisis year.

The Gypsy Foretold A Long Journey…

Memory has a peculiar tendency to bequeath one an equal share of happy and painful moments. Perhaps it does this so that the people who pack light as they set off on their journey do not curse the weighty baggage that accumulates by the end of the trip, as if it were a useless, unshakable burden.

Time and again the scene at the district attorney's office flashes before Klavdiya Ivanovna's eyes as if on a celluloid screen—a film in which all characters are real. Her passport is taken away. She is led up a wide stairway. She hears the term "deportation" for the first time in her life when an imposing man in uniform mentions it. She simply does not hear other words. He keeps talking about train cars, clothes. She feels so helpless, so depressed, so shaken by what is happening. On her way out she approaches a guard: "I want my papers back." He rolls up his jacket sleeve. His arm is covered in sores. "This is what your papers have cost me." (Apparently, the Great Purge was not easy on the guard, either.)

Vychegda (5). Rare missives from her husband would arrive from there (6). Soon even that came to an end. "He is in distant camps, with no correspondence privileges," she was told (7).

"I am writing with my blood, I write the truth," began the letter to Stalin she started in a rickety, cold train car. She had been given almost no time to pack. She took her son, took what little money they had, took just a few belongings. She grabbed the doll she herself had made for Levushka: A Gypsy—head from a stocking, bright lips, dazzling earrings. But this was a part of that other life. A life with a beautiful beginning. From now on the Gypsy would only come up with sad stories for her son. Still, for a very long time she concealed from him what had happened to his Daddy.

As part of her ethnography field work in Moscow State University, Klavdiya Ivanovna had traveled and had seen the Chuvash and the Udmurt of the Volga region of Russia. Of Central Asia, however, she knew nothing. Deportees arrived in Frunze almost daily. They walked from house to house looking for shelter. The locals pointed at them. "There they go, the enemies of the people!" She did not give up. She believed that her husband's arrest had been a mistake, that it would be looked into. Although an older man she met during her woeful wanderings said to her, "We are all non-entities," she continued to consider herself a [good] Soviet citizen.

A Home Regained

Klavdia and her four-year-old son slept in a barn. Haystacks served as their beds. She would faint from hunger and unexpected extreme heat. She looked for a job that would allow her to feed her son. The first position she took was fairly idiosyncratic. A car would arrive every morning to take her to the house of the local Minister of Communications. She taught him Russian. They would sit down on the floor, and the lesson would begin. For her, too, this was a school of sorts. She liked the Kyrgyz. They were polite, hospitable.

One day she was walking around town and bumped right into Nick Nick, who had arrived in Frunze on a research field trip. "Kalya, my dearest, I swear your days of poverty are over." The very next day she was hired by the Kyrgyz Academy of Sciences. Her first project was the Museum of History. It was dirt poor—or, more precisely, it was in ruins. Bit by bit Klavdia Ivanovna began to put together exhibits and to sort through the textual materials. Olga Maksimilianovna Manuilova, for her part, decorated the entryway with marble statues of male and female workers and a miner. All in all, not bad for a beginning. She registered the museum as her permanent residence. This was her home, her workplace, her spiritual buttress.

Once she was leading a tour of the museum. Among the visitors she noticed a young Orthodox priest.

He not only posed questions but elaborated upon her narrative. She listened to him, surprised. Who was he? Where did he come from? Such a young man, and yet he knows so much about Kirghizia's past—as if he had been born there. She then began to realize what a bottomless pit of information about this part of the world awaited her. Through personal acquaintances and through the collecting of artifacts and documents, she increased her knowledge. While reading, she would fall asleep long after midnight in the high-back armchair at the museum.

In 1952 she joined the first ethnographic expedition conducted in cooperation with several Moscow scholars. This was a much needed Kirghiz-organized reconnaissance mission into the most remote and the least examined regions of the Kirghiz Soviet Socialist Republic. Top-notch archeologists and ethnographers were invited. There she met and became a friend of the renowned ethnographer, Saul Matveevich Ambramzon. Many more of those missions followed, sometimes with colleagues, sometimes alone.

As she crisscrossed the Kirghiz Soviet Socialist Republic, she was a welcome guest—in fact, more than just a guest—in the most distant villages. As for the Kyrgyz language, she never studied it formally. However, she learned it without difficulty, absorbing it along with other elements of Kyrgyz traditional culture and folk art that had long since captivated her. She never advertised her knowledge of the language. (Sometimes this caused embarrassment for those who thought they could talk freely in her presence.) She slept in yurts. She became intimately familiar with every yurt cord, band, structure, and the birchwood dome wheel, the tunduk, that holds the whole construction together and is featured on the current flag of our Republic. And the Kyrgyz designs? Some have said that there were hundreds of them. In fact, they are countless. There are thousands of ways to embroider them on cloth and on felt.

The origins of the cheek-covering component of traditional women's headgear and the breast-covering part of the typical women's dress remain a mystery to this day. Ters kayik, a unique type of embroidery, had been found only here. Although the stitching pattern seemed familiar, the technology of its execution had been lost. With her own hands Klavdiya Antipina reconstructed the stitch. She had not seen that kind of beauty among any other people. The national style—the Kyrgyz pattern—is immortal. It is a whole scholarly field in its own right. It is ludicrous to see it only as an applied object. There is a direct connection to ethnogenesis here: How does an ethnicity come about? With whom has it merged? What direction does it choose for itself?

A Tale About The Master

Southern Kyrgyzia: There is not a family, not a village, where the folk arts would not have been practiced.

Northern Kyrgyzia: There is the same disposition toward creativity. The Kyrgyz have turned their felt design into an exquisite art form and their hands have been accustomed to spinning since childhood.

…[T]here was a […] Master in the region of Chon, respected and admired by all. From where did his craft come? There was no special teacher. There were, however, always people around—different ethnic groups lending and exchanging skills. Sometimes, however, there was self invention.

Manas (8), too, contains a paean to the Master. Kanykei, the protagonist's wife, knew well the secrets of domestic crafts. A long-held dream of Klavdia Antipina has been to put out a small book using Kanykei's texts as a manual for creating a shyrdak (mosaic felt rug) and a chiy (reed screen).

Klavdia Antipina came to admire the Chon Master. She often said that he belongs in a school environment. The idea did not appeal to the bureaucrats. They said, "He is not educated. What kind of teacher would he make?" "But on the inside he is remarkably sophisticated," Klavdiya Ivanovna argued. With every work he produces he creates a present from the bottom of his heart—a quality rare in people these days. Suddenly, now, they've decided to drown him in dollars. But he doesn't need the money. He needs materials, information exchange and, most importantly, a student he can train. The folk master complains that there is no one to follow him, and that the children don't listen. Artistic principles that have been refined over centuries are gradually being obliterated. And the craft is lost. When the exchange of ideas and information is constant, when the craft is an object of everyone's interest, then It flourishes.

Klavdiya Antipina has done what she could: she wrote a book about the Master and his hands, the hands that preserve the historical memory of his people.

The distinction between southern and northern Kyrgyz is specious, she wants to reiterate. Nevertheless here, in this tiny country, Southerners don't know how Northerners work. Meanwhile in the South they know how to put together classical designs and they have mastered the rare craft of ribbon embroidery. But even the large museum in the capital (in the North) has no specimens of that craft in its collections. And, on the other hand, there is no production of the shyrdak in the South. No exhibitions are organized in common. The Afghan and the Chinese Kyrgyz have come to visit; there are many similarities to us in their traditions, in their clothing. Political polarization is disastrous for the arts. But this is already a different topic for conversation—not her topic.

Chapter the Last, the Unfinished…

Klavdiya Ivanovna's narrative is part parable, part anecdote. There lived once in the mountains a tribe—isolated, self-sufficient. From generation to generation they passed on the same congenital disorder: fingers that have grown together. Nothing they did could remedy the hereditary affliction. And things kept falling from their ugly fingers. She laughs coyly: there was, of course, a solution, a simple one at that…

"I'd like to begin corresponding with the American Indians," Klavdvia Ivanovna relates wistfully. "It's amazing, but there are so many similarities between the designs they weave and those of the Kyrgyz masters. It turns out all of us in this world belong to the same race."

Meeting this eighty-eight-year-old woman instills in one faith in the enduring nature of existence—a neglected, forgotten notion these days. She has lost a great deal, but she has also gained a lot. There's her son Lev (Leo), like a little shining star in her past. "Mama, I remember: Nyusha (i. e., 'Mama') is holding me in her arms. You and Dad are skating." "But you couldn't possibly remember that. Even I have forgotten, and you were too young then." "But it did happen that way, right?"

In 1956 (three years after Stalin's death) her son called her from Moscow where he was studying at the time. "You're being summoned to the MGB (9)." She was given a paper that said she and her husband had been innocent. But only this year—1992—thirty six years after receiving that paper and with information now available—her son said to her: "Mama, it turns out Dad was shot back in 1938."

Through all the suffering she has endured she has not lost kindness, magnanimity, generosity. Young people flock to her, she is always surrounded by them. Counting her as a teacher and a life influence are famous artists, acknowledged virtuosos of the applied arts. Asyla Imanalieva, a graduate of Moscow State University, an ethnographer, complements my narrative:

> I can hardly call myself a student of Klavdiya Ivanova in the classical sense of the word. Although our all-too-infrequent meetings (there's never enough time) could be considered lessons, lessons in understanding and respect for one's own people, lessons in believing in oneself, in one's abilities.

When exhaustion, hostility, and pessimism accumulate, I come to her tiny cozy apartment and she, like a kind nanny, begins to tell me beautiful stories from her field notes. Stories about her visits to the Kyrgyz aul (10), about her fearless hiking trips up and down mountain trails. She tells me about the bright, wise faces she encountered, the skillful hands she saw. And, sitting in her armchair, I feel my strength returning, drop by drop, I am once again filled with the greatest admiration for my own people, filled with the desire to do good, meaningful things.

You leave, and again the everyday routine takes over, as rude, as mediocre, as incomprehensibly aggressive as ever. But you yourself harbor not anger but a desire to change something. It may sound paradoxical, but this Russian woman has truly taught me how to love my people. One can love in different ways. One can wave flags around, blame 'the foreigners,' and demand special rights for oneself. Or one can work, calmly and honestly. Klavdia Ivanovna prefers the latter.

It's difficult to measure love. But it seems to me that the love Klavdiya Ivanova feels for the Kyrgyz people—the love reflected in her books, her articles, in her advice and in her lessons, will outweigh the love of those who keep brandishing their slogans in the air. Many people, chuckling, call her works "unscholarly," "descriptive." It's strange for me to hear this from people whose works are full of her drawings, her photographs, from those who drew their "scholarly conclusions" from her "descriptive" books.

She has accumulated incredibly rich field data, and it won't perish in her file cabinet, as so often happens among the ethnographers. All of it is in her books. True, it is descriptive. But that is what "pure ethnography" is all about. What is all of scholarship built on, where do philosophy, history, psychology derive their data? She has saved hundreds of scholars many a field trip "to the aborigines." You can go to the library, get Klavdiya Ivanovna's books and make your scholarly conclusions in ten minutes. It was more difficult to collect and to describe the material objectively, not forcing one's own "scholarship" upon it.

Time passes, and the works of Antipina and of her colleagues become invaluable, the books become bibliographic rarities. Rarities because, unfortunately, there are more and more "scholarly works," and fewer and fewer "descriptive" ones. The day will come when Klavdiya Ivanovna's books will be the only sources of our knowledge about our art. So we should hurry to thank her now, while she's still alive, rather than much later, as has been the case with other non-Kyrgyz scholars who have left our country embittered or have passed away.

...In my hands is an exquisitely published volume, *The Turkish Dress*, given to Klavdia Ivanovna by Kyrgyzstan's new friends (The Turkish Government). We leaf through the glossy pages. What a terrible pity that for several years now Antipina's own attempts to publish a book about *The Kyrgyz National Costume* have led to nothing. The richness of *that* material, after all, may surprise even the Turks.

Notes

1. Dungan is the Russian name for the Hui (also spelled Hwei or Hui-hui), Chinese Muslims a large concentration of whom exists in the Talas oblasty (province) of Kyrgyzstan.
2. Karl Bernhardovich Radek (1885-1939?) was a leader of the Third (Communist) International in the 1920s and a member of the editorial board of Izvestiya, the official newspaper of the Soviet government, in the 1930s. Arrested in 1936, he was one of the defendants at the second major show trial of the Great Purge in 1937 and is believed to have died in prison or in a concentration camp.
3. Nadezhda Konstantinovna Krupskaya (1869-1939), the wife/widow of Lenin, had disagreed with Stalin in the 1920s, but remained formally aloof from intraparty struggles and high politics throughout the 1930s, devoting most of her time to her writings on public education.
4. Rabinovich's letters indicate unambiguously that he was already in the camps in January 1937. These events must have taken place in 1936.
5. Vychegda is a river in northwestern Russia, a tributary of the Northern Dvina, that crosses the Komi republic and the Arkhangelsk oblast' (The Archangel province).
6. The return address and the postmark on Rabinovich's postcard clearly indicate that he was writing from Chibyu/Ukhta. The site of Rabinovich's camp (the Ukhtpechlag) is some 150 km away from the Vychegda. It is possible that he was taken from the Ukhta to the Vychegda to work on some sort of construction or mining project, and wrote Antipina about it, which is why she believes that he was writing to her "from" Vychegda. Or this could be the journalist's mistake.
7. "Ten years of incarceration with no correspondence privileges" was one of the more severe punishments specified by the Soviet Criminal Code. Beginning in 1935, when the number of arrests and executions skyrocketed, the expression became the standard euphemism for capital punishment (death by firing squad) employed by the criminal justice authorities in official communication with the victims' families.
8. Manas is the heroic epic of the Kyrgyz people.
9. MGB is the Russian abbreviation for the Ministry of State Security (Ministerstvo Gosudarstvennoi Bezopasnosti), one of the many names of the Soviet secret police. The MGB had been dissolved in March 1953. In 1956, the secret police agency was known as the KGB, the Committee on State Security (Komitet Gosudarstvennoi Bezopasnosti), the name that it kept until the collapse of the Soviet Union.
10. A village.

II.

Vechernyi Bishkek, Wednesday 11 May 1994

Translation by Nathan Hodge

A Person Among People: Klavdiya Ivanovna in her 91st Spring

By C. Svetlakov *(with a photo by the author)*

I want to introduce you to this dear woman—Klavdiya Ivanovna Antipina, although I am quite certain that many already know her. Many readers of Vechernyi are her former students from the history faculty in the department where Klavdiya Ivanovna worked as an instructor, as well as those who have read her works on the history and culture of the Kyrgyz people. A candidate in the historical sciences, she dedicated her life to the study of ethnography at The Academy of Sciences.

Her fate was similar to the fate of many women whose husbands were "repressed." In the 1930's, she found herself in Kirghizia, exiled from Moscow, and had to begin her life over again from the beginning, as difficult as that was with the mark of "an enemy of the people." But her will, goodness and hard work aided her. She was not hard-hearted, but quite the opposite. Whenever she encountered someone whose lot was more difficult, she took on their pain as her own. A beautiful life!

Not long ago Klavdiya Ivanovna marked her 90th year. And she is full of energy and optimism. We wish the best of health for the many years still to come!

III.

Kyrgyzstan Chronicle, 24 May 1994

(An English language newspaper published in Bishkek, Kyrgyzstan. The following is an edited excerpt from the article.)

Your Majesty Suit

By E. Luzonova

"…the scientist, Klavdiya Antipina, is celebrating her 90th anniversary these days and the editorial staff of the Kyrgyzstan Chronicle congratulates her sincerely. Klavdiya Ivanovna Antipina devoted forty years of her life to the investigation of the Kyrgyz costume…

"She went through the whole republic…picking up unique information about fabric, styles, accessories, hats, shoes and all kinds of information about women's, men's and children's dress. It was material for the first album of Kyrgyz National Dress in Central Asia. This was to have been published in the Kyrgyz in the Russian and in the English languages by "Adabiat" Publishing House. Among the 244 illustrations there would have been archival photographs, color pictures and drawings by our artist, Temirbek Musakeev. Also, there were to have been commentaries by Professors K. Antipina and A. Kochkunov. Unfortunately, this valuable professionally-made work exists only as a model. The publishing house does not have enough money for printing this large work…

"The Editor in Chief, B. Alagushev, said, '…We'll be glad to cooperate with our possible partners on the available terms. I'm sure these materials are of great value to history and science and will be of interest to museums, theaters, modern dress designers and, even, to the children's goods industry.'"

Stalin

Isaac Deutscher, a biographer of Stalin, wrote the *Encyclopedia Britannica* article *Stalin, Joseph Vissarionovich (Dzhugashvili) (1879-1953)* (1). The following excerpts from that article tell of Stalin's rise to power and something of his ruthlessness:

The People's Commissar

... In April, 1922, after the 11th Party Congress, the last congress attended by Lenin, Stalin was appointed secretary-general of the party and relinquished his posts in the Council of People's Commissars. This was a turning point in his career: as secretary-general he soon came to control the whole machinery of the party and through it the government.

The Succession to Lenin

... In 1923 Stalin, Zinoviev, and L. B. Kamenev formed a triumvirate with the purpose of debarring from power Trotski, who was generally regarded as Lenin's successor. In his last will Lenin advised his followers to remove Stalin from the general secretariat of the [Communist] party on the ground that Stalin was rude and inclined to abuse power. But Stalin, supported by Zinoviev and Kamenev, retained his office. In constant struggle against his opponents he abolished whatever freedom of expression still existed within the party and transformed the party into a "monolithic" body. In the autumn of 1924 he expounded the theory of "socialism in one country", proclaiming the self-sufficiency of the Russian Revolution. This doctrinal innovation marked a departure from Leninist internationalism, although Stalin did his utmost to present his views as orthodox Leninism. ...

Industrialization and Collectivization

... Throughout the Stalin era the USSR's urban population grew by about 45,000,000. In order to free labor for industry and to secure food for the swelling urban population, Stalin collectivized farming. In 1929 there were about 25,000,000 primitive rural small-holdings in the USSR. In 1952 there were 100,000 large and highly mechanized collective farms. The peasantry at first bitterly resisted collectivization. Stalin broke its resistance and ordered the deportation of many kulaks into the notorious labor camps. Despite initial failures and famines, the new system of farming achieved a degree of consolidation in later years that enabled it to survive the shocks of World War II and its aftermath; but it did not attain a high productivity.

The Great Purges

At the height of the industrial drive shortly after he had introduced the quasi-liberal constitution of 1936, Stalin staged the great purge trials in which most of the old Bolsheviks and some military leaders were charged with treason, terrorism, and espionage and brought to "confess" guilt. In this way Stalin exterminated the men who might have been able to overthrow him and form an alternative government during a national crisis. The purges, carried out on a mass scale, imparted to the Stalinist regime its peculiar terroristic character.

In 1997 a free-lance foreign correspondent, Charles Digges, reported the recent finding of a mass grave containing the remains of over nine thousand bodies in a forest north of Saint Petersburg (2). He reported that this "haunting discovery" constitutes what historians have said is one of the largest mass execution and gravesites ever uncovered in European Russia.

He quoted Vyacheslav Kashtanov, the deputy mayor of Medvezhyegorsk, a town of 20,000 near the mass grave, as having said, "There are people in this town who have been looking all their lives for the bones that lie out there in that forest… [With the compilation of the names of the victims] we have the beginnings of their biographies, and relatives are coming forward. They still have fading photos, memories of those they lost."

Digges reported further that the "shattered skulls and twisted skeletons" in those trenches covering two and a half acres of isolated forest, had belonged to 9,111 political prisoners executed by the NKVD, Stalin's secret police. (The NKVD was the precursor of the KGB.) Stalin had signed NKVD order No. 00447 on August 5, 1937, mandating that all prison camps across the Soviet Union should be emptied. He, thus, set in motion a chain of events that led to this and other mass executions. Digges reported that Dmitry [sic] Volkogonov, an authority on Stalin's purges, has estimated that nearly fourteen million persons across The Soviet Union died in those two-years.

The KGB archives were opened in the late 1980s and early 1990s, however, by Soviet leader Mikhail Gorbachev. Subsequently, across the former Soviet Union there were discovered thousands of mass graves from Stalin's time.

Charles Digges quotes Venyamin Yofe of the historical society, MEMORIAL, as having said of those identified in the mass graves that they had been "the victims of The Bolshoi Terror (The Great Terror) of the Stalinist purges", which had been at their height in 1937 and 1938. "Lawyers, school teachers, scholars, professors, ethnic minorities, religious leaders, university students, even simple workers—anyone who had any standing in society or the ability to say the slightest thing to challenge the order—those are the ones in these trenches… This is what our society lost."

Princeton University Professor Stephen Kotkin, in a 1989 essay, wrote about Magnitogorsk (3), a steel manufacturing city that he knew well. (Magnitogorsk is situated at a distance of more than eight hundred miles from Moscow):

"... The terror of 1937-38 hit Magnitogorsk like a cyclone: midnight arrests, torture, hysterical informing, venomous secret and public denunciations, suicides, disappearances without trace, executions. Such things occurred both before and after 1937-38, but the scale of what happened in those years distinguishes them in the popular imagination. Virtually no one in a position of responsibility escaped arrest, although some were later released. Most of the city's leading cultural figures were deported. Every top-level party figure or factory executive who had ever worked in the city, with one exception, was shot or had already committed suicide. The police themselves, those who faithfully followed orders and zealously carried out the terror, were eventually arrested and shot. Few, if anyone, understood what was going on. The episode remains largely mysterious to this day. ..."

(By permission of the author.)

University of Washington Professor Daniel Chirot has written (4):

"In 1935, Stalin began a campaign of killing his loyal supporters and huge numbers of his own people who had nothing at all to do with politics, who had never been singled out by communist theoreticians as dangerous, and he continued even though he was securely ensconced in a position of absolute power. No attempt to explain this has been entirely successful, and no matter how many documents are uncovered from that period, there will be always be questions about why it happened."

"... once a tyrant is in power, whatever his original motivation, the tendency toward increasing isolation from reality, growing impatience and frustration at the reverses he inevitably suffers, and mounting intolerance of criticism, tend to make him suspicious of all those around him. We see this in the career of every tyrant, and in fact, of every individual who is in power for too long."

"...There must have been many who protested, but not enough to stop it, so that those who showed insufficient enthusiasm were packed off to camps and prisons. Denunciation and fear spread, to the point that local initiatives could often sweep victims up without having any direct orders from the top. And in this climate of growing fear and paranoia, officials from the center would visit outlying parts of the Union and order purges, not only to show the boss, Stalin, that they were loyal, but to secure themselves against potential rivals."

"...as the purges proceeded, those local officials who had failed to take the initiative and start to purge their own districts risked falling when the central authorities examined their actions."

(By permission of the author.)

Thus, two thousand miles from the Kremlin, citizens of the Khirghiz Soviet Socialist Republic also experienced Stalin's unspeakable ruthlessness. A once secret mass grave outside Bishkek, is now the site of a major Kyrgyz national memorial—Ata Beyit. Despite such present-day openness, many still are reluctant to speak of those times.

Notes

1. Isaac Deutscher: Stalin, Joseph Vissarionovich (1879-1953), Encyclopedia Britannica Volume 21, Encyclopedia Britannica, Inc., William Benton Publisher, 1968. (Pages 105 and 106).

2. Charles Digges: Mass Grave of Stalin Victims Found in Russia, San Francisco Chronicle, 17 July 1997, San Francisco, California. (Page one.)

3. Stephen Kotkin: Steeltown, USSR: Glasnost, Destalinization, and Perestroika in the Provinces. The Center for Slavic and East European Studies, University of California at Berkeley, Berkeley, California, the Regents of the University of California, 1989. (Pages 44 and 45.)

4. Daniel Chirot: Modern Tyrants, The Power and Prevalence of Evil in Our Age, Princeton University Press, Princeton 1994. (Pages 144 and 152.)

Cathedral of Christ the Savior

Fig. 1.31 The Cathedral of Christ the Savior. Moscow, 19th Century.
Downloaded from: http://www.cmp.ucr.edu/exhibitions/moscow/Cathedral/The_Cathedral_1.html

After the defeat of Napoleon's French armies in 1812, Tsar Alexander I ordered architects to design a new cathedral in Moscow—The Cathedral of Christ The Savior—to commemorate the great victory of the Russian people and their gratitude to God for the salvation of Moscow and Russia.

However, for a variety of reasons the actual construction of the cathedral was delayed to 1839, the reign of Tsar Nicholas I. By 1858 the exterior was completed, the scaffolding dismantled. The enormous building stood for all to see. It was bigger by far than anything else in Moscow. Its height was 330 feet and its area 73,500 square feet. Thirty-six columns supported its cornice. Five domes surmounted the church; the great central dome measured a full hundred feet in diameter. Finally, in 1883, in the reign of Tsar Alexander III, decoration and finishing touches now done, The Cathedral of Christ The Savior was complete (Fig. 1.31) and the building was dedicated. The size of the place and the wealth of the interior—the icons, the frescoes, the gold, all illuminated by the light of three thousand candles—was impressive.

After the Communist revolution of 1917, the new regime, which viewed traditional religion as "the opiate of the masses" and which "…recognized that religion was their main ideological competitor…" (1), saw The Cathedral Of Christ The Savior as a "breeding ground for addiction to the narcotic" of religion. Perhaps more than any other structure, it was a distasteful symbol of the imperial power of the despised Tsars and of the Church. There it was, just upstream from the Kremlin, a constant visual reminder.

On 5 December 1931, Moscow was rocked by powerful detonations. Then silence. A heavy cloud of dust hung above the city and a smoking pile of rubble lay where the cathedral had once stood (Figures 1.32, 1.33 and 1.34).

Joseph Stalin had ordered this demolition. He also had ordered that a film of this destruction be made exclusively for his personal viewing. Film-maker Vladislav Mikosha, who had been forced to do this documentation, returned to his home badly shaken and "forever after sought assignments that would take him far from Moscow." (2)

In the cathedral's place, Stalin had planned to glorify communism by building a giant Palace of The Soviets. It was to be taller than any other man-made structure in existence at the time—taller than the Empire State Building in New York City. It would be 1300 feet high, topped by a 300-foot statue of Lenin. Visible for many miles, it would be a building of pride, communist pride (Fig. 1.35).

Construction began, but engineers soon discovered that the soil would never support foundations for such a giant mass of stone. Plans were quietly dropped and in 1959, in its place, construction began on a heated, open-air swimming pool, the world's largest (Fig. 1.36).

In 1994, however, just three years after dissolution of the Soviet Union, this pool was closed and replacement of the mammoth church—The Cathedral Of Christ The Savior—was begun. Six years later—in August 2000—the re-built cathedral was consecrated. (Fig.1.37). Once again, it towers on the Moscow skyline.

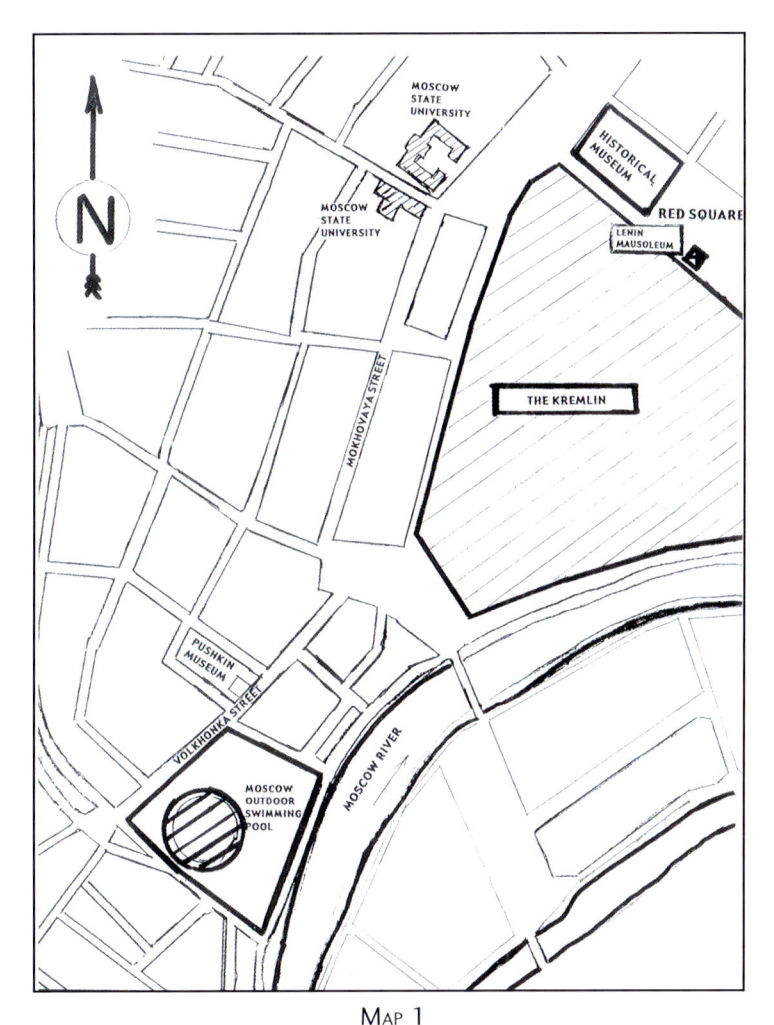

MAP 1
Map of Central Moscow, 1980s
The Moscow Outdoor Swimming Pool is on the site of the Cathedral of Christ the Savior. *(Note: Location of Volkhonka and Mokhovaya Streets and of Moscow State University.)*

Notes

1. Daniel Chirot: Modern Tyrants: The Power and Prevalence of Evil in Our Age. Princeton University Press 1994, page 58.
2. Leah Bendavid-Val: Propaganda & Dreams: Photographing the 1930s in the USSR and the US, Leah Bendavid-Val, Washington DC, and Stemmle publishers Gmbh/Edition Stemmle, Thalwil/Zurich and New York 1999.

Fig. 1.32 Demolition of the Cathedral of Christ the Savior. Moscow 1931. (Still from film by Vladislav Mikosha. From *Propaganda & Dreams, Photographing the 1930s in the USSR and the US* by Leah Bendavid-Cal, Edition Stemmle, Zurich & New York 1999. Used by permission.)

Fig. 1.33 Demolition of the Cathedral of Christ the Savior. Moscow 1931. (Still from film by Vladislav Mikosha. From *Propaganda & Dreams, Photographing the 1930s in the USSR and the US* by Leah Bendavid-Cal, Edition Stemmle, Zurich & New York 1999. Used by permission.)

Fig. 1.34 Site of the demolished Cathedral of Christ the Savior. Official rally in 1932. The slogan is interpreted as "In place of the breeding ground of the narcotic [of religion], The Palace of Soviets!"
Downloaded from http://cweb.middlebury.edu/bulgakov/aram.html

Fig. 1.35 The Palace of Soviets. Artist's conception of the unbuilt structure. *Downloaded from http://cweb.middlebury.edu/bulgakov/xram.html*

Fig. 1.36 The Moscow Swimming Pool built in 1958 on the site of the demolished Cathedral of Christ the Savior. (From V. Berezin, et.al.: *Moscow Metro Photoguide*, Planeta Publisher, Moscow 1986.)

Fig. 1.37 The re-built Cathedral of Christ the Savior, consecrated in August 2000. *Downloaded from http://www.duran-audio.com/DDC_Projects/ChristSaviorMoscow.htm*

Ata Beyit & Chinghiz Aitmatov

Ata Beyit

An archway over a staircase descending to a plaza, a granite monument on which are inscribed over a hundred names, a large sculpture, a museum—these are elements of a major national memorial to the victims once secretly buried here on a gentle grassy hillside southeast of Bishkek. This is where a mass grave in which the bodies of executed Kyrgyz intelligentsia—the society's leaders—were discovered. The site, snow-covered in winter, is on the Chong Tash Ski Resort.

In the 1994 guide book, Bishkek Handbook, Inside and Out (1), Daniel Prior, under the heading Chong Tash (Ata Beyit), states the following:

" … In 1991 television viewers in Kirghizstan witnessed the sensational excavation of a secret mass grave in the foothills south of Bishkek. On the grounds of the Chong Tash ski resort, in a small underground brick kiln, victims of Stalinist repression were found heaped together in a solid mass of human remains only 40 cm below the ground surface. The approximately 4 x 4 x 4 m chamber yielded 137 (by some counts, 138) skeletons. [They] had clothing, identity papers, and personal effects, such as toothbrushes. The backs of all the skulls were perforated with bullet holes."

"Chong Tash [Ata Beyit] is believed to be the resting place of the entire Supreme Soviet Central Committee of 1938. The kiln also…contained the bodies of the renowned linguist Kasym Tynystanov (his portrait is now on the 10 som note) and Torekul Aitmatov, the father of the author Chinghiz Aitmatov. …"

" … in 1991 an elderly woman from a nearby village came to the police with a story she had kept to herself for many years and only dared to tell after the communist regime was no more. Her father had been the caretaker of the property in 1938 and was the only unofficial witness of the mass murder and burial. The KGB swore him to secrecy, but on his deathbed he entrusted the burden to his daughter in the hope that the story could one day be told. …"

(Daniel Prior: Bishkek Handbook, Inside and Out, Literary Kyrgyzstan, Bishkek, 1994, page 130. Used with the permission of the author.)

Recently, when the authors visited Ata Beyit, there in the museum was a photograph made at the time of the re-burial of the victims. This photograph shows the distinguished writer Chinghiz Aitmatov with Askar Akiev, President of The Kyrgyz Republic, lifting a box containing the remains of Torekul Aitmatov, the writer's father. Chinghiz Aitmatov is quoted as having said on that occasion, "Father, I looked for you for 53 years. Now I have found you…"

Also, there in the museum is a photograph of Joseph Stalin, looking rather pleased. Below it is a second photograph, this of a skull and some bones. Round holes—bullet holes—perforate the back of the skull.

When the authors had first visited Ata Beyit, things had been simple. There had been steps up to a walkway surrounding the open-air, brick-lined pit.

However, five years later (2001) when we visited Ata Beyit, things had changed. A protective building with a glass barrier had been constructed over the pit. And a museum building, a monument, a plaza, a sculpture, a descending stairway—all were now in place.

Chinghiz Aitmatov

Following are excerpts from the book *Time To Speak* by Chinghiz Atimatov. This book is a collection of writings, speeches and at least one interview. In it, Chinghiz Aitmatov in *Notes About Myself* wrote this short cryptic paragraph in 1972:

> " ... In 1937 my father, a Party worker, who at that time attended the Red Professorship Institute in Moscow, was purged. Our family moved to the village. That is when the real school of life, with all its complexities, began for me. ..."

(Note: Chinghiz Aitmatov, who was born in December 1928, would have been nine years old in December of 1937.)

In 1987 during perestroika and fifteen years after writing that, there was this exchange during an interview with the reporter Felix Medvedev:

A: "... A person poisoned with hatred, envy and malice becomes a slave of the night, not the creator of light.

M: Is it true that your father, Torekul Aitmatov, and his brothers, village activists Ryskylbak and Alemkul, were subject of repressions in 1937? I learned about this only recently.

A: Yes, it is true. This happened half a century ago but the memory still rankles. I never mention this in public; this is in fact the first time I have spoken of it. I do not want it to be misinterpreted by some people. But even if it had not happened, I would have opposed the personality cult with all my might. Even today many people fail to understand what immense damage it inflicted on Soviet society. The personality cult dealt an irreparable and disfiguring blow to the image of socialism. We were caught for much too long in the trap of the authoritarian regime established by Stalin and it is only now, almost thirty-five years after he died, that we have begun to free ourselves. This is not a simple task, for there are still many adherents of the past. They do not wish to see anything and do not seek change. If we succeed in putting an end once and for all to this legacy of the past, that will be a great achievement of perestroika, politically and spiritually."

Chinghiz Aitmatov: *Time To Speak*, International Publishers, New York 1989. (Pages 6 and 184.)

Klavdiya Antipina

Part 2: Interviews

Introduction to Part Two

Edited transcriptions of recorded interviews form the basis of Part II of this book.

Fourteen persons acquainted with Klavdiya Antipina have been interviewed, most of them in Bishkek in June 1997. Bibira Akmoldoeva arranged for these interviews and was the interpreter. Two interviews occurred in the Washington DC area.

Klavdiya Antipina's friends sometimes referred to her as "Klavdivana", using a shortened form of her name, informal and convenient. Some of the interviews, as transcribed, are the usual "give and take", some are conversational, some are almost "streams of consciousness", and some are nearly monologues.

Among those interviewed are academic colleagues, an ambassador, artists, neighbors, students, and friends. For some, Klavdiya Antipina was a confident, a counselor, an adviser, a teacher. And, for some, she was a mother, even a grandmother. They believed Klavdiya Antipina had been an exceptional person, who was wise, friendly, optimistic, approachable, knowledgeable, precise, and very private. Klavdiya Antipina was respected by all, and, for many, she was the inspiration of a lifetime.

The euphemism "difficulties" was used by many persons interviewed when referring to Klavdiya Antipina's exile from Moscow, during Stalinist times, arriving in Frunze (Bishkek) with a small son, as an "enemy of the people." One senses a lingering reluctance to speak openly about those matters, even a decade after Glasnost, Peristroika, collapse of the Soviet Union, and independence of The Kyrgyz Republic. (Apparently, this is an ingrained habit from earlier years when, for one's own personal safety, one did not speak of such things—even privately or in confidence.) Repeatedly, persons expressed "amazement" that, despite the "difficulties" in her life, Klavdiya Antipina could be the person she was and accomplish what she did.

Without exception, persons interviewed gave explicit permission for the use of these recorded statements as well as any photographs in publications or elsewhere. In the process of editing the transcripts, some have been reduced, rearranged, and rephrased. Sometimes the comments of a person interviewed more than once are combined into a unified transcription. In one case the "interview" is translated from a prepared written statement. It is our hope that the inevitable shifts in meaning and shades of meaning—which result from interpreting, transcribing, and editing—have not been so great as to affect the validity of the original statements. Any errors of interpreting, transcribing, and editing rest solidly with us.

—Bibira Akmoldoeva and John Sommer

Persons interviewed:

Kushbek Usenbaev (deceased)
Professor of History.
Academic colleague. Friend.
Interviewed in his office in The Academy of Sciences, Bishkek.

Bibina Omurzakovna Orusbayeva
Professor of Philology.
Academic colleague. Friend.
Interviewed in her office in The Academy of Sciences, Bishkek.

Svetlana Dunovskaya
Retired mathematics teacher of architects and structural engineers.
Friend.
Interviewed in her apartment, Bishkek.

Roza Otunbayeva
Ambassador of The Kyrgyz Republic to The United Kingdom.
Friend.
Interviewed in Washington D.C. and in The Embassy of The Kyrgyz Republic, London.

Dinara Chochunbaeva
Director, The Kyrgyz Style.
Former Director of The National Center of Aesthetic Education for Children.
Artist. Colleague. Friend. Student.
Interviewed in her office, Bishkek.

Toktosunova Gulchahra
Art Museum Administrator
Former teacher in The Academy of Art and in The Academy of Sciences.
Artist. Friend. Student.
Interviewed in her apartment and in her office, Bishkek.

Akylai Sharshenalieva
Chief Curator, The Kyrgyz Historical Museum
Colleague. Friend. Student.
Interviewed in her office, Bishkek.

PART TWO — INTERVIEWS

Rysbubu Abdieva
Director, "Babushka Adoption"
Former Director, The Kyrgyz Film Studio
Friend.
Interviewed in her office, Bishkek.

Stella Mateeva
Former Researcher, The Kyrgyz Historical Museum.
Friend.
Interview is a written statement. Visited in her apartment, Bishkek.

Kalipa Asanakunova
Artist. Friend. Student.
Interviewed in her apartment, Bishkek.

Bolotbek Karakeev
Artist.
Interviewed in his apartment-studio, Bishkek.

Temirbek Musakeev
Artist.
Interviewed in his studio, Bishkek.

Kathleen Kuehnast
American Cultural Anthropologist.
Friend. Student.
Research Associate, Institute of European, Russian, and Eurasian Studies at The George Washington University, Washington DC.
Member, The Advisory Council of The Kennan Institute for Advanced Russian Studies at The Woodrow Wilson Center for Scholars, Washington DC.
Interviewed in her home, Alexandria, Virginia.

Bibira Akmoldoeva
Country Program Manager (The Kyrgyz Republic), Humanitarian Assistance Program of Counterpart International, Inc.
Former Professor of Ethnography, Kyrgyz State University.
Former Head of The Humanities Department, Kyrgyz State University.
Colleague. Friend.
Interviewed in her apartment, Bishkek.
Co-author of this book.

Photograph by John Sommer

Fig. 2.1 Professor Kushbek Usenbaev (deceased)
Bishkek, June 1997

PART TWO   INTERVIEWS

Interview with
Kushbek Usenbaev (deceased)

Academician, Professor of History, Colleague, Friend
Interviewed in his office in The Academy of Sciences, Bishkek, Kyrgyzstan
June 18, 1997

Professor Kushbek Usenbaev, along with Klavdiya Antipina, Abramson, and Galitsky, had founded the Kyrgyz Historical Museum in Bishkek.

JS: Please tell of your acquaintance with Klavdiya Antipina.

KU: I have known Klavdiya Antipina since 1947. I began post graduate courses at The Academy of Sciences and she had been working there already. (It was about 1945 when she began to work at The Academy of Sciences in Bishkek.) I have known her at least since 1947.

She was kind, modest and sincere. She was a good looking woman and people were attracted to her. She was ready to help when people needed help. She readily sympathized. She was responsive to perceived need, even without being asked.

She had a love affair with the Material Culture of the Kyrgyz people. She was a devoted friend of people and was enthusiastic about her work. The Kyrgyz people had one other person like Klavdiya Antipina. That was Abramson, who also had a love affair with the Material Culture of the Kyrgyz people. Abramson was called a "Kyrgyz Nationalist" and was severely criticized.

Abramson was a founder of The Kyrgyz Museum of History. In 1927, he began his efforts. He knew Klavdiya Antipina, who had her own unique approach to the Material Culture of the Kyrgyz. She was really dedicated to the investigation of Material Culture. Abramson lived in Leningrad, but Klavdiya Antipina lived here among the Kyrgyz. She devoted herself to the national Kyrgyz culture, including rugs and reed screens (*chiy*).

Klavdiya Antipina was the greatest optimist I have ever known. She always smiled. She was such a nice person and it was pleasant to talk with her. She was sociable and communicative. Usually she could support people when they were in a bad mood.

Her own life was hard. Her husband had been arrested and taken away, and she herself had been exiled, experiences that affected her entire life. She had no reason to be happy. She was a political immigrant and it was difficult for her to establish herself. In her life she really didn't have any choice. Still, like a judge, she was basically objective and distant from these things. The Kyrgyz people really loved her and I think she responded to this love and acceptance by the people. She dedicated herself to her beloved

Kyrgyz people for whom she had a sincere respect. She wanted to do something important for these people.

One thing I want to say: I had never known Klavdiya Antipina to be pessimistic. On the contrary I'd seen her being optimistic and excited, enthusiastic. Not something artificial, but genuine.

Once, however, she came to me absolutely crying. [Professor Usenbaev had been Director of The History Museum at the time.] Down, down. And I was seriously concerned about her emotional state. I asked who had offended her—if not a secret—and she told me what was bothering her.

She had brought a reed screen (*chiy*) from Aktallar, where the best *çig* grows. The moths were eating it. She cried and cried and didn't stop. I told her there was money for a new one, that we could ask the woman to make another one, that we would buy it. We went to see the *çig*. The moths had eaten only some of it, not everything. (I don't know what ultimately happened to this *çig*.) But I told her, "I can't stand this—please stop crying." This episode gave me insight into her feelings about her work.

Klavdiya Antipina was a special friend of Bibina Orusbayeva. They were about the same age. Professor Orusbayeva was responsible for The Kyrgyz Encyclopedia and assisted Klavdiya Antipina in writing the article on traditional material culture for it. All the authors—including Klavdiya Antipina—were honored with The State Laureate Prize for that undertaking. I think it was Bibina who nominated Klavdiya Antipina for the Presidential price—and stipend—which she also received. She received several other prizes as well. When Kyrgyz costumes were made—as for the National Theater—Klavdiya Antipina was the person consulted.

Klavdiya Antipina would give money—to her neighbors, for example—and wouldn't get it back. The same with books. I heard that many people borrowed her books which are now lost. Scholars trust people. Klavdiya Antipina was a scholar. She was too open. A scholar, not a housekeeper. She was not concerned about the things she had at home.

We were really friends. We would invite her to our home and she would invite us to her place. Once, most of her guests were Kyrgyz and the meal was Kyrgyz food. Another historian, Jamgerchinov, Vice-President of The Academy of Sciences, was invited. We went together. When we arrived, we saw only Kyrgyz people and a table full of Kyrgyz food. And I just thought, we the Kyrgyz, don't think to make *kattama* (baklavah without honey and nuts), but Klavdiya Antipina did. That's why she didn't want to move to Moscow.

As for me, my way to science was complex. I entered the postgraduate courses in 1947 in The Institute of History in the Academy of Science and began my research in the history of the Kyrgyz Republic. (After finishing, I began my research in Kyrgyz History [prior to the October Revolution].) I was present with Abramson and also I was a friend of Bernstam. I knew these two people. They were dedicated to the themes of history, especially to the history of the Kyrgyz people, their traditions and costume. They did a lot for the history of Kyrgyzstan. We had much in common. We were all devoted to our profession.

We were all spied on during the totalitarian regime in our country. But I don't have any resentment of Soviet power. I would say that that period gave a lot to my country and to my people. After investigating events of 1916—especially the Kyrgyz uprising—I would say that the Soviet Power and The October Revolution helped Kyrgyz people and if it hadn't happened, the Kyrgyz people would have perished and disappeared.

History has its own peculiarities. My comments are based on facts. As a result of the uprising of 1916, the Kyrgyz population was reduced by 41%, that is, 41% of the Kyrgyz people died or were killed. In 1916, the Czar had ordered all men to the front. The remainder of the Kyrgyz people (60%) were to die off. There had been a decree by order of Czar Nicholas II to establish a Kyrgyz region only in Naryn, a non-agricultural area. By the Czar's order, all remaining Kyrgyz people were to move to Naryn where, knowing only agriculture, they would die out. This order had led to an uprising. Then the October 17th Revolution removed the Czar from power. No one moved to Naryn and the Kyrgyz people survived. All these facts say that Soviet Power helped.

I'm not saying the Soviet system was ideal. The Soviet system had its own disadvantages.

The most important disadvantage of the Soviet system was that everything was dictated. Everything was done according to dictatorship. Those who wouldn't obey the Soviet dictatorship, were punished severely. Such persons were forced to leave their jobs and were thrown out of Communist Party membership. There were special decrees of the Communist Party Central Committee on such people who disobeyed the Soviet power.

Such fate was experienced by the late Bernstam. He had been spied on because he published a book in which he had written of the structure and function of nomadic society. He described the destroyed nomad society as having been politically well-organized, socially united and well run. He stated that nomadic society was well arranged militarily. He wrote that they had lived by livestock breeding. He really wrote a very objective thing.

Abramson had written a genealogy of the Kyrgyz people. The system didn't like this story. He was spied on and arrested. He also was spied on and criticized. He was spied on and outlawed because of his book, *The Kyrgyz and Their Genetic Cultural Ties*. He wrote that in some regions of the Tien Shan, nomads used horse sleighs to move from one place to another. He also had written that some nomads in Tien Shan used trailers and wagons to transport their houses and bags from one place to another, that people still used this means of transportation. This was seen by the authorities as insulting to the nomads.

And I had written that the Kyrgyz in the south had been partially conquered. In the 1860's Russia conquered the Kyrgyz people. This was accomplished by the Russian General Skobelov ("The Conqueror Skobelov"). I also wrote that the eldest son of Kurmanjan Datka ("The Queen of the Alai Kyrgyz") was the leader of the uprising in southern Kyrgyzstan. From 1873 through 1876, the Kokhan Khanate was headed by him.

What I wrote was not the official line and for this I was persecuted.

Klavdiya Antipina had a similar fate. Usenbaev [the interviewee], Abramson, Bernstam and Antipina were *all* criticized as "Kyrgyz Nationalists."

JS: Thank you very much.

Photograph by John Sommer

Fig 2.2 Professor Bibina Omurzakovna Orusbayeva
Bishkek, June 1997

PART TWO   INTERVIEWS

Interview with
Bibina Omurzakovna Orusbayeva

Academician, Professor of Philology, Academic colleague, Friend
Interviewed in her office in The Academy of Sciences, Bishkek, Kyrgyzstan
June 1997 and September 2000

JS: Please tell about yourself and your acquaintance with Klavdiya Antipina.

BO: I'm not accustomed to speaking about myself. I come from an ordinary family, from the Issyk-Kul region. I spent my childhood in Karakol (Przwalski). (1) Since 1944, I have been in Bishkek.

As for Klavdiya Antipina, I guess no one knows her better than I. I know her character and her family relationships. She began working in The Academy of Sciences in 1953. We were close friends, almost like sisters.

She was born in 1904, in Morshansk, near Moscow. That she started her career so late—1953—had its own reasons.

Klavdiya Antipina was born into a large family. She was the fourth child. Her father came from Russian nobility, an aristocrat, a "blue blood." After the revolution, however, titles of nobility were eliminated and such status alone became reason enough for later being spied upon.

Most of her brothers and sisters lived long lives. An older brother was a well-known medical doctor, a surgeon. The eldest sister, Nina, lived in Tashkent and had been a Communist Party leader working with the General Secretary and the First Secretary of the Central Committee of the Communist Party of Uzbekistan. An older sister lived in Moscow. Two elder sisters and a brother and then Klavdiya. At least these, I know. There was also a younger sister who lived in Moscow. There was a still younger sister, Larisa, who died several years ago. One sibling is still living.

The family moved from Morshansk to Moscow in 1922. Klavdiya Antipina was in a variety of positions. In 1927 she entered Moscow State University, studying in the special Section of Anthropology. She is a graduate of that University. There she studied with prominent anthropologists, one of whom was Tatiana Zhdanko, who had been head of The Central Asian Institute of Ethnography at the Academy of Sciences. Another classmate was the well-known Nicholai Nicholayevich Cheboksarov. These people studied anthropology and graduated together from Moscow State University. They were classmates and room-mates. They all became well-known scholars.

In 1929 Klavdiya Antipina married a fellow student Mikhail Rabinovich. He was a construction engineer. He also edited a newspaper, the newsletter of The Academy of Sciences. He had been educated as a construction engineer. After she graduated from Moscow State University, Klavdivana had worked with him as a proof reader. They had lived a nice, happy life.

In 1937, however, mass repression began.

Then it happened. Her husband, Mikhail Rabinovich, was arrested and taken away. Their son, Lev (Leo), was only a little boy then. Later, Klavdivana was ordered into exile. On twenty-four hours notice, she and her young son were taken to the Kazan RR station and sent to Frunze (Bishkek). Can you imagine! At that time Frunze (Bishkek) was a small provincial town and the journey by train from Moscow required perhaps ten days.

She got off the train in Frunze (Bishkek), with her little son, and looked for a place to stay. She found some Russian-speaking people who allowed her to stay with them. They gave her a room, a storage room, a pantry. She would hang a cloth over the doorway. The floor was earth, but she polished it. At that time all kinds of people were being sent from Moscow. Some were sent to Kyrgyzstan, some to another place. Klavdivana adapted to the living conditions in Frunze (Bishkek).

After about a month she found a job in the laboratory at a sanitary epidemiology station. It was like "washing dishes." Later, the head of this laboratory gave Klavdivana the position of laboratory worker and his secretary. (She typed for him.) He, too, had been exiled to Kyrgyzstan. (His family had been well known in Russia, one of his ancestors being the genius of Russian poets, Pushkin.) He became a well-known, respected biologist.

In her early years in Bishkek, Klavdivana was eventually allowed to work in the homes of teachers as an expert on curriculum development, methodology, and syllabi. Later, she also taught Russian language and literature in schools, now the 6th and the 28th schools.

JS: Do you know who took care of her little son, Leo?

BO: She, herself. No one else.

And for punishment he had to take off his shoes and sit down. That's all. She never used harsh words or physical punishment. He feared the situation in which Mama would tell him, "Take off your shoes…"

He was an excellent student, but because he was the son of "an enemy of the people," he was not given the medals and awards such good students would usually have received.

Klavdiya Antipina had been exiled as an "enemy of the people." Such exiles had been required to report every month to the local office of NKVD (later known as KGB). This requirement had changed to every 2 to 3 months, then to every 6 months and then to every year. Until 1953, she had been required to report every year.

In that year, 1953, Stalin died. Persons who had been political exiles were amnestied.

It was a remarkable time for Klavdivana. She was invited to the NKVD agency and told that she was no longer a political exile. (The label was removed.) She was free to stay in Bishkek. She was free to return to Moscow. She was allowed to do anything she wanted to. She was allowed to work as a scholar. This is how, step by step, she moved into her professional position.

Then she took a position at the Historical Museum. The position was that of a subordinate worker, not a scholar. She became involved in ethnography. This is how she began her career in humanities. She became "Junior Scholar Scientific Worker" of the Historical Institute of The Academy of Sciences.

She began to participate in the Museum's activities, and she took part in several expeditions to southern Kyrgyzstan.

In 1962, she published a book, *Osobennosti Materialnoi Kultury I Prikladnogo Iskusstva Iuzhnykh Kirgizov* (Characteristics of the Material Culture and Applied Art of the Southern Kirghiz), her major research. This book became her doctoral dissertation which she defended in Moscow at The Institute of Ethnography.

Klavdivana helped to establish Ethnography as a science in Kyrgyzstan, as Abramson had done.

She began her scholarly life late.

There is something I want to add. When she would send a letter asking about her husband, she would get a reply from the agency to the effect that political exiles had no right to correspond, that her husband had no right to receive or to send messages.

After 1953, when Klavdivana began to work in The Institute of History and the Archives, she wrote again, asking for information about her husband. They told her lies. They told her he'd return—if he were amnestied. They told her that he had died in 1952--53. But she continued to inquire. Finally, she was told that in 1943 her husband had died (or was killed).

She was shocked by the lies she had been told. She lost her hopes that her husband would return. (In her memories, he was a young handsome man.) This influenced her health, and her health deteriorated.

She developed an enlargement in her neck. Her eyes became prominent. Physical ailments. A mental depression. She spent eight months in a hospital. She had an operation on her neck. Her voice changed. It became hoarse. (2)

Then in 1962, after all this, she defended her doctoral dissertation in Moscow.

In the following years she took part in expeditions to various parts of Kyrgyzstan. (I also took part and wrote part of the report.) She wrote another book, published in Vienna—in English. (The general secretary of the Communist Party of Kyrgyzstan helped greatly in getting this published.)

Though *she* would say she began her scientific work very late (and, thus, did not accomplish so much), *I* would say she accomplished a great deal. She succeeded. Even more, I'd say that most of our present [day] ethnographers would not be the ethnographers they are today without the instruction and advice they received from Klavdivana.

KLAVDIYA ANTIPINA

For 30 years she had been compiling an album of Kyrgyz national costume. If she had not been so exacting, it could have been published earlier. She was keen about accurate detail.

She would help everyone in everything—everyone who asked for help. Though she herself didn't publish a great deal, she was greatly helpful to anyone who needed her advice and consultation. She would edit papers of the post graduate students who asked for her help. She was an exacting person, and she expected the same from others. She made her own contribution to what we now call Applied Art, promoting the Kyrgyz pattern to this rank.

She would advise the cabinet ministers about Kyrgyz ornament and pattern. She contributed much to the improvement of standards. She contributed to *The Kyrgyz Pattern*, which was published and printed in DDR (The German Democratic Republic, East Germany.) She helped greatly with her advice and editing skills. As for museums, whenever ethnography or applied art was the subject, Klavdivana was to be found there advising on the content and design.

Klavdivana was a modest and exacting person. She was highly educated and graduated from the best university in our country. She knew details. She was active and took part in everything. She would read and adjust her literary style. She worked to her last day. Some persons lose their abilities, but Klavdivana was creative to her last days. She was in her nineties, but active. I would say she was interested in almost everything. She lived here in a provincial city and I was happy to help her as a friend over many years. We were often together at Christmas. She would stay with my family. Sometimes, after guests would leave, she would stay and we'd talk for a long time into the night. She knew interesting stories.

She trusted almost everyone and some persons took advantage of this. She was generous and would give people money. There was one man to whom she gave 500 to 1000 dollars "to help organize a funeral." She didn't tell me she gave him money. It was not a funeral. It was to open a workshop for making rugs. She'd say, "I'm sorry I didn't tell you, but I gave money."

All my relatives knew her and were her friends. She had many young friends. She had something of a rule: to know young friends and to support them. She would give them books, knowing some wouldn't be returned. It was a way of life for her. She had a title, "The Honored Worker of Science & Culture of Kyrgyzstan." She also had a medal and other honors.

Klavdiya Antipina was the person chiefly responsible for the high quality of the storage, conservation, exhibition and record keeping in the Bishkek museums. She would intervene with the political authorities on behalf of the master artisans, emphasizing the importance of the Kyrgyz material culture. It was because of Klavdivana that College number 17 was founded in which students could study the traditions and techniques of the Kyrgyz material culture.

Many young persons would come to her from the museums and the institutes just to learn from her. Sometimes, however, people used her ethnographic materials without giving her credit, publishing her material as their own.

Klavdivana was always telling about Kyrgyz carpets. They were something special, her favorite example of the Kyrgyz material culture.

Klavdivana would say, when you get older, you have to do it beautifully. Dress well. You have to look beautiful at that age.

JS: That was, perhaps, why she did not like the word *babushka*.

BO: Yes, it's true. She did not like this word *babushka*.

Now we have another word, a Kyrgyz word, *Baibichya*. [Say: "Bye BEE Chiya"] Baibichya. A Kyrgyz man used to have several wives and the *first* was "Baibichya." Later the meaning of the word came to be "respected older woman," a woman who was a wise and very respectable person.

She knew the most outstanding Kyrgyz persons.

One such person, for example, is Rosa Otunbaeyeva, Ambassador to the United States and Canada, then the Kyrgyz Foreign Minister. [Now she is ambassador of The Kyrgyz Republic to The United Kingdom with her offices in London.] She was helpful in expediting the making of the film *Fate* and in seeing that Klavdivana was represented among the scholars. She arranged for Klavdivana to be hospitalized and she visited Klavdivana there. Later she took her to her country place (dasha) for an extended rest.

Another such outstanding person was Chingiz Aitmatov, the well-known writer and the organizer of The Issyk-Kul Forum. He invited Klavdiya Antipina to make a presentation. People here really respected her very much. I think that's why she didn't want to move to Moscow.

Also *she* respected everybody, because she loved everybody.

When Klavdivana was doing field work in Chichkan and Darkhan, she visited certain families to learn about Kyrgyz traditions. In one family a woman was very knowledgeable about funeral songs and traditions. She visited her everyday and she would see a sick girl lying there. When she finished with her work she took that girl to Bishkek. Klavdivana, who was not a wealthy person, took the girl, ill with tuberculosis, to the children's tuberculosis sanitarium near Bishkek where the girl stayed for nine years, graduating from the school there. Klavdivana would go on weekends to talk to the doctor and to take the girl some food. Klavdiya Antipina did such things.

Later when this girl graduated from school, Klavdivana took her back to her own apartment and helped her prepare for the examination for the Kyrgyz Women's Pedagogical Institute. This girl, for four or five years, was studying in the University. She met her future husband, an agricultural student. Klavdivana prepared the wedding party and reception for her. The husband was a senior specialist on a collective farm and this girl began teaching Russian literature and language in a secondary school. They had six children.

Those kids grew up and Klavdivana helped them prepare for the university exams. They would come to her as to their own Kyrgyz grandmother. If they needed to shower, for example, they used her apartment. If they had problems, they went to KA. One of the daughters has now married and has a family.

Klavdiya Antipina is not buried in the proper place. We can't change it now; what happened, happened.

We have a number of persons who have established themselves as scholars. All had great difficulties. Their lives and their careers have not been smooth and easy. Karl Marx once said, "In science there is no light and easy way; one must go through stony roads to get to the top." There are different kinds of research scientists. Our knowledge is not yet complete in all things and there is still much to know. We need science.

Notes

1. Issyk-Kul is a large lake in northeastern Kyrgyzstan. A city at its eastern tip again has its old name, Karakol. During the Soviet period the city was called Przewalski, for a prominent Russian naturalist.

2. Probably she had developed hyperthyroidism with goiter (enlargement of the thyroid gland) and exophthalmos (prominence of he eyes), and had undergone thyroidectomy. Since her voice had become subsequently "hoarse," it is likely that one of the recurrent laryngeal nerves had been injured during the operation, paralyzing a vocal cord.

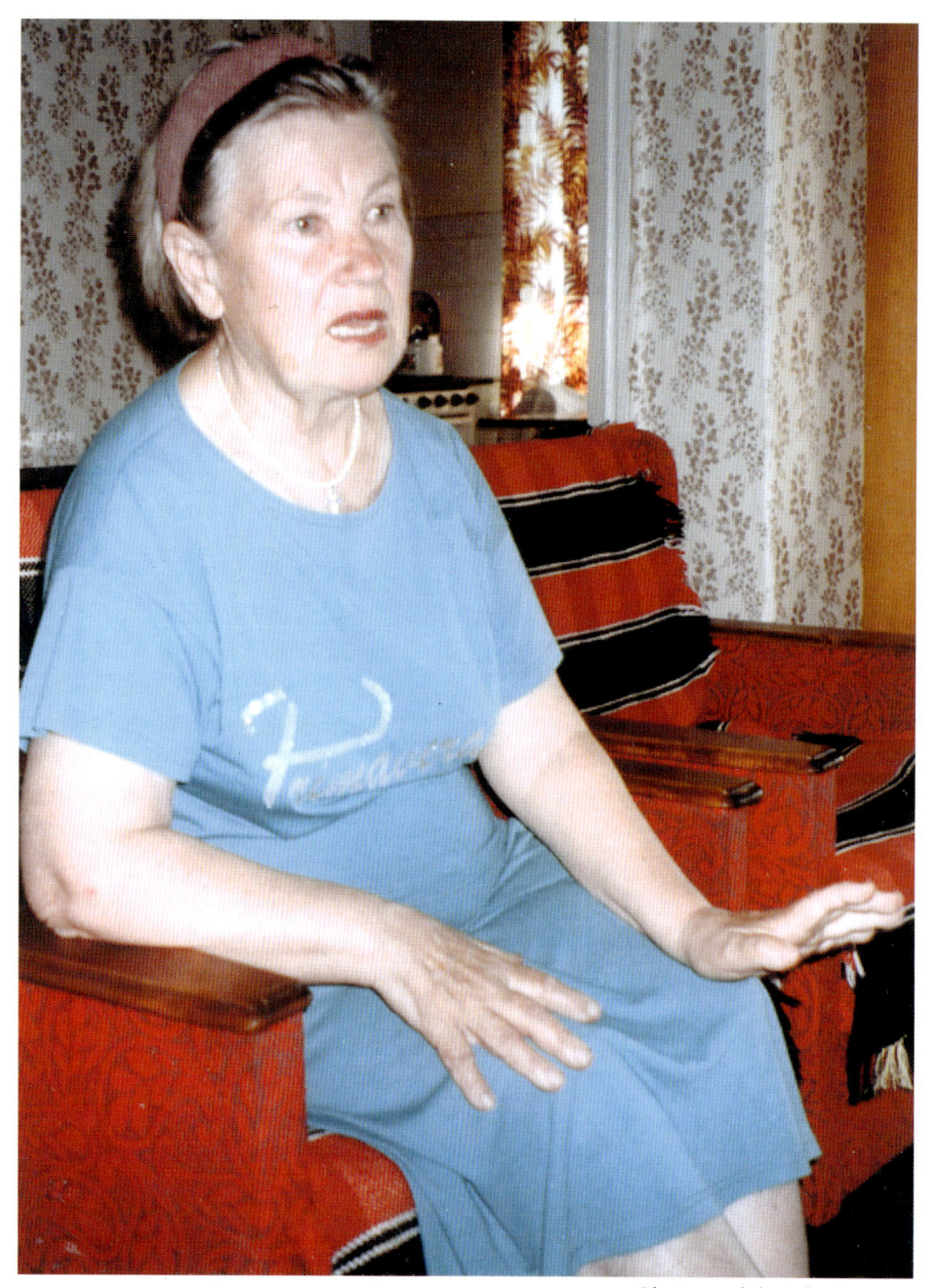

Photograph by John Sommer

Fig. 2.3 Svetlana Dunovskaya
Bishkek, June 1997

PART TWO   INTERVIEWS

Interview with
Svetlana Dunovskaya

Friend, Retired Mathematics Teacher
(for 32 years she taught architects and structural engineers)
Bishkek, Kyrgyzstan
June 17, 1997 and September 2, 2000

JS: Please tell me about Klavdiya Antipina.

SD: I met Klavdiya Antipina almost 40 years ago—in 1959. We were good friends.

I met her in the home of her friend, Sophie Petrovna, who was Korean—Sophie Petrovna Choy, her Korean name. (Sophie's husband was Kyrgyz.) Sometimes people would take advantage of Klavdivana's kindness and Sophie Petrovna would suggest how to deal with such people.

Sophie had a strong personality, a strong character. She had been a nurse in a kindergarten, then the director of that kindergarten. Sophie Petrovna went back to Moscow but Klavdivana stayed in Bishkek. Sophie Petrovna asked me to please look after Klavdivana. After that, it was up to me.

Sophie Petrovna and Klavdivana had become best friends; they each had a similar fate. They were nearly the same age (Sophie Petrovna Choy was two years older but also died at age 92). Each had lost her husband during the Stalin era of Soviet rule. Klavdivana's husband, a fellow student, was two years younger than she. Their son, Lev (Leo), was born in 1932. Sophie's husband—Shorukov—had been a deputy of the Soviet government. He was arrested, taken away and executed in 1937. (1) Each had a son. These sons were the same age and were classmates in Bishkek.

I loved Klavdivana, I loved her very much…

When we first met, we spoke for a long time and didn't stop talking. The main thing in her life was her work. Klavdivana wanted to write about the things Kyrgyz people take for granted. She was not interested in politics, only in her work.

She loved the Kyrgyz people so much. Even, sometimes, when she had been offended by someone, she'd say, "I love them." At first Klavdivana had been told Kyrgyz people were bad. But when she came to Kyrgyzstan she loved the people she met. Sophie Petrovna, who became her best friend, was one who helped her at that time. Later, she would go to those families and take them gifts. She stayed in touch with the children and the grandchildren of those families.

JS: Please tell me a little about yourself.

KLAVDIYA ANTIPINA

SD: My mother was Russian. My father was Polish. When my family moved to Kyrgyzstan, my father became ill. When he regained his health, our family decided to stay. I have lived here in Kyrgyzstan since 1946. My late husband was Kyrgyz.

Sophie Petrovna's son, who lives in Moscow, came to Bishkek almost every year. Once he visited relatives in the Karakol region and was amazed at how many relatives he has there. Earlier an aunt and an uncle had been afraid to speak of their relationship because his father—their brother—had been a "political enemy." When the son came last time, we took him to the memorial, Ata Beyit, which is not far from where Klavdiya Antipina is buried. 139 bodies were found in that mass grave. One was that of his own father, Shorukov. One was that of a woman who has never been identified. Some other bodies have not been identified. We held a mass funeral for those 139 victims.

Klavdivana played a great role in establishing the museums in Bishkek. She contributed to all of them. She was the stimulus, the idea person. Accuracy was her great concern. She knew everyone in the museums, and they would seek her opinion and advice.

She was exact and accurate in all things. People—for example, Olympic teams or delegations to Moscow—would come to Klavdivana to consult her about what to wear, how to wear it and what to do. And she gave very good advice. She knew everything about Kyrgyz people. Nobody knew as much.

Klavdivana would see just the bright side of things. She worked with people and had a very good psychological understanding of them. She would *never* say anything bad about a person.

Klavdivana was a modest person. She would go hungry for several days at a time while working on a project. When she worked, she didn't think about food. I remember once asking her whether she had had anything to eat. Her reply was that, no, she had to finish her project. All her friends knew this. They used to bring food for her. Some brought soup. All her students brought food. (I used to be a student and brought food like this. I would to see other students very often in Klavdivana's place. We students were quite a family.)

When Klavdivana felt herself sick, she advised her students to write short booklets, pamphlets rather than books. Then they began writing pamphlets on the Kyrgyz people, the Kyrgyz national etiquette, the Kyrgyz national costume, the Kyrgyz traditions and the Kyrgyz customs—small things.

Klavdivana was old. She wanted to write, but her eyesight failed. During these times, she dictated and I wrote for her. In 1994, she underwent two eye operations.

Klavdivana had used the camera and took the archival photographs, herself, during her field studies in the 1950's and 1960's.

Klavdivana so loved people. She appreciated everyone. She would speak only of the good things even if she knew negative things about a person. If someone asked her for money, she would give it to them, never asking for its return. She used to offer money, knowing it would not be returned. She was so generous.

She was interested in everything. I would tell her everything and would speak about my own [personal] problems. And she was interested. She liked for me to visit and would say I was "a good influence" and gave her "a good feeling" of being more energetic. "Tomorrow I'll start a new book." We had a good relationship.

Klavdivana's son, Lev (Leo), would call and write, "Come to Moscow." She was 60 or 70 years old then. Three years ago—when she was ninety—we had the idea she should go to Moscow to live. Her son agreed. However, he also recognized that this place, Bishkek, "feeds her and gives her life" and how could he make her move to Moscow? She visited him in Moscow and returned after forty days, deciding to stay in Bishkek.

As a child, Klavdivana lived in a two storied house. On the second floor there was a piano. The children would entertain themselves playing recital pieces. Their mother would make them practice, but would invite them down to tea. They would write poems… interesting times… an intelligent family.

JS: Did Klavdiya Antipina speak of Moscow?

SD: No. Her friends were here in Bishkek. She had no friends in Moscow.

Notes

1. His body was found in the secret mass grave at Ata Beyit.

Photograph by John Sommer

Fig. 2.4 Ambassador Roza Otunbayeva
London, June 2001

PART TWO   INTERVIEWS

Interview with
Roza Otunbayeva

In 1975, after graduation from Moscow State University, Roza Otunbayeva joined the faculty of the Kyrgyz State University where she worked six years.
She had been the Kyrgyz Ambassador to the United States and Canada
She then became the Foreign Minister of the Kyrgyz Republic.
Now she is the Ambassador of the Kyrgyz Republic to the United Kingdom.
Interviewed in Washington, D.C. and in The Embassy of The Kyrgyz Republic, London
June, 2001

JS: Please tell about your acquaintance with Clavdiya Antipina.

RO: When I came to the Government in 1987, Clavdiya Antipina was the person with whom I worked very closely to set up the national union of handicrafters. Her very first advice was: "You should keep folk handicrafts. You should preserve that for the next generation."

Clavdiya Ivanovna was already retired. Although she didn't work closely with the National Academy of Sciences, she was still associated with it. She initiated nationwide exhibitions of handicrafts. And because of ideas and inspirations of many people like Clavdivana in the final Soviet days we accomplished important things to preserve our traditional culture, folk crafts.

Clavdiya Ivanovna brought many persons to my attention. She was the idea person, who worked behind the scenes in all of this.

JS: When did you first meet her?

RO: It was in early 1986, when I invited her several times to my office to talk about development of folk arts. She was a beautiful and handsome person. She had such a noble and aristocratic sort of bearing and breeding.

Since that time we became friends. I was close to Clavdivana in her last years. I tried to look after her as much as I could. She was living alone and couldn't move independently. We used to bring her regularly food.

Once my driver took her literally in his hands from her third floor apartment in the car to my dasha, a beautiful place close to Bishkek. She was desperately eager to walk and walk. She was so excited and impressed with trees and birds around that she walked so far away, we couldn't find her for a while. She lost her way back home. At last we found her and first she was saying she was so happy... Also, I remember, she had her glasses, 4 or 5 pairs, in my home, and she would lose all of them at the same time.

KLAVDIYA ANTIPINA

She really liked the place there. She breathed the good air, she ate regular meals and she was looked after. I hope that in the last three months I was able to give her some good feeling and memories. Otherwise I felt that all of us, friends, public were sort of guilty.

At evenings when I came from office back home she told me how, when she was strong, she had gone to the southern part of the country, talked with the people and gathered old things.

In 1986 I brought to my home a woman named Anara-apa, a master, an artist from Batken. She was extremely poor and had been severely beaten by her husband because she couldn't give birth. She was a great *kurak* maker. (*Kurak* is like an American quilt with many small fabric pieces sewn together.) Clavdiya Antipina emphasized that *kurak* patterns are unique; and she knew the context and meaning of each of them.

JS: Some of the people interviewed have told me that Clavdiya Antipina "taught me to see." She was from Moscow, a Russian, an outsider to Kyrgyzstan. I think that sometimes the outsider sees things that insiders do not. The outsider has a place. What are your thoughts?

RO: That's true. It's always true. Alongside the sculptor Olga Manuilova and the painter Lidiya Iliyna, Klavdiya Antipina helped the Kyrgyz nation to see itself from outside. Iliyna has done more for Kyrgyz women than any other ethnic Kyrgyz woman. She knew so well hardships of women's life and you will see in her famous paintings the inspired images of women in mountains and fields.

Clavdivana never liked to talk about herself. Even if she's in trouble. Even if she's hungry. She was so noble. She never told anybody such things. She was so independent, so strong.

For all of us who knew her so long and so well, she never gave the impression that she would speak bad things about anyone.

She had great integrity. This was, I guess, her main characteristic.

She was self-aware, an independent woman. She didn't like to depend on anybody.

In her last years of her life I took her to the concert of classical music; at another time we brought her to The Ministry of Foreign Affairs for a poetry evening, the eighth of March, Women's Day. She told me, "Oh, I should do my hair, I should have a manicure." She used to do all of this herself. She always had as I recall well-dressed hair. And she looked really very, very good.

[…]. John, did you see her book? The book which must be published. Before and after the collapse of the Soviet Union I tried to help publish her book on Kyrgyz costume, which was prepared by her properly. A very gifted Kyrgyz painter with movie painting background, Temirbek Musakeev, had drawn all the pictures.

JS: Temirbek, at the time of our interview, had some very good pictures left over from that book.

RO: I do believe this book is unique. The book was ready to be published. It was a full maquette of the book.

In the very beginning of 1992 I came back from Moscow where I had worked in the Foreign Ministry for the last years before the collapse of the USSR. And again Clavdivana told me she would like to publish this book, that it was an important book for the newly independent nation. I completely realized that it was very important.

The Turks were supportive of our emergence as a sovereign country, of our search for our identity. I have asked the Foreign Minister [of Turkey], our good friend, Hikmet Chetin: "Help us please to publish this book. This is really an important book for the nation". He immediately endorsed the idea. The publishing house "Kyrgyzstan" started to negotiate with their counterparts in Turkey, including the translation of the text into Turkish. The book is in Turkey somewhere and it has not been published, yet!

JS: This would be an important book.

RO: Very important. In order to get this book published today, there are thousands of difficulties to overcome. But the book is ready. This was her book, her monument. It is an accomplished book, a real monument for her life.

It is a desirable book. I think a lot about this book.

In 1986 she frequently mentioned she should finish the book but she should still do "this," she should complete "that" and yet another thing. I think she was a perfectionist. She was like Marx, writing, writing and re-writing. Never happy with it, never satisfied.

JS: When I first met Clavdiya Antipina in 1992, I very quickly realized that this was a very important lady!

RO: I am sure the nation eventually will give her due honor.

JS: Such simple things as the translation of her writings. A start.

RO: Yes, yes. She was fully devoted to this small nation. We are happy that we have had such a person like Antipina, who gave order to the roots, to the sources, to the soul of the nation. What Clavdivana did is extremely important for a new nation. She was a mother of Kyrgyz anthropology.

She was not a lady of race or gender. She was human. A great human. For her I was like a daughter. There are some other artists, researchers, crafts people in my country who have exactly the same feeling.

JS: Clavdiya Antipina is unknown in the western world. She deserves to be known.

Thank you very much.

Photograph by John Sommer

Fig. 2.5 Dinara Chochunbaeva
Bishkek, September 2000

PART TWO   INTERVIEWS

Interview with
Dinara Chochunbaeva

Director, The Kyrgyz Style
Director, The National Center of Aesthetic Education For Children
Artist. Colleague. Friend. Student.
June 1997

Dinara Chochunbaeva is the Director of The Kyrgyz Style and The National Center of Aesthetic Education for Children, where Kyrgyz traditions and material arts are taught. She manages, produces, plans daily unit projects, paints, goes to government to seek support, and represents Kyrgyz women abroad in art and in social work.

Note: Dinara Chochunbaeva's transcribed, edited interview from June 1997 was deemed unsatisfactory. A statement was then written in Russian, here freely translated with the assistance of Natalie Cherry. *This statement is substituted for the original transcribed interview.*

Statement

In my life I have met three women who I would call "teachers of life." They were my grandmother, the artist Olga Manuilova, and the ethnographer Klavdiya Ivanovna Antipina.

My grandmother, who raised me, was a genuine teacher. She was a capable and courageous woman who could handle anything. For thirty years she had participated in the state campaign to overcome illiteracy in southern Kyrgyzstan and during the war she received a medal "For brave work."

Olga Manuilova was an artist, a sculptor, a person of miraculous simplicity with an incredible devotion to art. She lived in her studio near my school and, after lessons, we children would run to see her. We went out of curiosity, to look at her sculptures and to sense the atmosphere of freedom and creativity. Some of those students eventually studied with her.

Then there was Klavdiya Ivanovna Antipina. I had heard of her in the mid-70's. Once when I had returned on a vacation from Moscow where I was studying in the Polytechnical Institute, I met the artist Bolotbek Karakeev in the street carrying a large portfolio of drawings of traditional Kyrgyz costume for Klavdiya Antipina's monograph. They were pencil drawings reminiscent of Persian miniatures.

After I finished the Institute, fate brought me to Klavdiya Antipina. We were "like family." Her eyes were a remarkable bright light blue; they were wide open and alert. Even to the end, she cared about her appearance. She never liked being sick and didn't want to think about old age. She boiled with energy. She liked helping people. She was impractical, naïve, and trusting. As a result, sometimes she was victimized by the unscrupulous.

However, she did not complain or mention this.

Klavdiya Antipina almost never talked badly or spoke ill of anyone. Just once I heard her say something negative about a woman who, through deceit, had caused her to live in a one-room apartment. ("I do not like her. She is not good…") In that apartment there were a desk, two chairs, and a bookcase. Because of the shortage of space, Klavdiya Antipina's bed was placed on the glassed-in balcony.

Nevertheless that tiny apartment attracted a great variety of people. In the course of a single day, if Klavdiya Antipina felt well (and wishing was always enough), one could meet the intellectual elite; members of the highest artistic and political circles; and simple craftsmen from remote villages. I very much loved to sit with her on that self-made divan in that miniscule kitchen and discuss life.

When I was the young, beginning director of the *National Center Of Aesthetic Education For Children*, she guided me. She advised on the organization of studios for training in the traditional arts. She helped to attract the best teachers and educators to the Center. Although I didn't always follow her advice, both of us received true pleasure from our relationship.

She also tried to interest me in research work, but I was not ready at that time. I remember her enthusiastic description of *kurak* artwork and the symbolism of its patterns. Another project which Klavdiya Antipina and I discussed many times, but never realized, was the production of an album of Kyrgyz patterns on felt rugs, flatwoven rugs, pile woven rugs, and head dress. (Klavdiya Antipina had many colorful sketches from her field trips over the years.) I was too overloaded with other work and Klavdiya Ivanovna also had a very busy schedule. To this day I'm really sorry that, at the least, we did not do the album for felt carpets.

Regarding the book *Kyrgyz Costume*, Klavdiya Antipina worked on it with Bolotbek Karakeev for a number of years. However, for some subjective and objective reasons, this effort did not bear fruit. Klavdiya Antipina came to me, as the book designer, for advice. I recommended Temirbek Musakeev, who was engaged in animation and the illustration of children's books at the time. In my view, he was suited to Klavdiya Antipina's needs for the scrupulous reproduction of the national costume. This was successful. Musakeev made wonderful watercolors from old photos and sketches from Klavdiya Antipina's field work. The book was nearly complete. But, because of funding shortages at *Kyrgyzstan*, the government publishing house, publishing the book was set aside. Turkish investors were involved. I don't know what happened, but the book was not published.

In 1993 I showed some of Musakeev's watercolors to my friend Philippe Labreveux, who was working at that time in the Tashkent office of the United Nations High Commissioner for Refugees. He was helpful in organizing my exhibition of traditional and contemporary arts on a regional level. He had a burning desire to publish this book and he obtained part of the necessary funds from the French government. He bought some watercolors of Musakeev, Klavdiya Antipina wrote the captions, and an eminent French photographer arrived in Kyrgyzstan to make photos of modern Kyrgyz clothing. But, with this, the money was finished, the funds were exhausted. Trying to interest publishers, Philippe organized two exhibitions of traditional Kyrgyz costume, presenting some actual pieces but mostly photos and watercolors. These exhibitions were held in Hungary and in the British Museum, London.

Time has passed. Philippe Labreveux has retired and now lives among the vineyards in the Bordeaux region of France. Investors are in not so interested in arts that are disappearing. Although dozens of people have waited, thousands would have benefited. Nevertheless, friends and admirers of Antipina, scientists, ethnographers, anthropologists, and simple patriots of our country have not lost hope of finding interested foreign or domestic investors for this worthy enterprise.

Klavdiya Antipina, initially, had been forced to come to Kyrgyzstan. She had been exiled as the wife of "an enemy of the people." But she developed a love for the Kyrgyz people and stayed to do ethnographic work. In a 1992 newspaper article she was described as "the *babushka* (grandmother) of Kyrgyz ethnography." She was hurt. "Why a grandmother? I am a scientist." Klavdiya Antipina would not leave Kyrgyzstan even during the years of instability following the collapse of the Soviet Union. Once on her return from Moscow, we talked and I realized she was a master at communicating "between the lines."

On the rare occasions when Klavdiya Antipina spoke about her husband, Misha, she cried. In Moscow Misha had been arrested and taken away. He then disappeared in prison—through "repression." To her last days she felt keenly the pain of losing this dear person and the injustice of it. However, even about Stalin, who was responsible for the end of her family, she did not say bad things. Perhaps she developed the habit of fear. Perhaps, like many Soviet people of that time, she didn't feel a connection between the tyrant and the troubles. She would say only, "The time was such …"

In my memory there will always be the image of Klavdiya Antipina with her silvery halo of gray hair and with her naïve and wide-open light-blue eyes, always ready to be surprised and to trust…

Photograph by John Sommer

Fig. 2.6 Toktosunova Gulchahra
Bishkek, June 1997

PART TWO   INTERVIEWS

Interview with
Toktosunova Gulchahra

Art Museum Administrator, Artist, Friend, Former Student
Former teacher of Art History in the Academy of Art and the Academy of Science
Interviewed in her apartment and in her office, Bishkek, Kyrgyzstan
June 15, 1997 and September 1, 2000

JS: What sort of person was Klavdiya Antipina?

TGI: She was a very different and amazing person. She had a habit of being interested in everything. She was a very important person and very keen. She was a new person. She was quite unknown and at the same time a very important person but modest. Very private, but courageous. It was amazing to me how she could keep to herself all the difficulties she had in her life. She was very open, but still kept inside her "something secret", "private", "never known", "alone."

I've known Klavdiya since 1967—already thirty years. At that time she was younger than when you saw her in 1992 and more energetic, full of ideas. Very active, creative. Also, she looked younger then.

JS: Why would a woman from Moscow come to Kyrgyzstan? Why was she interested in Kyrgyz people and Kyrgyz culture?

It was a very difficult time for her. She came to a different country. She began to live among different people. It was her wish at that time to learn about people and to learn about their history and culture. It was a difficult time for her and she needed something like that.

… In 1937, her life changed. As if from white to black. In Moscow she had had a lovely husband. Klavdiya Antipina grew up in a large family, a religious family. … She was not a religious person, but she always mentioned that her grandfather was a person of the church.

JS: Did she ever talk about the time she arrived here?

TGI: In 1938 she already was in Kyrgyzstan. Frunze at that time, not Bishkek. She was sent here with a little son.

When Klavdiya Antipina came here from Moscow—even though she arrived with a little child—the officials didn't pay attention to her. Nobody paid any attention to her. And some people would throw rocks at her.

JS: Why was that?

TGI: She was considered to be an "enemy" of Soviet Power. It was common knowledge that persons who came here from Moscow had been sent here. When she arrived the authorities did not provide for her. It was her own business to find a place to live.

Simple people, who understood her situation, helped her and took her in to live with them. Very simple people, not highly educated. They talked openly with her, understood her situation and supported her.

So, living among the simple Kyrgyz people, she decided herself she would study Kyrgyz life. She would spend her life among the Kyrgyz people because she really appreciated the Kyrgyz who supported her. After she arrived in Kyrgyzstan, she taught the Russian language in secondary schools. And after a few years, she learned Kyrgyz language enough to understand.

She started her career as a research scientist very late in life. She was fifty years old when she began her work in The Academy of Sciences.

JS: Do I understand correctly that she taught Russian language in the secondary schools shortly after she came here?

TGI: Yes. Klavdivana Antipina was a very active person, you know. When she arrived in Kyrgyzstan, she was frustrated by not being allowed to pursue her training and her career. Later, however, she began working actively as a teacher of Russian language and literature.

She believed that her husband was *not* an enemy of the Soviet system. She waited for him to return, expecting to receive from the government the recognition that he was not an enemy. During all these years, she sent letters and packages to her husband, believing they would reach him. In fact, he had been executed shortly after his arrest in Moscow, but she did not know this. She continued to send letters and waited.

Eventually she realized that he had died, but when and under what circumstances she never knew. The topic was painful and she wouldn't readily talk about it.

When she was asked, "Who are you?" or "Where are you from?" or "How did you come to Kyrgyzstan?" her answer would be, "I'm from 1937." But she gave this answer *only after* the establishment of Kyrgyz independence in 1991. Before that, she would *never* give this answer, perhaps because it was too painful or because people misunderstood.

JS: When she first arrived here, she was identified as an "enemy of the people?"

TGI: Yes. In the early years you had to be very careful what you said.

Klavdivana found the main goal of her life, something that helped her continue to live without her lovely husband. She developed a great interest in the traditional Kyrgyz material culture. She was impressed that the people made such beautiful things.

JS: When you began working with her in 1967, what did you do?

TGI: Artists were going to school here in Bishkek. At that time, I took the examination for the Leningrad Art Institute and I went to study there. But each summer I came back here to Bishkek and went with Klavdivana on field work. One year we worked in the Issyk-Kul and the Talas Regions. I worked closely with Klavdivana. I would draw or paint whatever she asked.

JS: Klavdivana had many photographs in her archives. Who used the camera? Who made the photographs?

TGI: All these pictures were made by Klavdivana. All of them were developed and processed in the laboratory of the Academy of Science.

JS: Often in a picture there is a person with a rug or with a reed screen (chiy). I have the impression that this is the person who made it. Is this correct?

TGI: Yes, yes. You are right. Sometimes the person who made the thing has died and it belongs to the children. So these younger persons display it for the camera.

JS: Did Klavdivana ever talk about her early life?

TGI: She gave little information about her life. That part was for her.

I was in Leningrad/St. Petersburg and in Kalmykiya for 17 years, from 1968 to 1985. [Kalmykiya is in the Rostov region, the heart of Russia.] But I kept in touch with Klavdivana.

JS: You were away for seventeen years? Why was that?

TGI: I was in Leningrad for five years and I married there. My husband was from Kalmykiya. We lived in Kalmykiya.

JS: You worked with Klavdivana. What sort of work did you do?

TGI: I worked as her assistant during the time of her field work. Later, during those years, I came to Bishkek occasionally, but only for short periods. It was a time when Klavdivana collected a lot of research materials and a lot of data. I often worked with other people, other painters. I would send postcards, holiday greeting cards, gifts and books.

Since 1985 I have lived in Bishkek. I am teaching in the Academy of Art. At the same time I am working in the Academy of Sciences. And, to some extent, I continue the work I started with Klavdivana.

KLAVDIYA ANTIPINA

JS: Was Klavdiya Antipina active in 1985? Was she writing?

TGI: She was always working, she was always writing something.

JS: Was Klavdivana important in your life?

TGI: It was amazing and a great surprise to me what I saw: A Russian woman who was involved in all things Kyrgyz. A good combination—amazing. A Russian lady.

It was unusual that I met this Russian lady. All this traditional Kyrgyz stuff, and she's doing it very correctly, very professionally. After this, I myself began to look more carefully for my traditions and for my things. Klavdiya Antipina taught me to see in this way. I became interested in these things and began studying them. Klavdivana was a great influence.

In about 1970, Klavdivana asked me to draw pictures from other places to prepare a costume book.

In Kalmykiya, I would draw traditional men's and women's costumes and send these pictures to Klavdivana. She would inquire of the style and cut of costumes and the names of each part. She asked about all such details. I would collect this material and send it to her.

What a great person she was! How unbelievably important for many people. You begin to realize how each word, each part of her work and speech held deep meaning. Klavdivana was different from anybody else. Anyone could see this. She was unusual.

Photograph by John Sommer

Fig. 2.7 Akylai Sharshenalieva
Bishkek, June 1997

PART TWO   INTERVIEWS

Interview with
Akylai Sharshenalieva

Chief curator, The Kyrgyz Historical Museum, colleague, friend, former student
Interviewed in her office, Bishkek, Kyrgyzstan
June 1997

JS: Please tell me of your acquaintance with Klavdiya Antipina.

AS: I had known Klavdiya Antipina since the mid 1960's, when I started at the University. My husband [earlier had] participated in expeditions to the Toktugul Region, where they went annually for three years. My husband would interpret for those expeditions (Russian to Kyrgyz and Kyrgyz to Russian.) He is a doctor of History and now is in the Humanities Department of the university. Sometimes he would take pictures for Klavdiya Antipina, who was the expedition director. So, I had been acquainted with her at a distance.

In the museum, however, I had closer contact. I came to the Museum first as a translator. Then, I was given a topic to develop into a large exhibition on the life of the Kyrgyz people. I went to Klavdiya Antipina for advice and consultation.

Klavdivana loved the museum. Ever since coming to Kyrgyzstan—even in her last days—she was in contact with The Historical Museum. Even after she retired, we were all in close contact with her. Almost every week we would go to see her at her place.

We all loved her and she seemed to love us too. She had done everything in the museum. Klavdivana had the official position of "Consultant to the Museum." The founders of the museum were Abramson, Antipina, Galitsky and Usenbaev. No one here knows that these four people were the founders of the museum. They were the experts, the museologists, the researchers, the consultants. They were the heart of the museum. We, ourselves, did not have special education in museology, therefore, we asked them. In recent years, Klavdivana was our consultant in all things.

Generally, we'd ask how to bring together the items for exhibition. She knew how to create exhibitions and I think all the best that I know in museology, I learned from Klavdiya Antipina. Although I have gone to professional workshops in Leningrad and Moscow, Klavdiya Antipina was the best. She had been consulting since the museum's start. All the museum worker experts would go to her place. She advised us on how to acquire, how to store and how to display. She advised us on how to get material for research and how to write papers. Everything, Klavdiya Antipina!

I'm a historian, an ethnographer. I think of the ethnography I learned at this museum thanks to

Klavdivana. Details of pattern and embroideries, for example, for the first time in modern times, that "ters kayuk" has been analyzed and authentically reproduced. I learned from her, for example, that women who lost close relatives usually did this embroidery during the mourning period. All these things I learned from Klavdivana, who told us about it with great love.

JS: How is it that Klavdiya Antipina, an ethnic Russian, came here and learned so much about Kyrgyz culture?

AS: In this, she was genetically inclined, gifted, talented. Also, when she came to Kyrgyzstan, she worked with gifted co-workers in the museum and in the Historical Institute. These colleagues represented something more and they all influenced her with their good methodology. It was a good experience for her to work with Abramson, who was methodologically advanced and exact. I think she also met excellent friends.

The Kyrgyz loved her. They would send her butter and honey by courier from all parts of the country. I remember she often had guests from the southern regions of Kyrgyzstan. She would invite them to stay with her and she would treat them as if they were her relatives. She would ask them about such things as the making of felt and the technology of foods. All this knowledge made her a pre-eminent scholar and people treated her with respect.

JS: Please tell about yourself.

AS: I have two grandchildren: 7 years and 2 years.

Ever since graduating from the University, I have been working at the Historical Museum. I was out for 7 years—far from the museum. I went to study in Moscow. Our family moved to Talas to live with my husband's family.

In Moscow (1978-79) my husband wrote several books on Kyrgyz history and published them. In 1955 when Klavdiya Antipina went on expedition, my husband was "too young." He did participate, however, in her later expeditions. In Toktogul, my husband would translate—from Kyrgyz to Russian.

The last time we formally consulted Klavdivana was when we were organizing the museum of Manas in Talas. Not only did we, the curators, consult with her, the artists did also. She consulted with love.

Photograph by John Sommer

Fig. 2.8 Rysbubu Abdieva
Bishkek, September 2000

PART TWO INTERVIEWS

Interview with
Rysbubu Abdieva

Friend, former student, Consultant and Director, Babushka Adoption
Former Director, The Kyrgyz Film Studio
Interviewed in her office. Bishkek, Kyrgyzstan
September 1, 2000

Rysbubu Abdieva is the administrator of Babushka Adoption, an organization, sponsored by Europeans, which supports elderly women who live alone without other support. This non-governmental organization was established in June 1999 in Bishkek with the financial support of the Swiss Coordination Office. The objective of the NGO is to assist specific hardship cases of the most vulnerable old people by providing regular monthly financial support, not to replace the work of the social security institutions of the Kyrgyz Republic.

JS: Please tell about yourself and Klavdiya Antipina.

RA: I have three children and three grandchildren. My husband introduced Klavdiya Antipina to me many years ago and we became close friends.

My husband, Musa Abdiev, had been born and raised in south Kyrgyzstan. In the 1950's when Klavdiya Antipina was doing work in that area, she met him when he was a secondary school boy. When she saw his drawings, she arranged for him to come to Bishkek (Frunze) to study in the art school. My girl friend, whose husband was Musa's friend, introduced us. The third time I saw Musa, I married him.

I would like to tell you of my gratitude to Klavdiya Antipina. She had a great influence on the professional level and skill of my husband, Musa Abdiev. She was a very good influence.

My husband maintained friendship with Klavdiya Antipina throughout his life. When he began working as a film maker at The Kyrgyz Film Studio he would invite Klavdiya Antipina to consult on matters of Kyrgyz crafts and traditions. For example, my husband invited her to be a consultant for the two-part, four hour film *Snow Leopard*. They discussed Kyrgyz traditional life, traditions, customs, everything. She also consulted on other films.

Always she helped young families. There would be difficulties, of course. She would give advice. We thought of her as a member of our family, a *babushka*, not just as a friend.

In 1993 Klavdiya Antipina was very sick. She had a problem with her leg.

She called me and told me she felt bad. "Can you come and help me?" It was a great pleasure for me to assist Klavdiya Antipina.

When I arrived there I saw that the whole apartment was in need of attention, and that routine housekeeping had not been done. The toilet didn't work properly and many things were broken. The apartment needed some repairs. At first I asked if I could arrange for some repairs, not just to show up and prepare some lunch or breakfast or dinner. I also asked her approval for doing a bit of cleaning and painting in her apartment. I arranged for the repair of the bathroom and the toilet and for the apartment to be painted.

Roza Otunbayeva was very helpful. It was she who arranged for Klavdiya Antipina to be hospitalized. (Roza Otunbayeva at that time was the Minister of Foreign Affairs of The Kyrgyz Republic.) Then Klavdiya Antipina went into the hospital and spent two months there. The doctors were very good and they helped her. After discharge from the hospital, she spent time in Roza Otunbayeva's dasha, a summer place, outside of Bishkek.

She never liked to tell people about her health problems. The main goal of her life was her research.

She would tell her students that she would like to publish the book *Kyrgyz Traditional Clothing*.

She always helped young researchers, people who were interested in this field. She would give to them pictures, articles, books, monographs, and manuscripts. She always shared her experience with people who were interested.

Sometimes I would ask her, "Why are you so open? Some people are very good, but some will never return these treasures. Why do you give them to everybody?"

And Klavdiya Antipina would tell me. "Yes, you're right. I know that some of my materials are walking around. On the one hand, it may be not so good, but, on the other hand, I'm glad that there are people to do this research. If people are not returning [things] to me, *they* are responsible for that."

JS: Everything I've heard about this lady is good. In the past, I have asked others whether there was anything bad about her. I have received two answers, usually after lengthy hesitation on the part of the person questioned. One "bad thing" was that sometimes she would borrow books and not return them. The other "bad thing" was that she would lend money to people who would not return it. Those were the two "bad things" about Klavdiya Antipina.

RA: Yes, I know of a situation where she gave a lot of money to somebody to invest. That person had come

to her and she decided it's better to use this money and maybe have some income. She invested in this man's project. This man took the money and that's all. She never received it back, nor did she receive income.

I talked to Klavdiya Antipina and said, "Why do you give such a large amount of money to this man? The situation in the country now is very difficult and who knows what happens with your money? You should *not* give him money."

And Klavdiya Antipina's answer was, "I know this man. I trusted him and I believed him." Sometimes

Klavdiya Antipina would ask me to go to him and ask for the money which I did several times. He did say that he remembered that he took the money, that he would pay it back, that she would receive money for everyday living expenses. But Klavdiya Antipina told me that she never received any money.

JS: Did Klavdiya Antipina ever talk about her early life? Also, there is a period—1937 to 1951—that I know very little about, because, I think, Klavdiya Antipina didn't talk about those years.

RA: Actually, it's true. She never talked about that time.

However, she often did speak of her childhood and her family. They had good traditions and strict rules. For example, they never ate a meal (breakfast, lunch, or dinner) unless their father, as head of the family, first said a prayer. Only then would they begin to eat.

She told of when she graduated from the secondary school, went to Moscow, took the exam and enrolled in the School of Forestry.

Klavdiya Antipina was like my own mother. I loved her very much. She was always interested in my kids and she would tell me what nice children I have. You know she had much experience.

She lived alone, an old lady.

I was looking at her life and I began to understand the life of an old lady. I decided to organize a charity fund which will help them, these elderly women who live alone. We created a fund which helps poor families and elderly people. I am a consultant to the organization and head of this division.

Right now we support fifty (50) women. Most of our sponsors are from Europe. These sponsors transfer money for a year and they get the name of the *babushka* who receives the money.

JS: And this came from your acquaintance with Klavdiya Antipina?

RA: Yes. It was after my experience with her, that I got the idea for this.

Photograph by John Sommer

Fig. 2.9 Stella Mateeva
Bishkek, June 1997

PART TWO   INTERVIEWS

Interview with
Stella Mateeva

Former Researcher at The Kyrgyz Historical Museum
Not an interview, but a written statement
Bishkek, Kyrgyzstan
June 29, 1997, 6:30 p.m.

People know Klavdiya Antipina as a respected scholar and ethnographer who devoted her life to the investigation of the history, life, and applied art of the Kyrgyz people. She had founded The Museum Foundation in Kyrgyzstan. She made her greatest contribution, however, by organizing the ethnographic section of The Kyrgyz Historical Museum. (She had been responsible for the first Kyrgyz exhibition of the socialist society *The Soviet Period In Kyrgyz Ethnography*.)

Klavdiya Antipina had been at The Kyrgyz Historical Museum from 1947 to 1963, a time when the museum concentrated on gathering archaeological and ethnographic materials. She participated in the archaeological-ethnographic expedition in the 1950's organized by S. Abramson, the museum's founder. The museum now takes pride in its Kyrgyz collections acquired by Klavdiya Antipina. These collections include decorative arts and crafts and Kyrgyz material culture from the end of the 19th century through the early 20th century.

Klavdiya Antipina, during those years, had also assembled and had given scholarly descriptions to the ethnographic collections through the mid-twentieth century. In 1963 she moved to The Academy of Sciences, but had kept in touch with The Kyrgyz Historical Museum, having been a member of that museum's Academic Council, also. She advised young museum workers. She would teach the research, the organization, and the description of interesting collections.

We always loved and respected Klavdiana. I remember her as a kind, gifted, highly educated, and very cultured person. I was greatly impressed by her consultations and by her advice.

(Signed) Stella Mateeva

Photograph by John Sommer
Fig. 2.10 Kalipa Asanakunova
Bishkek, June 1997

PART TWO   INTERVIEWS

Interview with
Kalipa Asanakunova

Artist, friend
Interviewed in her apartment, Bishkek, Kyrgyzstan
June 1997

JS: Please tell about Klavdiya Antipina.

KA: Klavdiya Antipina had many friends. She loved people. Many people took advantage of her. I would go to people and ask them to give the money back to her that she had handed them. She had some people she supported financially for many years. She would give money and other things.

JS: Was there anything bad about her?

KA: Klavdiya Antipina would not return books she borrowed.

She was very talented, very gifted. I have no way to explain in words what kind of person she was. She was kind.

I was really lucky to know such a person as Klavdiya Antipina. And I thank God that I met her. Thanks to her I became an artist. I'm happy that for the many years I worked with Klavdiya Antipina. The things I achieved in my life were thanks to her. I learned much from her.

JS: Klavdiya Antipina was an important lady. I met her through Bibira Akmoldoeva.

KA: I heard a lot from Klavdiya Antipina about Bibira. She loved Bibira. Both of them were working on the same topic. She also loved Gulchahra [Toktosunova Gulchahra].

Klavdiya Antipina would say, "Katusha" (for Kalipa). She would say, "Do for your children. Don't be afraid to waste your money for your children. Entertain them. They will remember all these things forever."

Klavdiya Antipina would tell me about her family in which she was brought up—sisters, brothers.

She was my teacher—and in all the events of my life she took an active part—the valleys and the peaks in my life, and Klavdiya Antipina helped me with my family problems. I would say the existing mountain in *her* life was when she came here to Bishkek.

Photograph by John Sommer

Fig. 2.11 Bolotbek Karakeev
holding the first drawing
Bishkek, June 1997

PART TWO   INTERVIEWS

Interview with
Bolotbek Karakeev

Artist
Interviewed in his apartment/studio
Bishkek, Kyrgyzstan
June 1997

JS: Please tell about your acquaintance with KA.

BK: I met Klavdiya Antipina in 1972 at my parents' place. That was 25 years ago. I had some vague idea of what ethnography was. My sister, an ethnographer, advised me. When I became mature, I was gradually involved in making reed screens (*chiys*). That was many years ago. In a trivial way, I was involved in art.
I began working with Klavdiya Antipina as an artist, a painter. At that time Klavdiya Antipina had been working on Kyrgyz National Costume in Moscow.

The first test picture I made I showed her and she seemed pleased. She had seemed to like it. We had decided to work together. However, it had not been so easy as I had thought. The work went slowly.

Photograph by John Sommer
Fig. 2.12 Bolotbek Karakeev's first drawing

It is one thing to like the thing you do, but another thing when you don't. When one deals with science and scholarly work, one must limit one's artistic inclinations. And on this point, the scholarly vs. the artistic, we differed.

We could not have made the book together. Klavdiya Antipina was very exacting. She didn't like most of what I liked.

And we decided we couldn't work together.

Fig. 2.13 Temirbek Musakeev
Bishkek, June 1997

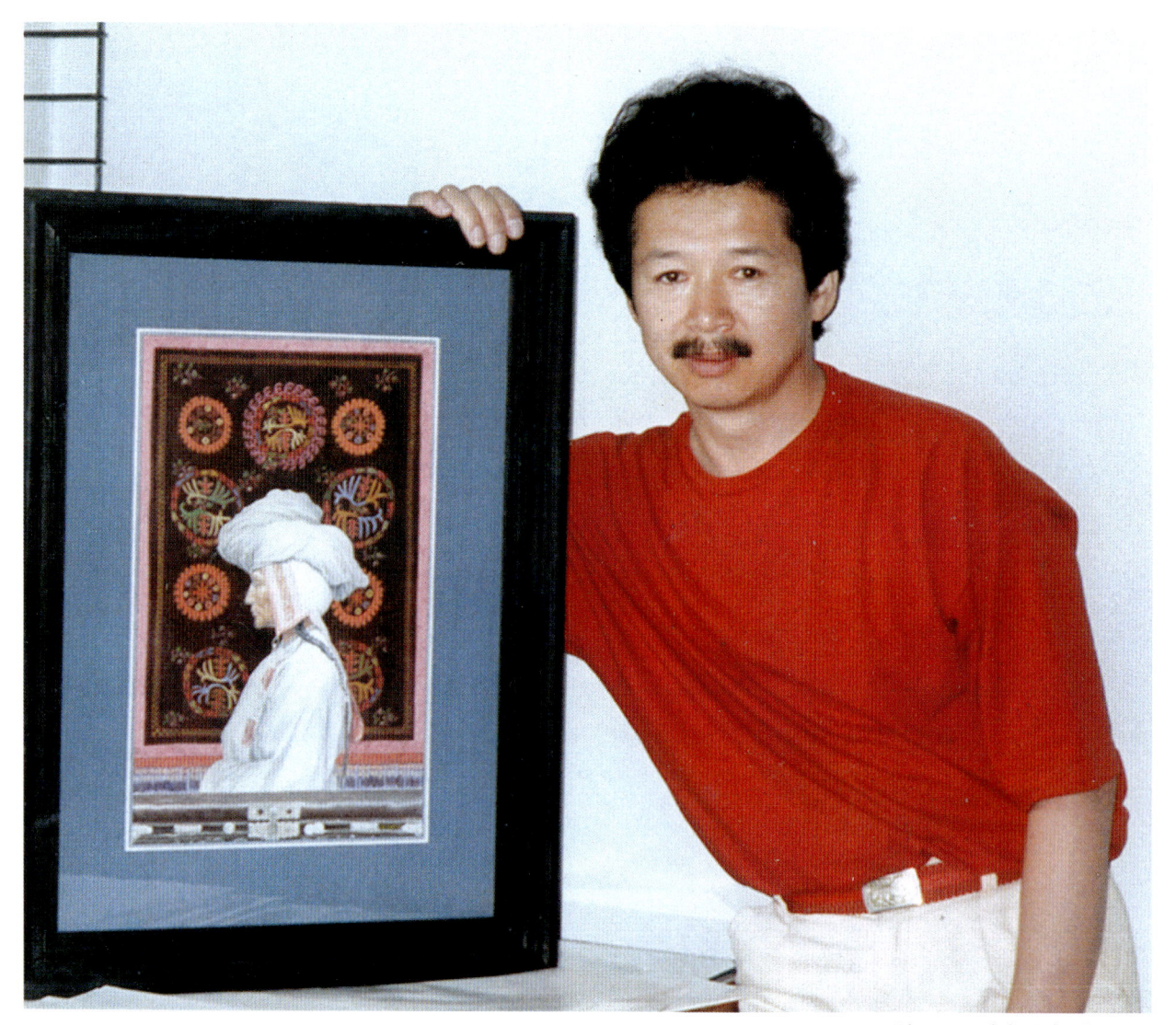

Photograph by John Sommer

PART TWO   INTERVIEWS

Interview with
Temirbek Musakeev

Artist
Interviewed in his studio, Bishkek, Kyrgyzstan
June 1997

This artist had worked with Klavdiya Antipina to the end of her life. His work had pleased her. His studio was a large, sparsely-furnished room located in an industrial area of Bishkek. Parts of bronze statues lay in the building's courtyard. Initially, he spoke briefly about himself. In Moscow, he had studied in The Cinematography Institute and in an art school.

JS: Please tell of your acquaintance with Klavdiya Antipina.

TM: I had known Klavdiya Antipina for 5 years. I had become acquainted with her—I think by chance—and had begun this book on Kyrgyz costume.

Klavdiya Antipina had been looking for someone at the time. I had been working at a publishing house making children's books. It was the main publishing house of Kyrgyzstan, the State Publishing House. The Soviet Union was still intact at that time; it was a crucial period. I began working with her in 1990. She had worked with many artists. They had tried to complete the book, but had not been successful. Work on it had begun more than ten years earlier.

I talked with the other artists who had worked on this album, asking for more details. Some told me it would be impossible, that Klavdiya Antipina wouldn't like anything I'd do. Others told me, "Remember, she doesn't like anyone."

But, when I met Klavdiya Antipina, I liked her. It was really pleasant to talk with her. Despite the opinions of other people, I found she was intelligent, possessed of a great knowledge—a spiritual knowledge—and a nice person. I could see this and I liked her. I thought of her as *babushka*, as my own grandmother.

We talked for a long time, that first day. She told me about her ideas and shared some pictures, showing me how the album was to be done. She wanted exact costumes. I realized what I was to do. I caught the ideas about the album. When I saw all these things and talked to Klavdiya Antipina, all the impressions from other artists disappeared. Klavdivana was really a sincere, warm-hearted person. I liked her.

So we started to work. No misunderstanding, no complaints, no problems. She was very easy. We discussed. We each had our ideas, and occasionally came close to conflict. But it worked. A good working relationship. We discussed differences, some were very hard. I tried to withdraw myself from these conflicts. She was right; it had to be the way she said. I really joked on these things and tried to find common understanding with Klavdivana, and I think she liked this. I would joke so as to withdraw from that situation. She was very exact, precise, fastidious.

I think I was successful. I had worked with children, and I drew on some of that experience.

We would meet informally. I'd call her on special occasions and holidays. On her birthday, I'd call her and I'd go there and talk for a long time. We would drink tea. She would tell me her new ideas. All this we did after the album was finished.

She reminded me of my own grandmother. She treated me like a grandson. She used to say we really did a good job because we had a common sense of what we were doing together. She said, "Psychologically, we have a good balance."

I liked her as she was. I liked the way she lived, the way she thought, and the way she knew many things. She was creative. Whenever, I would arrive at her place, she would be working, doing something, creating something. I liked her creativeness. I'd never met such a person.

Sometimes I would go there in the evening when it was already dark. Sometimes she would call late in the night. "Where are you? I have rolls. Come now. I have something to tell you. A brilliant idea, come right now." I also was the kind of person who worked at night. And I'd drop my work and go. When I went, I'd see her working. She would be absorbed in writing something, always creating. She would start telling me about her new ideas.

She would never say that she worked. She never called it work. Amazing. I compare her with children at play. Klavdivana was like children who never sense that they are doing something worthwhile. I said to myself that she had been just playing—a kind of general image of Klavdivana playing with ideas. This is what I planned to tell you about her, that she had been playing with ideas all her life.

Now, I realize why it was that she lived a long life. She never told others she'd been working hard. She, herself, seemed to have no idea she was doing hard work. She would never say that she'd been working all day. *But I would say that I had worked all day.* She had been working this way her whole life. I really think she had a good schedule and system. That is why she lived long.

In our book, I made the illustrations like actual persons wearing costumes from the end of the 19th century and beginning of the 20th century. There were 160 Illustrations. You couldn't imagine that we could have done this job so quickly! (1)

Klavdiya Antipina would say that contemporary Kyrgyz forget their past life, their unique culture of the past—even the elementary things. For example, how people dressed fifty years ago. These things are being forgotten. The city has no national face, and it doesn't show the uniqueness of the Kyrgyz culture. She was always thinking of how to represent our unique Kyrgyz culture to current society.

We were planning to make one more book about *current* national costume, showing various layers of society, to show the archaic life of the past and how it relates to the present. If she had lived only ten years more, we could have done this.

My *babushka* died and I was left. We lost our ideas as well. She had such ideas! It is a pity. I'm so sorry it happened.

Notes

1. This important book on Kyrgyz Costume, written by Klavdiya Antipina and illustrated chiefly by this artist, Temirbek Musakeev, is not yet published. In fact, its very whereabouts is currently not known.

Fig. 2.14 Traditional Kyrgyz man's costume
See also Photograph No. 60 (KA 2675)
Artwork by Temirbek Musakeev

Fig. 2.15 Traditional Kyrgyz man's costume
Artwork by Temirbek Musakeev

Fig. 2.16 Traditional Kyrgyz woman's costume
Silk ikat and *elechek* headdress, probably from the Fergana Valley area.
Artwork by Temirbek Musakeev

Fig. 2.17 Kathleen Kuehnast
Alexandria, Virginia, 2001

PART TWO   INTERVIEWS

Interview with
Kathleen Kuehnast

Alexandria, Virginia
March 31, 2001

Kathleen Kuehnast, an American anthropologist, received the Doctor of Philosophy (Ph. D.) degree in 1997 from the University of Minnesota. Her dissertation, Let The Stone Lie Where It Has Fallen: Dilemmas Of Gender and Generation In Post-Soviet Kyrgyzstan, concentrates on Kyrgyz women, their traditions, the impact of Islam, the impact of the Soviet communism, and the present situation in the post-Soviet period. Dr. Kuehnast, who lives near Washington DC, is a Research Associate at the Institute of European, Russian and Eurasian Studies, The George Washington University. She is also a member of the Advisory Council of The Kennan Institute for Advanced Russian Studies of the Woodrow Wilson Center for Scholars. Her relationship with Professor Klavdiya Antipina began in 1991. Her geologist husband, Dr. Kenneth Rasmussen, studies Kyrgyzstan's Lake Issyk-Kul. They have three children—a six year old son and infant twin daughters. They live in Alexandria, Virginia.

This edited transcript of a brief interview is followed by excerpts from records of her own interviews of Klavdiya Antipina. In addition, there are excerpts from the dissertation. (The language is English.)

JS: Please tell of your acquaintance with Klavdiya Antipina.

KK: I met Klavdiya Antipina in 1991 when I was beginning my field research in Kyrgyzstan for my doctoral dissertation. My relationship with her was formal, that of student to teacher. It seemed to please her to have an American student. During those early days, I was typically accompanied by my research assistant and interpreter, Almash Naizabekova, a Kyrgyz specialist of the arts. Antipina always enjoyed when we came together, as she would call us "sisters with twin spirits", or "of the same soul," even though we were from very different cultures. We would typically bring lunch to share, and this is where our three-way friendship really blossomed.

Klavdiya thought that the nature of my dissertation on Kyrgyz women and change (or what I would call "post-modern") was far too complex to document. Instead, she conceived material culture of the Kyrgyz as the only dependable lens in which to do ethnography. So, she decided that if I was going to be her student that I should acquire expert knowledge about the *elechek*, the unusual headdress of the Kyrgyz married woman.

Over the course of 1994 when I lived in Kyrgyzstan for eight months, Klavdiya tutored me on the unique role of the *elechek* in the material culture of Central Asia. The headdress, made up of yards and yards of white cotton cloth, was meticulously wrapped around the married woman's head each morning. According to Klavdiya, it was also used as a shroud when a woman died.

The *elechek* and its origins greatly interested me, and I would repeatedly ask Klavdiya to speculate as to where it came from. She would always reply with the same answer, "Some things we will never know." To me, as an outsider, the *elechek* seemed to have the appearance of a head wrap that a mullah wears. But Klavdiya didn't see this resemblance. I then began asking others about the *elechek* and their impressions of this odd headdress. One Kyrgyz woman responded that it was a very practical addition to a nomadic woman's garments, so if she should fall off her horse, it protected her head, like a helmet would. Others speculated that women wore the *elechek* to stay cool in the summer and to stay warm in the winter.

What was fascinating to me was that every part of Kyrgyzstan had its own distinctive way to wrap the *elechek*, both in the way the headdress was placed on the head and how it was tied off at the end of the fabric. As our tutorials progressed, it became a game with Klavdiya and me. She would show me one of her fabulous photos of a woman in an *elechek* and I would tell her which region it originated. By year's end, I had become pretty proficient at recognizing the regional differences of *elecheks*. It pleased her, and I loved pleasing Klavdiya, as I saw her work as so important to the memory of the Kyrgyz and their material culture.

JS: I have heard it described that the Soviet order for Uzbek women to expose their faces in public by *not* wearing the *paranja* was like a federal order in this country for women to go topless. Unthinkable.

KK: Also, it was an intentional Soviet effort to divide the family and the household. The Soviets thought it criminal that women should be required to wear these heavy and hot *paranjas*.

JS: Cultural insensitivity?

KK: Oh, sure. There was a missionary quality to the Russians, you might say.
But the wearer's of the *paranjas* themselves, had their reasons, too. There were some practical ideas behind the wearing of the *paranja*. The city was dirty. A woman felt more privacy when she was covered. She didn't worry about how she looked to others.

JS: Repeatedly, I have heard the expression of amazement that a woman from Moscow, an outsider basically, would come to Kyrgyzstan and then become *so interested* in the Kyrgyz people and their culture—beyond the interest of the Kyrgyz people themselves. The role of the outsider. Do you have any comments about that?

KK: It seems very natural to me, being an outsider, myself. That's where Klavdiya Antipina and I found common ground. We were both outsiders with this intimate love for the Kyrgyz culture. It is quite remarkable that she recovered from what happened to her in her young thirties. At that time, she had no choice but to live in Bishkek.

PART TWO   INTERVIEWS

Excerpts from Dr. Kuehnast's records of her own interviews of Klavdiya Antipina

In 1952 Klavdiya Antipina was allowed to do field work in ethnography. She began to study the Kyrgyz, going to the Issyk-Kyl region where no Russian ethnographer had ever been. As a specialist, she wrote about the culture. A book resulted. *("You need this book very much. The bibliography is correct and important. You can choose definite references. Nobody in Moscow understood Kyrgyzstan.")*

She also studied the history and the religion of the region and came to be regarded as a real scientist. She was then assigned the entire Osh region (Oblast) for her ethnographic field work. ("For three years I studied alone in Osh. I love that oblast. I tried to be an objective anthropologist, not a 'Russian', not an 'American', but an objective anthropologist.")

The *elechek*, she said, is the headdress of a married woman. An unmarried woman would never be seen in it. In her opinion the *elechek* is a garment that emphasizes the face, makes a woman look more attractive, outlining the face in white cloth. "Women aspired to be attractive." [This struck me as opposite to the veiling among Muslims, where the face is hidden so as not to attract attention. KK]

She commented on how comparable was such headgear to that worn by a Mullah. [How is it that the holiest of men's clothing could become an honorary garment for women? Klavdiya Antipina did not have an answer for this. KK] Rich women wore as much as fifty meters of white cloth wrapped around the head. Someone would help the woman every morning to put on the *elechek*. [Almash told me that her own grandmother had worn an *elechek*. KK] With the development of Soviet socialism, however, the *elechek* disappeared.

She would speak of the Kyrgyz tribal distribution, listing more than thirty groups by name.

"Ethnography is a young science right now. I am old, but you can study still."

Excerpts from the Dissertation

Acknowledgments

"… I recognize the tremendous contribution which the late Professor Klavdiya Ivanovna Antipina (1904-1996) made to my fieldwork experience and scholarship. Even at the age of 90, Klavdiya graciously welcomed me into her small apartment in Bishkek and schooled me in the Soviet ethnography of the Kyrgyz. Klavdiya shared histories and stories, photos and references. But moreover, she constantly and unknowingly reinforced my decision to become an anthropologist, especially as I watched her work[ing] diligently […] even in the last years of her life. Klavdiya's remarkable work continues to be a daily inspiration…" (page xii)

Preface

"… As it was conveyed by my Kyrgyz friends, my research in Kyrgyzstan had been determined as my fate, and not as any sort of choice that I had made… In their estimation, the stone had fallen, there it should remain. This outlook of fatalism permeated many interactions during the course of my early fieldwork experiences…" (Page 6).

Part One

"… Kyrgyz tradition that persisted throughout the Soviet period, including the syncretism of shamanism and Islam. …"

"… the Kyrgyz have maintained a focus toward their traditional past while continually adapting to the new ideas, behaviors, and ideals presented by Sovietization, as well as the recent influx of gender ideals gleaned from globalization, a stance that could be called 'collaborative conservatism'…" (Page 52)

Part Two

"… Between 1935 and 1960, the use of yurts was strongly discouraged by the Communist Party, since they represented to the Party an outmoded way of life. However, in 1961, Soviet leader Nikita Khrushchev once again championed the yurt as an efficient dwelling for shepherds and went on to recommend improvements for the mass production of the portable housing…"

"… As he had done in Ukraine during the same period, Stalin…, using devious tactics, had essentially caused a famine in which seven million people reportedly died between 1932 and 1933… After that, collectivization rapidly took hold because people were hungry and they were living in terror for their lives…" (Page 210)

Conclusion

"Almash [Naizabekova]…offered me a useful analogy about how Kyrgyz women had integrated Sovietism and Kyrgyz traditionalism into their identity.":

> Think of the chiy screen… It is made from the thinnest of reeds, bound together by woolen threads. It is firm and strong enough to keep the winter winds out of the yurt. It is an essential framework into which beautiful designs are then woven. There is no choice about the frame, it is necessary. But the colors that the wool threads are dyed and the design that comes from these colors, are all in a woman's mind. She can choose freely. This is like the life of a Kyrgyz woman. And, like the frame of a reed screen, we have our ancestors, their knowledge and their customs. And, now we also have seventy years of Soviet mentality when we had the opportunity to make many more choices. Nevertheless, we never forgot the origin of our lives—the framework. Even though there was an attempt by the Communists to erase our ancestors from our minds, we couldn't erase patterns. In the same way now, we shouldn't forget "Papa Lenin." He is a part of us. His statue should continue to stand on Chui Prospect. He is naturally a part of our future. As we say in Kyrgyz, *Ötköndü bilüü-kelechekti körüü* ["If you know the past, then you can shape the future."] (Page 374)

"The central argument of this dissertation is that the Soviet-Kyrgyz identity was significantly shaped in the everyday lives of Kyrgyz women and that the forging of such an identity took place more in a complex spirit of collaboration than of simple one-dimensional resistance." (Page 376)

Photograph by John Sommer

Fig. 2.18 Bibira Akmoldoeva
Bishkek, September 2000

PART TWO   INTERVIEWS

Interview with
Bibira Akmoldoeva

Colleague, friend
Co-author of this book
Country Program Manager (The Kyrgyz Republic) Humanitarian Assistance Program of Counterpart International, Inc.
Former Professor of Cultural Anthropology, Kyrgyz State University
Former Head of The Humanities Department, Kyrgyz State University
Interviewed in her apartment, Bishkek, Kyrgyzstan
May 2001

JS: Please tell about your acquaintance with Klavdiya Antipina.

BA: I was sixteen years old. It was a time of life when one begins to think seriously about career and the goals of one's education. I met Klavdiya Antipina and she channeled my interest into ethnography.

I studied in Moscow State University. It was a great honor to be a student of that university. I had very good professors who influenced me greatly. Nicholai Nicholayevich Cheboksarov was one of them. Tatiana Alexandrovna Zhdanko was head of The Central Asian Ethnography Department at The Academy of Sciences. Years before, both had been Klavdiya Antipina's classmates. I was not aware, then, that they were such illustrious persons, such famous people. I thought that *all* scientists were like them. As ethnography students from Moscow State University, we would visit The Academy of Sciences to hear about research and to participate in seminars.

Whenever I came back to Bishkek, as for the summer holidays I *always* went to talk with Klavdivana and to bring her greetings from her colleagues, who were also my teachers. She would inquire about their health, what they were doing, what kinds of publications they were preparing, and what kinds of field work they were conducting. She always wanted to know the details of what was going on. She herself, of course, was involved in research in Kyrgyzstan and was collecting materials. Sometimes I would take small packages from her to her son, who lived in Moscow, and also to her professional colleagues there. In this way, I became acquainted with those persons in Moscow close to Klavdivana.

I recall that, as a third year student, my research was done with the participation of Klavdiya Ivanovna. I worked on the subject *Women and Islam*. My diploma work was on *Felt Ornaments of the Kyrgyz*. My Ph. D. dissertation dealt with the subject of *Horse Breeding Within The Traditional Kyrgyz Economy*. Klavdiya Antipina advised me in my field work. She recommended that I pay special attention to funeral rites, advised me to visit certain villages, and acquainted me with legendary seamstresses who worked with felt.

Klavdiya Ivanovna Antipina could talk for hours about Kyrgyz carpets and of how little work had been done on this most interesting subject. I was always amazed by her capacity to ignite interest. After meeting with Klavdiya Ivanovna I always wanted to create.

She was interested in young people. She advised them, and they were her friends. I'm grateful to Klavdivana that she paid attention to a young student like me.

When I would visit her, I expected we would talk perhaps for an hour or two at most. But sometimes we would talk into the night. On such occasions, she worried about my getting home. I would tell her not to worry, that I would call her from home. Whenever I forgot, *she* called me.

We talked about *everything*, not just ethnography. We talked about the theater, about life, about friends. Her influence was good. I didn't feel an age difference. I felt she was my friend. I think that she made me as I am right now.

I should say that she was a very professional ethnographer. Also, she was a skilled educator. What I learned from her was important for me later, when I started teaching in the University.

I also realized that, although my students knew her wonderful book *Osobennosti Materielnoi Kultury I Prikladnogo Iskusstva Iuzhnykh Kirgizov*, they didn't realize that Klavdiya Antipina was still active.

When I told them that she was working, most of my students could hardly believe it. Sometimes I would arrange for Klavdivana to talk to them. Her enthusiasm impressed them. Many of the ethnography students then visited her, developing their own true friendships.

The students were truly amazed that this legendary, almost god-like figure could be such a simple, warm, and nice person who made them feel comfortable. They learned much from her.

Although I was her friend, I would always call her before visiting. If she had free time to meet, she would say yes, you can come at this time or that time. Now, I realize she wanted to get herself ready. She always was beautiful. Every time I visited her she was dressed nicely, her hair fixed, and her nails manicured. I think Klavdivana was not just a great professional and a good scientist; she was a very beautiful lady. She could not have any other image.

Klavdivana was always making plans, preparing a book, writing an article. She wanted to know about conferences, when and where they were held, and the results. I don't know where she found the time for everything, but it seems to me she always did. She kept herself informed. She would call my attention to newly-published ethnographic books and where they could be obtained.

When somebody gave her various books to read—non-scientific novels, even—she would share them with me. Afterward, we would discuss them. She would say that the more you know, the easier to understand other things. She had wide interests and was widely educated.

Because Klavdivana promoted them in an address to the Union of Artists, simple people who could make the traditional things began to be recognized as artists in their own right. We have a Union of Scientists, a Union of Writers, and a Union of Artists. She said that not just painters and sculptors should belong to this latter organization, but also makers of the traditional arts—makers of *shyrdaks*, *woven carpets*, *chiy*, and such things. She was also concerned about their living and working conditions. She created an organization and a fund named **Kyayl**.

This organization produced Kyrgyz national souvenirs using traditional designs. In Soviet times our delegation went to different countries, showing these **Kyayl** souvenirs. Many were used as official gifts.

Klavdivana built up the ethnography collection of the Historical Museum here in Bishkek. She advised the museum staff on proper methodology, labeling, the documentation of each item in the collection, and such things.

JS: From many people I've heard that she *never* said anything negative or bad about *anybody*.

BA: And she never talked about the hard times in her life. I learned that she didn't want to talk about that. It was also like a sign that you don't ask about that.

JS: Please tell me about Sophie Petrovna.

BA: Sophie Petrovna had been Klavdivana's very good friend here in Bishkek. Her husband had worked in the government. His name was Shorukov. He was Kyrgyz, from Issyk-Kul.

JS: Do you know whether Klavdiya Antipina was here when Sophie Petrovna's husband was arrested, taken away, and executed? [That was in November 1938, if I recall correctly. His body was one of those identified in the mass grave at Ata Beyit].

BA: Yes. She would have been here then, and she would have known about Sophie Petrovna's husband. But she wouldn't have known about Ata Beyit. Prior to 1991, almost no one was aware of what had happened at Ata Beyit.

JS: Both Sophie Petrovna and Klavdiya Antipina were "enemies of the people." Each had lost a husband. They each had a son. It seems they had much in common?

BA: Yes. Klavdiya Antipina and Sophie Petrovna became closest friends. They had similar destiny. Both were intelligent, educated, and completely vulnerable. They were supportive of each other. Their sons were friends.

JS: I sense that among the older people there were certain things they did not talk about even with their family, their friends, their neighbors—nobody. Some things were not discussible.

BA: We didn't talk much about the Stalin time. It was as if the people had forgotten about that time or that they didn't want talk about it. Younger people, like me, didn't know much about those times. All that we knew from the books appears to have been half lies, and some pages of Soviet history are appallingly tragic.

JS: I've heard it said that the present generation is the first living generation not to know "fear of government." You were of a transitional generation. Did you know this "fear of government?"

BA: Yes. I was growing up at that time. The Communist Party was strong.

I was a student in the History Department [Moscow State University]. After graduating, I came back and started to work in the History Department of Kyrgyz State University. I was told that if I would like to make a career, I had to be a member of the Communist Party.

But I told them that I was not from the Communist History Department, I was from the Ethnography Department. It didn't matter. They told me I *had* to be a member, and that if not, I would never have a career. I would never grow as a specialist. My career would stop. Moreover, only one person per year could qualify for membership in the Communist Party. As a result of such pressure and such limitations, there was high competition among the people who worked in the History Department for such membership. A worker from a plant, a factory, or a collective farm, however, could readily qualify.

I was young. I said, "Why?" It seemed strange that I, who had been to the university and had been teaching, should now go to work in a factory or on a collective farm so I could add a line to my *curriculum vitae* and thus more easily qualify for membership in the Communist Party. It was strange for me, as well as for others. A lot of people couldn't understand.

JS: Is it correct that you were *never* a member of the Communist Party?

BA: Never. That is why sometimes I had difficulties working in the History Department. If you did work in that History Department, the Communist Party's history department, you had a very good career.

JS: Tell me about Professor Kushbek Usenbayev. He was a member of the Communist Party, I think, for a time, and then he was expelled because of his work?

BA: Yes. He was a member of the Communist Party and had some background as a worker. When he started as a scientist in The Academy of Sciences he was a very good professional historian. He worked hard in the archives and wrote a wonderful monograph about the uprising of 1916. His conclusion about that event was correct, but it was not the official line.

He had trouble with that. He was expelled from the Communist Party and was no longer allowed to do his research. Then he had to "confess" that he was wrong, and he was highly criticized publicly. Only that part of his book, which agreed with the official line, was published. The rest was suppressed. With Kyrgyz Independence, however, this book was finally published.

JS: In his interview, Professor Usenbayev suggested that Abramson also had been expelled from The Communist Party.

BA: Yes.

Abramson was from Leningrad. During the second World War and the Leningrad blockade, scientists were sent to Central Asia. They just tried to save their lives and a lot of people were moved to Central Asia. Whole institutions moved here. That is the reason that we have the Academy of Sciences here in Bishkek.

Saul Matveevich Abramson devoted his whole life to the study of the Kyrgyz. Under his leadership, some of the best ethnography was done. His monograph, *The Kyrgyz And Their Ethno-genetic And Historical-Cultural Connections,* summarized his research. This work, which today is an outstanding source for Kyrgyz history, had stirred a negative reaction among the local party chiefs at the time of its appearance. For this remarkable monograph, Abramson was subjected to an undeserved criticism.

JS: Professor Kushbek Usenbaev referred to Klavdiya Antipina and her work. He said also that Abramson, Antipina, Bernshtam, and he were *all* criticized for being "Kyrgyz Nationalists."

BA: Yes. Because they wrote the truth, they were called "Kyrgyz Nationalists."
You know, it was the time when we were the "younger brother", and "younger brother" was expected to follow "older brother" and listen.

JS: "Older brother" lived in Moscow?

BA: Yes.

JS: Thank you very much for this interview.

BA You're welcome.

Klavdiya Antipina

Part 3: Photo Archive

KLAVDIYA ANTIPINA

Introduction to Part Three

Klavdiya Antipina was interested in nearly everything. Many persons who had known her personally told us this, and all agreed that her interests were wide.

Over the years, wielding her camera among the Kyrgyz people, Klavdiya Antipina built a vast photographic archive, an ethnographic treasure. Except when she had an assistant, she herself made these photographs. Her cameras were the FAD, the KIEV and the ZENIT. All photographic film had been processed in the laboratories of The Academy of Sciences in Bishkek, Kyrgyzstan. In her photographic archive she included a small number of drawings by artists, a few pictures clipped from periodicals, and several photographs by others. Her own camera work, however, makes up the bulk of this vast archive, an archive that contains thousands of her photographs.

Klavdiya Antipina was interested in people, people of all ages, infants to oldsters. She was interested in all aspects of how the Kyrgyz people lived, in what they did and in what they made. She was interested in *how* they did things. She was interested in clothing, in costume. It was she who chose the subjects and the moments for the photographs. She, an ethnographer, saw and studied what others took for granted.

This is a selection of photographs from the Antipina Photographic Archive. But how can the several dozen selected from thousands be representative? We, the authors, concluded that no such selection could be truly representative of the whole. Thus, we chose to concentrate on Klavdiya Antipina's clear love for people. People are depicted in many of our selections. Where possible, we have chosen to show costume as well. In one case, we have included a short series of photographs of a woman donning the *elechek* headdress (3.31-3.40). These unique photographs are of a subject dear to Klavdiya Antipina's heart. Although we have included several photographs of looms and weaving, no attempt has been made to include photographs of yurt construction, of animal husbandry, of felt making, of metal work, of leather work, or of wood carving. Also, other activities are not included.

Words in quotation marks are translations of the words, in pencilled Russian longhand, found on the backs of some of the photographs. Generally we have avoided additional captions, allowing the photographs to speak for themselves.

To some extent, the viewing of photographs, acquaints one with the person *behind* the camera. Through the viewing of our selection of photographs from the archive, the reader is invited to make further acquaintance with this ethnographer of the Kyrgyz, Klavdiya Antipina.

— Bibira Akmoldoeva and John Sommer

PART THREE
PHOTO ARCHIVES

Fig. 3.1 "Tian Shan"
(KA 1564)

Fig. 3.2 (KA 0725)

Fig. 3.3 (KA 1372)

KLAVDIYA ANTIPINA

Fig. 3.4 "Suzak Area, Collective Farms Karl Marx" (KA 0682)

Fig. 3.5 "1969" (KA 0751)

Fig. 3.6 "Toktogul Area, 1967" (KA 0805)

Fig. 3.7 "Toktogul Area, 1967"
(KA 3796)

Fig. 3.8 "Kulanai Village, Tian-Shan"
(KA 2354)

Fig. 3.9 "Batken Area, Collective Farms Andreeva, Barzun Village" (KA 0757)

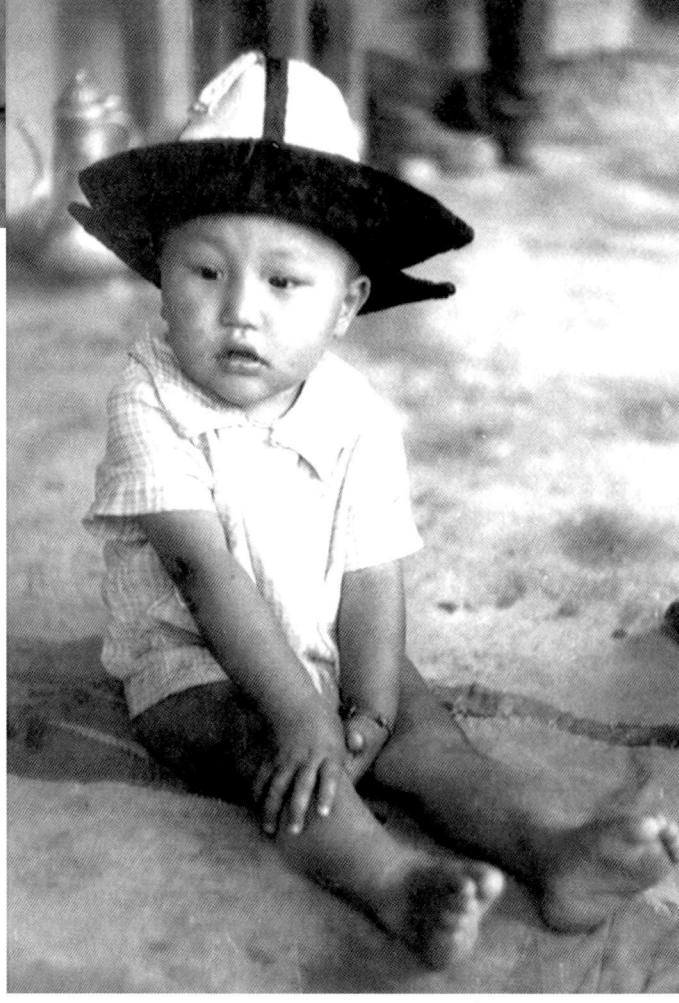

Fig. 3.10 "Kyzyl Uran, 1966" (KA 0770)

Fig. 3.11 "Molotov Area, Collective Farms Voroshilov"
(KA 0888)

Fig. 3.12 "Toktogul Area, 1967"
(KA 0797)

Fig. 3.13 "45 4-1-6"
(KA 0778)

PART THREE — PHOTO ARCHIVES

Fig. 3.14 "Suzak Area. Collective Farms Karl Marx" (KA 3337)

Fig. 3.15 "Archa Village, Tian Shan" (KA 1495)

Fig. 3.16 "Egat, Daki, Amanchik, Omurakhan, Saken, Abla, and Aitvai. Toktogul, 1966 (KA 0870)

Fig. 3.17 (KA 3886)

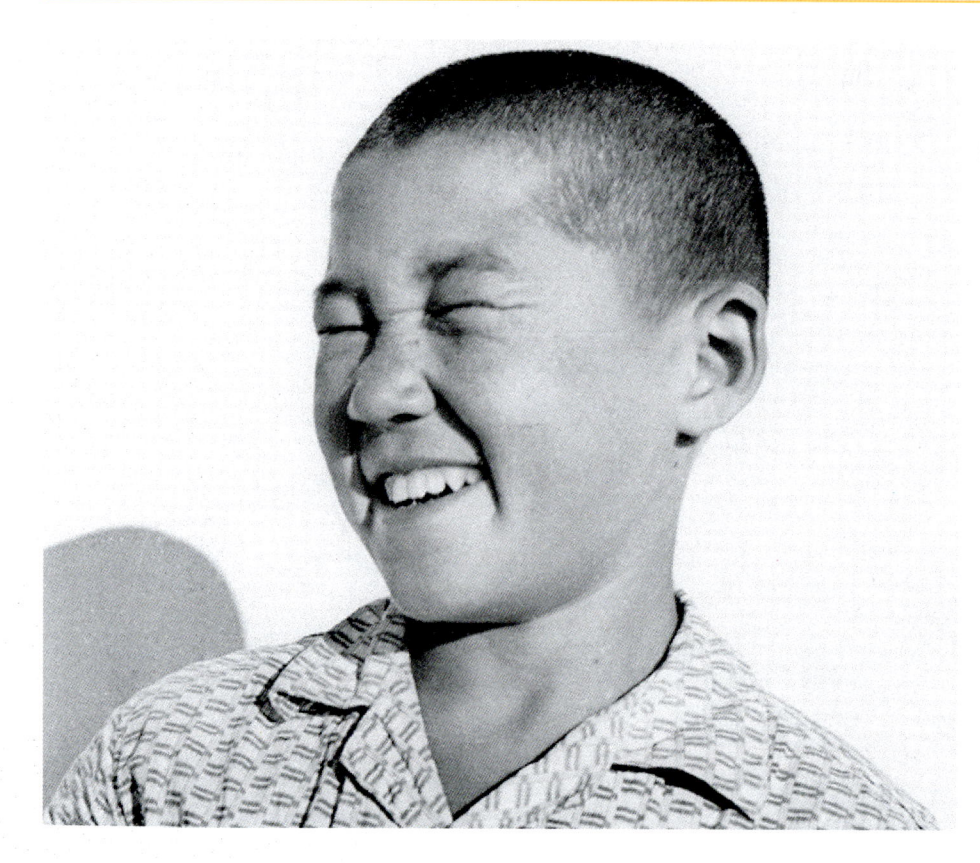

Fig. 3.18 (KA 0884)

Fig. 3.19 "Choi-Kra, 1969" (KA 0883)

Fig. 3.20
"Frontier Village, 1954"
(KA 0686)

KLAVDIYA ANTIPINA

Fig. 3.21 (KA 0845)

Fig. 3.22 (KA 0820)

PART THREE

PHOTO ARCHIVES

Fig. 3.23 (KA 0826)

Fig. 3.24 "Djangadjolskii Area, Collective Farms Jdanov, 1963" (KA 0833)

131

Fig. 3.25 "1954, Atbashi District"
(KA 0734)

Fig. 3.26 "1954, Atbashi District"
(KA 0735)

Fig. 3.27 (KA 0839)

Fig. 3.28 "Molotov Area, Karakul Village, Collective Farm Voroshilov" (KA 0904)

Fig. 3.29 "Toktogul Area, Collective Farms Karl Marx" (KA 0902)

PART THREE   PHOTO ARCHIVES

Fig. 3.30 "1954, Leninopol District" (KA 0847)

Fig. 3.31 "Emgen, 1963" (KA 2708A)

KLAVDIYA ANTIPINA

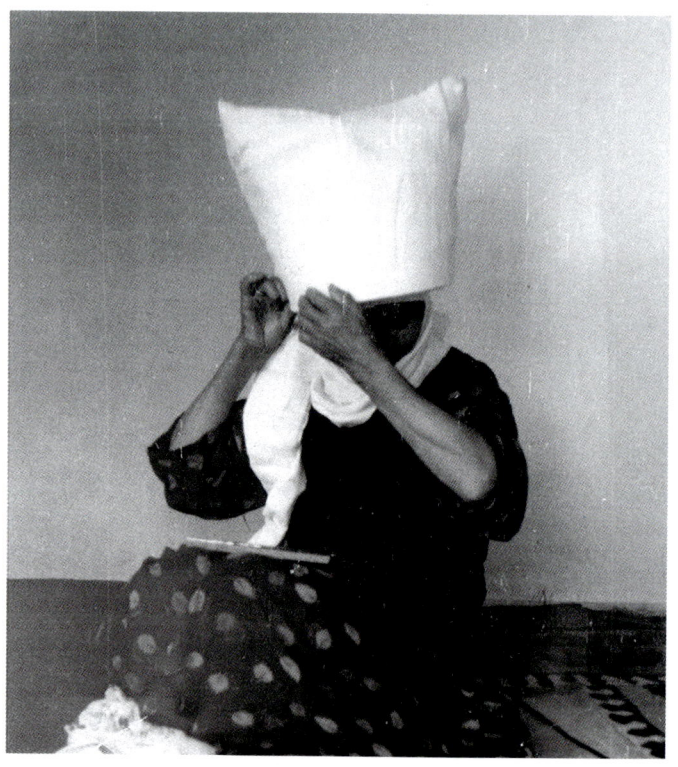

Fig. 3.32 "Emgen, 1963" (KA 2709)

Fig. 3.33 "Emgen, 1963" (KA 2710)

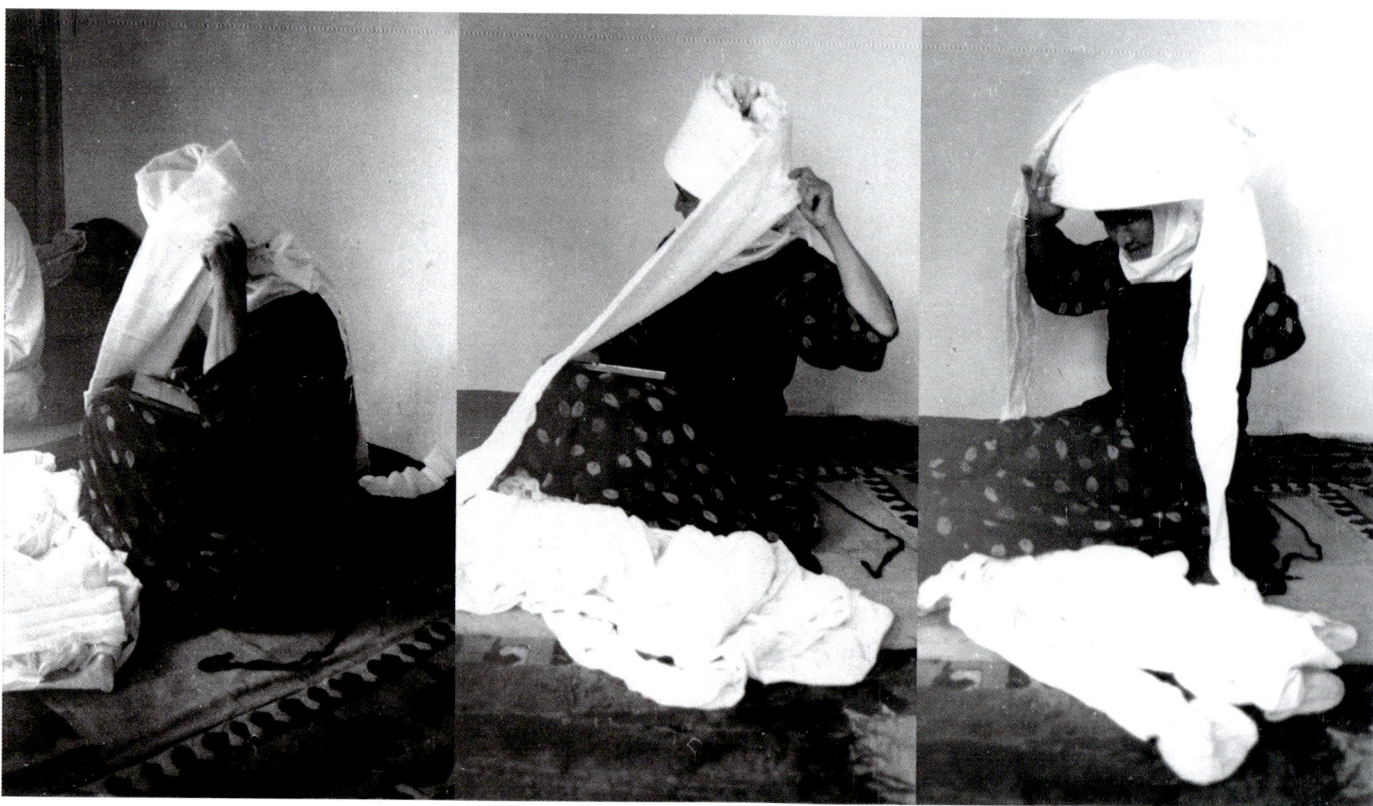

Fig. 3.34 "Emgen, 1963" (KA 2711 B)

Fig. 3.35 "Emgen, 1963" (KA 2714)

Fig. 3.36 "Emgen, 1963" (KA 2716)

PART THREE — PHOTO ARCHIVES

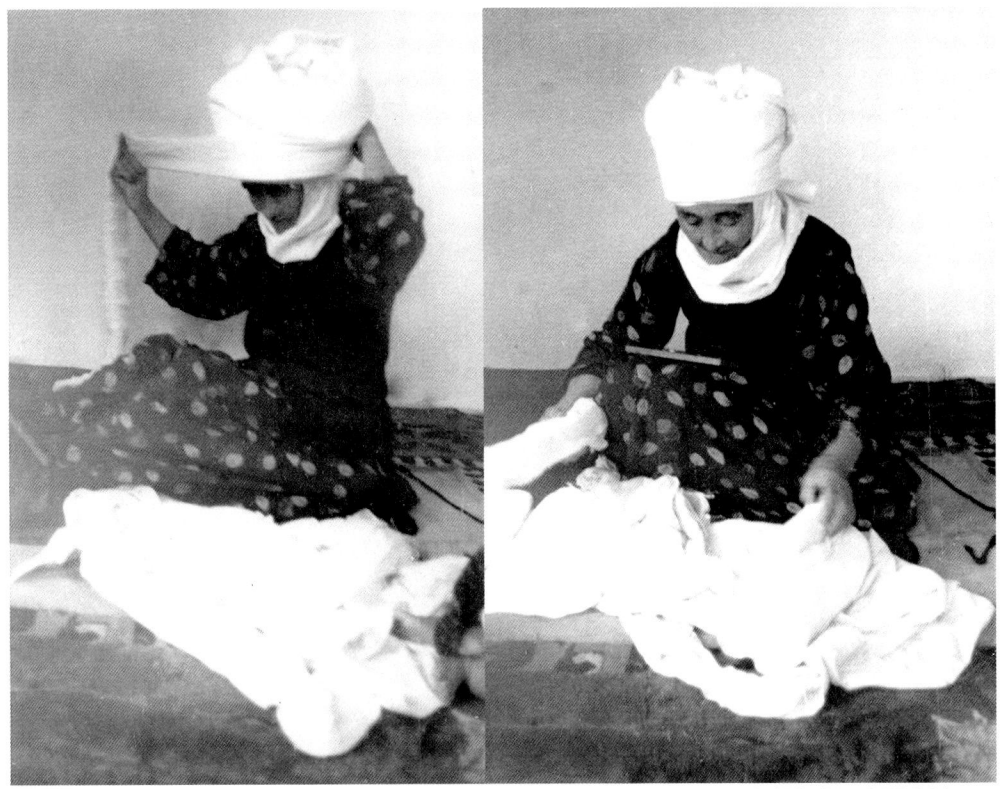

Fig. 3.37 "Emgen, 1963" (KA 2717)

Fig. 3.38 "Emgen, 1963" (KA 2722B)

Fig. 3.39 "Emgen, 1963" (KA 2724A)

Fig. 3.40 "Emgen, 1963" (KA 2725B)

Fig. 3.41 Antipina Archives
(Photograph by S. M. Dudin, early 20th century)

Fig. 3.42 "Pile Carpet, Batken Area, Collective Farms Malenkov, Karabulak Village" (KA 0927)

PART THREE PHOTO ARCHIVES

Fig. 3.43 "Bazaar, Kyzyl-Kia City (Noukat), 1969" (KA 0428)

Fig.3.44 (KA 3210)

139

Fig. 3.45 (KA 0930)

Fig. 3.46 "Carpet. Kurshabad Area, Collective Farms, Kyzyl October, Kara-Suzak Village." (KA 0929)

Fig. 3.47 "Djangidjolskii Area, Byimom Village, 1969" (KA 0640)

Fig. 3.48 (KA 0920, Detail)

Fig. 3.49 "Suzak Area, Collective Farms Karl Marx" (KA 0177)

Fig. 3.50 "Weaver Baibushan Bailieva (date of birth: 1942), Osh Region, Soviet Area. Kok-Art Village, 1977" (KA 1769)

Fig. 3.51 (KA 2835)

Fig. 3.52 "No. 28 Chon-Alay District, Village of Chak, Jailoo Kom Kaiyn" (KA 1360)

Fig. 3.53 "Detail of interior of yurt, Lylyak Area. Collective Farm: Tralina, Togua, Julak Village." (KA 1538)

PART THREE PHOTO ARCHIVES

Fig. 3.54 "Uzgen Area, Kara-Kuldjuk Village, 1969" (KA 0663)

Fig. 3.55 "1969" (KA 0749)

Fig. 3.56 "1962 Kyrt" (KA 0003)

The master *chiy* maker, *chyrmakchy*, seated on a mosaic felt, *shyrdak*, is wrapping dyed, but unspun, wool onto an individual dried *chiy* grass stem. She then will lay it in place on the cloth in front of her with the group of stems before her which previously have been wrapped in accordance with the design which she carries in her memory. (From the *Kyrgyz And Their Reed Screens*, with permission.)

Fig. 3.57 (KA 0001)

A plain reed screen [ak chiy] being woven on an outdoor "weaving frame." (The ends of the grasses are still untrimmed.) The weaving frame is seen from the front with fewer than half the stone weights visible, suspended on their binding cords. Upright bundles of chiy grass (*Lasiagrostis splendens*) stand at the sides. (From *The Kyrgyz And Their Reed Screens*, with permission.)

Fig. 3.58 (KA 0045)
"Batkenskii Region, May First Collective Farm. *Ashkana*."

Interior view of yurt with close-up view of *ashkana chiy* (space divider reed screen) in use. In the foreground are two large iron cooking kettles, one supported by stones over the fire pit and the other (partially seen at the far right) on an iron tripod. There are two buckets. Because the outer wall felts have been lifted a little, the shadows of the lattice wall behind this *ashkana chiy* are visible due to the outdoor light. (From *The Kyrgyz And Their Reed Screens*, with permission.)

Fig. 3.59 "A 34/68, Suusamyr" (KA 0025)

A *kanat chiy* surrounding the lattice wall (*kerege*) of the yurt. The outer covering felt of the yurt has been lifted and tucked under the tensed reinforcing ropes, allowing the *kanat chiy* to be seen. The design is of stepped rhombs or diamonds. (From *The Kyrgyz And Their Reed Screens*, with permission.)

Fig. 3.60 "Gulchinskii Area, Toguz Bulak, Socialism Village, 1956" (KA 2675)

Fig. 3.61 "The Kuibyshev Area, 1963" (KA 0806)

Fig. 3.62 "Frontier Village, Tian Shan, 1968" (KA 1568)

Fig. 3.63 (KA 1574)

Fig. 3.64 "No. 56 Kurshab District, Village of Kara Taryk, the Karl Marx Collective Farm" (KA 3082)

Fig. 3.65 "Kalanak Village, Tian Shan, 1968" (KA 2643)

Klavdiya Antipina

Part 4: Writings

Introduction to Part Four

In 1962 Klavdiya Antipina, at age 58, published *Osobennosti Materialnoi Kultury I Prikladnogo Iskusstva Iuzhnykh Kirgizov (Distinctive Features Of The Material Culture and Applied Art Of The Southern Kirghiz)*. This book served as her dissertation for the doctoral degree granted her in Moscow. This information-filled work was based on her field research conducted during the latter half of the decade of the 1950's following her release from the obligation to report periodically to the police.

She had felt that her husband's arrest (and her own exile?) had been a mistake and that, in time, this would be recognized and corrected. But, gradually, she came to see that this would never happen. She recognized her widowed status and came to accept what, for her, was inevitable. With Stalin's death in 1953 her life began to change. She was no longer labeled "an enemy of the people."

For the first time in her life, she was able to pursue her primary interest, ethnography. Without openly complaining, for fifteen years she had lived a life of frustration and terror. Decades before, she had studied ethnography. Now, after extensive field work among the Kirghiz people conducted during the late 1950's, she wrote this towering ethnographic work. The introduction to the book and the chapter on pile weaving are reproduced here. One senses her considerable admiration and respect for the Kyrgyz people she had grown to love. One sees evidence of her ethnographic skills and thoroughness.

In that book she gave detailed information about wool processing, felt making, felt carpets, plaiting, reed screen making, spinning, plying, band weaving, "flatweaving," animal trappings, yurt furnishings, and stitchery (on felt, leather, and fabric). She described leather working and blacksmithing, the tools, the techniques, the designs, and the resulting products. In remarkable detail, she described the yurt, its parts, its construction, its set-up, its furnishings, and something of its symbolism. She gave details of construction, floor plans, and furnishings of non-portable (permanent) dwellings. She gave detailed descriptions of the design and use of outdoor ovens, of storage sheds, and of animal shelters. She gave similar detailed information on urban dwellings. Costume was a prime interest of Klavdiya Antipina. In this book she gave detailed, patterns, and illustrations of the costumes of men, women, and young people. She dealt with footwear, headwear, and jewelry. From that book, we have chosen to include here, in translation, her Introduction and her chapter on Pile Weaving.

Klavdiya Antipina had been the co-director of the archaeological-ethnographical expeditions in Kirghizia during the 1950's, and eventually she would be the co-editor (with S. V. Ivanov) of the fifth volume in the report of those expeditions, *Narodnoe Dekorativno-Prikladnoe Iskusstvo Kirgizov (Popular Ornamental Art Of The Kirghiz People)*, published by "Nauka" Publishers, Moscow, in 1968. In addition to editing, she also wrote various parts of the book. Her chapter on Pile Weaving is reproduced here in translation.

Through reading these excerpts from these two books, we gain insight into Klavdiya Antipina's thinking, her attention to detail, and her ethnographic thoroughness. We have made an effort, despite redundancies, to reproduce these excerpts of her writings as closely as possible to the originals, including original notes, figures, and plates.

Klavdiya Antipina avoided the limelight, often operating "behind the scenes." She was an "idea person"

PART FOUR   WRITINGS

who gave credit to others. All who had dealings with her, respected her. By many, she was much loved.

In English dictionaries, "ethnography" is defined as "descriptive anthropology." Much of Klavdiya Antipina's field work is descriptive. Had she not gathered and recorded it, this information would be lost to us today. Often she spoke with elderly persons, obtaining insights into remembered pastoralist life. (An elderly person in the 1950's might have remembered the nineteenth century.) She wrote:

> … where possible, we study the earlier forms of material art, the characteristics of which differentiate in everyday life the basic tribal and clan group organization along which the Kirghiz population had been divided in the past …

But a Soviet ethnographer also studied the present. Klavdiya Antipina also wrote:

> Soviet ethnographic science is not limited to the study of past cultures. It is also concerned with present changes resulting from socialist reconstruction of the economy and the growth of domestic production and material culture. The task of a multifaceted ethnographic historian is to study these phenomena. [This] is the task for modern ethnographers of the Kirghiz.

In isolated paragraphs of her writings, Klavdiya Antipina refers to "The Great October Revolution", to "Socialist principles", to "Marxist-Leninist principles", to "vicious class struggle", to "penetration of capitalist relations", and to "exploitation of workers." She also uses other stock words and phrases of the communist party line. Following her own personal experiences, did Klavdiya Antipina really have such admiration and loyalty for the Soviet regime? One might wonder.

We may be certain, however, that Klavdiya Antipina wanted to do ethnography. For the hope of publishing a book, the express approval of the Soviet system was necessary and expected by the Moscow review committees whose approval was essential for publication. Whatever Klavdiya Antipina's true thoughts, that was a small price for publishing this book. She felt that the material was important ethnographically. She also knew that this book could make a difference in her own career. If she was to continue to do high quality ethnography, this was the route. The book was published, in Frunze, in 1962. Five hundred copies in Russian. (At the time, in the United States, the book and its author had been unknown.) Thirty years later, in Bishkek, she apologized for not having a copy to give us, directing us instead to the Lenin Library in Moscow.

Klavdiya Antipina wrote on a variety of subjects. We have listed in the Bibliography some of the works she authored or co-authored, edited or co-edited. A book on costume she had been working on for at least three decades was finally completed but never published. This would be a major work, including many dozens of artworks (by Temirbek Musakeev) depicting actual persons and actual clothing. One of the disappointments of her life was that this book never was published. Regrettably, even the whereabouts of the manuscript is now unknown.

Generally in the present book, we have given names and terms in use at the time the material was written or at the time referred to. Thus, Petrograd or Saint Petersburg is used in nineteenth century references, Leningrad during the Soviet era, and now again Saint Petersburg. The system of transliteration of Russian words follows, in general, the system of the United States Board on Geographic Names. Well-known Russian names, however, if they occur, are given in the form that has become familiar to English-speaking readers. Inconsistencies in transliteration result from such differences. Other apparent inconsistencies result from Russian and Kyrgyz words that refer to the same thing. Insofar as possible, these inconsistencies have been eliminated, but inevitably some remain.

In the notes to translated material, there are sometimes references to parts of the book which do not appear here. We have allowed these to remain, although clearly it is not possible for the reader easily to use such references.

The translations have sometimes been rephrased and polished. We sincerely hope that essential meanings have not been altered by this effort to improve readability. For any errors of any kind, the authors assume full responsibility.

—Bibira Akmoldoeva and John Sommer

Introduction

Osobennosti Materialnoi Kultury I Prikladnogo Iskusstva Iuzhnykh Kirgizov (Distinctive Features of the Material Culture and Applied Art of the Southern Kirghiz), Frunze, 1962 pp.3-15

This edited translation is by Nathan Hodge and Sharon Weinberger.

Among the sources available for addressing the matter of the ethnic origins of a people and the emergence of their national customs, ethnic descriptions of material culture and native decorative art are of particular importance. In turn, the most valuable ethnographies devoted to this aspect of native life must employ detailed study of domestic handicrafts and products as a part of the larger material economy, which in the past served to satisfy the demands of everyday life as well as serving the people's aesthetic needs.

Soviet ethnographic science is not limited to the study of past cultures. It is also concerned with present changes resulting from socialist reconstruction of the economy and the growth of domestic production and material culture. The task of a multifaceted ethnographic historian is to study these phenomena. It is the task for modern ethnographers of the Kirghiz.

Until recently the material culture and domestic handicrafts of the Kirghiz were not specifically studied. The prerevolutionary ethnographic literature on the Kirghiz is fragmentary. The approach is not systematic. Most authors neglected to employ examples or illustrations of the tribal affiliations of the populations they described. They also failed to note the unique characteristics in the development between the cultures of the southern and northern Kirghiz. Nevertheless, among the works which hold valuable information of the questions raised above and which pay particular attention to the Kirghiz settled in Northern Kirghizia, several articles and selections should be mentioned, including those by Ch. Ch. Valikhanova (1), M. I. Venyukhova (2), L. F. Kostenko (3), G. S. Zagryazhsky (4), G. Bardasheva (5), A. P. Khoroshkhin (6), N. L. Zeelanda (7), and V. V. Radlova (8).

Interesting details about the Kirghiz people of Osh oblast can be found in the works of A. P. Fedchenko (9), G. E. Grum-Grzhimailo (10), B. Ya. Grombchevsky (11), V. I. Kushelevsky (12), V. A. Parfentieva (13), N. S. Lykoshina (14), N. L. Korzhenevsky (15), G. V. Pokrovsky and N. I. Stogova (16), A. A. Kushakevich (17), A. Uspensky (18), and others.

Immeasurably useful and notably better documents and detailed reports on material culture and handicraft production of the Kirghiz found a place in the labors of Soviet scientists, the majority of which are based on the principles of Marxist-Leninist methodology.

The valuable published works of F. A. Fielstrup (19), who travelled through Kirghizia, are supplemented by the well-described collection of ethnographic material gathered for the GME (20).

The works of S. M. Abramson (21), beginning with his publications following his complex expedition to Alai in 1927 (22), are notable for their breadth and diversity. From that time forward there has also been undertaken intensive work on additions to the ethnographic collection organized in 1926 at the Kirghiz Regional Museum (23), formerly the Historical Museum of the Kirghiz SSR.

The material culture of the northern Kirghiz has been the focus of much more literature than that of the southern Kirghiz. Thus, the Kirghiz of the Issyk-Kul region have been the subject of works by M. Aitbaeva (24) and E. I. Makhova (25). P. I. Kushner's book (26) appeared as a result of journeys by the author to the area of the Talas Valley. The dissertation by A. F. Burkovsky (27) *The Technology of Contemporary Handcraft Production of Kyrgyz Collective Farms,* published as a series of articles, devotes attention to the northern Kirghiz. The author, in devoting his study to the technical aspects of the forms of production, almost entirely neglects to assess the artistic side. Also, one has little idea of the actual items produced, the craftsmen who made them, or of the ethnic group itself.

An article by M. R. Ryskulbekova (28) is of interest in the study of Kirghiz domestic handicrafts. There is good ethnographic reporting and the economic side is revealed as well. S. Ilyasov (29) fixes his attention on the development of handicrafts and the cooperation with small-industry producers in the chapter on "Cooperation of Handicrafters and Tradesmen." Both authors note the differences between the southern and the northern Kirghiz.

Beginning in the twentieth century Kirghiz decorative art began to draw the attention of researchers. The first publications to appear were those of the Hungarian scientist Almashi (30) and of A. Felkersam (31).

Soviet art historians also developed an interest in Kirghiz art, as did ethnographers and artists themselves. This enriched the literature. The ethnographer and artist S. M. Dudin (32) gives interesting reports on native art. However, the value of some works is reduced by his not making a distinction between the Kazakh and the Kirghiz.

The articles by V. Chepelev (33) and A. Romm (34) give an overview. It is also important to include the works of M. S. Andreev (35) and M. F. Gavrilov (36), who gave their work scientific value by publishing their collection of ornamental art.

Among the research reports written, a special place belongs to the seminal work by the artist M. V. Rundin (with an introduction by A. N. Bershtam) which is dedicated to the Kirghiz ornamental art he collected over ten years (37). In a valuable review of the work, S. M. Abramson (38) reveals some of its inadequacies, enters into a highly debatable argument between the authors over the narrative character of Kirghiz pattern design, and points out the lack of scientific documentation of some of the ornaments published. In our view, these omissions reduce the value of the work as does the absence of characteristically southern ornamental forms.

Contributions to strengthening and broadening our ethnographic research were made between 1953 and 1955 by the Kirghiz combined archeological-ethnographic expedition organized by the Institute of History of the Academy of Sciences, Kirghiz SSR, in conjunction with Institute of Ethnography and the Institute of the History of Material Culture of the USSR Academy of Science. This and a scientific conference devoted to the theme of ethnogenesis of the Kirghiz people, led to the publication of a four-volume summary: *Works* (39). Its conclusions reflect the contributions of the expedition, including material culture of the Kirghiz (40, 41, 42) and their ornamental art. A fifth volume, devoted to the decorative arts of the Kirghiz, is currently underway.

The present work is based in large part on materials gathered by the author during her expeditions through the southern part of the Osh oblast of the Kirghiz SSR (1955-56), as well as in the Batkensky and Osh regions of the Oblast (1958). The participation of the author in the first stage of the information-gathering and research in the regions of the Osh region studied in the above-mentioned expedition undertaken in 1955, as a member of the ethnographic team, played a fundamental role in the direction of the present work. The task of this study is to place this in an ethnographic context and to reveal the original aspects and the ethnic singularity of the southern Kirghiz. We note the best ethnic traditions, and, where possible, we study the earlier forms of material art, the characteristics of which differentiate in everyday life the basic tribal/clan group organization along which the Kirghiz population had been divided in the past (43). Likewise, our mission is to show the whole complex of southern Kirghiz material culture as a part of the larger Kirghiz material culture.

The completion of our first two expeditions allowed us to speak with assurance not only about the uniqueness of the material culture of the Southern Kirghiz as a whole (having many remarkable features in contrast to the Kirghiz of the north), but it also enabled us to distinguish in the south of Kirghizia the existence of two clearly different traditions. One of these followed from the historical conditions among the tribal group of the Ichkilik people, and the second among a group of tribes, the Adgine and Mugush (explained below). Out of that observation grows the task set before this author, and which should enable us to solve one of the most important problems in Kirghiz historiography, viz., the question of the ancestry of the Kirghiz peoples.

As called for by socialist principles, and beginning with the second half of the nineteenth century, we have included in this scientific framework the systematized ethnographic material characteristics of the domestic handcraft, of the material culture, and of the decorative art of the southern Kirghiz. We have attempted to follow the historical changes in these areas of Kirghiz culture and to give a few observations on the contemporary forms of lifestyle among the southern Kirghiz.

In addition to the available literature, we availed ourselves of the physical artifacts—the ethnographic collections of the GME, MAE, the Historical Museum of the Kyrgyz SSR, the Historical Museum of the Uzbek SSR, and the Art Museum of the Uzbek SSR. Many illustrations and photographs employed in the book are of the objects stored in these museums. Particularly valuable among these are the photographs of S. M. Dudin, who at the beginning of our century visited Southern Kirghizia and Eastern Turkestan. S. M. Dudin also left us an account of his trip which is stored, along with his photographs, in the archives of the GME. They have enabled us to account for many of the important features of the material culture of the southern Kirghiz and to verify and refine reports received from our informants.

Also employed were short entries from the ethnographic encyclopedia of Kirghizia by S. M. Abramson and the ethnographic notes of K. Miftakov during an expedition in 1947 to the Alai Valley, which are stored in the archives of the Department of Social Sciences of the Kirghiz SSR.

Most of the material, however, on which the present work is based derives from notes taken during wanderings, study of items of contemporary life, and interviews with collective farmers. The interviews were with persons of varying age, but those with the older age groups told of life in previous generations. In using retrospective scholarship, we are aware that many everyday objects of previous centuries have been lost in the storm of historical events and socio-historical changes. We no longer come upon them. They are preserved only in collective memory (44).

In studying the household handicraft and artisanship which existed at an earlier time, it is vital to fix the primitive technology employed, because thanks to this technology, the ethnographic particularity of the southern Kirghiz was able to arise.

A valuable source for the study of the material culture and decorative art of the southern Kirghiz has been the innumerable color and pencil sketches of everyday objects and ornaments, as well as photographs made during field studies by the artist V. N. Lazarevskaya and the photographs of Y. V. Neskvernov and of D. Bakeev (45). In the work of the expedition, laboratory technicians K. Mambetalieva and A. Maksutova were very helpful.

In the process of collection, particular attention was paid to establishing a systematic use of terms. Such data may help to resolve a few ethnographic problems. (For the transcription of Kirghiz terms appearing in the text, please refer to the "Glossary of Local Terms" which is attached at the end of the book.) [Note: This glossary referred to by Klavdiya Antipina appears in *her* book *Osobenossti Materialnoi Kultury I Prikladnogo Iskusstva Iuzhnykh Kirgizov.* It in *not* the same glossary as that in the present book.]

The present work does not pretend to be a conclusive account of the material culture of the southern Kirghiz (46). It is merely the first attempt at their ethnographic study. Included in this book are materials and information which we have examined. This constitutes only a basis for the further and more detailed study which each theme demands. Only the gathering of a great volume of informational material and the comparative assessment of historical-ethnographic data will allow us in the future to resolve scientific problems which in the present study have been barely covered. We hope that the material here offered, when put in an anthropological, a linguistic, and a historical context, may help to resolve some issues connected with the ethnic history of the Kirghiz people, as well as the ethnography of Central Asia as a whole.

During the preparation of this book, many persons and institutions assisted, advised, furnished materials, and composed the illustrations. Valuable criticism was offered by colleagues from the Institute of History of the Kirghiz SSR, the Central Asia Sector of the Institute of Ethnography of the USSR (I. M. Peshcherova, E. I. Makhova, G. P. Vasilievna), scientific colleagues at the GME, MLE, the Uzbekistan Museum of Art, and the Historical Museum of the Institute of History of the Kirghiz SSR. All cooperated in acquainting the author with museum collections. The majority of illustrated materials were realized for the book by the artist Z. I. Kriuchkova; additional illustrations were by M. M. Korchakova and M. Abdulaev. The author would like to express her gratitude to all these persons and institutions.

The territory of the Osh oblast occupies the southwestern part of the Kirghiz SSR. The area covers 75,500 square kilometers. The southernmost part of this area covers 46,000 square kilometers. The rural Kirghiz population which lives here is the object of our study.

In the past, the Osh region was entirely under the territory of the Kokand Khanate, but after the latter's liquidation and formation of the Turkestan region, this territory became part of the Fergana region (1876), and until the new demarcation of Central Asian lands (1924), it was divided among Kokand, Skobelev (Margelan), Andizhan, Namangan, and Osh districts. The boundaries of these districts were notably wider than the boundaries of the present-day Osh region. They included the Pamir and a large part of the Fergana Valley. After the delineation of new national boundaries the name of the territory was joined with the Kirghiz autonomous region (which together would later become the Kirghiz SSR.)

The Osh region, subdivided into 17 districts, was formed in 1939, at the same time as the Jalalabad region, which occupied the northern part of the territory of Southern Kirghizia. In 1959, one region was created in the place of two—the Osh region, into which the entire territory of Southern Kirghizia was incorporated. At the same time the districts were consolidated, resulting in the 17 districts that encompass the Osh region today.

The Southeast of Osh region borders the Xianjian-Uighur autonomous region of the People's Republic of China, an area formerly known as Eastern Turkestan. On the south and southwestern edge runs the border of Osh region with the Tajik SSR (Gorno-Badakshan autonomous region, Leninabad (Dushanbe) regions and the Jargatalsk district. On the west of Osh region is found the Andizhan and Fergana regions of the Uzbek SSR. The territory extends for the largest part along the border of the Tajik SSR.

According to the statistics of the All-Union Population Survey of 1959, the Osh region had a population of 869,108 inhabitants, comprising 42% of the total population of the Kirghiz SSR.

In its ethnic composition the southern part of the Osh region is not much different from the northern part. According to the 1939 census, Kirghiz people comprised about 60% of the population, Uzbeks 22%, Russians and Ukrainians about 12%, and Tajiks approximately 2%. Other significantly less numerous nationalities and ethnic groups in the territory of the southern part of the region are Uighurs, Dungans, Turks, Tatars, Arabs, Armenians, and others.

Russian and Ukrainian settlers in the south began to arrive at the end of the nineteenth century, that is, later than in the northern regions of Issyk-Kul and in the Chui Valley. The largest numbers settled in the territories of the Northern part of the Alai, in the Uzgen and Suzak districts, principally in valley country best suited to the parcelling of land.

The more compact Kirghiz populace correspondingly lived in the territory of the Uzgen, Soviet, Alai, Naukat and Batken districts. In the majority of other regions the Kirghiz also predominated (47).

The Osh region was populated by Kirghiz who in former times had belonged to various clans and tribal groups. On the so-called right wing were situated the tribes of Adigine, Mungush, and Mongoldor. Alongside them was a series of tribal groups known by the name of the Ichkilik. The ethnic history of these tribes, however, differs (48). They probably appeared at different times in different migrations through the Fergana Valley. According to information related by elders, it appears that the Adigine tribe settled the land they presently occupy in the northern regions around 350 years ago (49). The Mungush tribe is genealogically connected to the Adigine and apparently settled simultaneously with them. They were neighbors. The Mongoldor tribe is of mixed Mongol and Turk origin. It was formed in the post-Mongol era and had lived continuously within the boundaries of northern Kirghizia (50).

Legend has it that the Adigine, the Mungush, and the Mongoldor shared ancestry with other tribes that belonged to the "right wing" and called Tagai their forefather. These tribes (the Bugu, the Sarybagysh, the Solto, etc.) have resided in Northern Kirghizia since time immemorial (51). Legends portray the Adigine and Tagai as brothers.

Their descendants—the Kirghiz themselves—relate to the three tribes named above, and largely populate the eastern and southeastern districts of the Osh region (Uzgen, Sovietsky, and Alai), and they can be found to an extent in other regions as well (in the Naukat, Osh, Aravan, Ala-Bukin, Chatkal, and Toklogul districts). In addition to these areas they also live in a few population centers in neighboring regions of the Uzbek SSR, particularly in the Andijan regions (these groups are descended from the Adigine and Mungush tribes), as well as in isolated parts of the Xianjian-Uighur autonomous region of the People's Republic of China (PRC).

The designation "Ichkilik" extends to the following tribes: Teyt, Naiman, Kypchak, Kandy, Avagat (Avat), Toolos, Kesek, Jookesek, Boston, and Noigut. Those Kirghiz descendants who count themselves as part of these tribes live largely in the southeastern region (in Lailak, Frunze, Batken, Naukat, Aravan, and Osh districts).

Groups also known by the name "Ichkilik" live in other regions of the Osh region, including Suzak, Uzgen, Kara-Su, Bazar-Kurgan, Ala Buka, and Lenin districts (52). A considerable number of Ichkilik settled in neighboring areas of the Fergana and Andijian regions of the Uzbek SSR, and in the Murgabsk, Gorno-Badakhshan autonomous regions, and the Jirgatal district of the Tajik SSR, as well as in the above-named districts of the Xianjian-Uighur autonomous region of the People's Republic of China.

The ethnic history of the tribes carrying the name "Ichkilik" has as yet not been studied adequately. Historical data and the accounts of elders suggest that the majority of these tribes emigrated from the territory of eastern Turkestan. Also it is clear that some groups included in the make-up of this tribe are also of local origin (53). The recently published source document, a manuscript entitled "Mojamu at-tavarik", gives us a basis for asserting that, by the sixteenth century, some of these tribes resided within the boundaries of their current dispersal (54).

Those Kirghiz who designate their ancestry as Ichkilik settled in compact local groups, and in these places they neighbor other tribes. In the Uzgen district, for example, these other tribes are the Adigine, the Kandy, the Bostons, the Mungush, and others. Differences in culture and way of life—so distinct in the past among each of these once entirely separate ethnic groups—are breaking down. However, we do find ethnic groups that have stabilized and preserved their traditions. For example, in the village of Tengizbai a long-resident group has preserved some characteristics of its tribe, characteristics corroborated by the oldest accounts.

The change from a rural, herding economy to that of land cultivation, a continuing process among the Kirghiz, intensified during the nineteenth century and proved dramatic. Such change depended on socioeconomic factors as well as natural geographic circumstances (55).

The environment of the southern part of the Osh region is rich and varied (56). Its geological relief, demarcated by the mountain ranges of Pamiro Alaya and Tien-Shan, includes the southern part of the broader Fergana basin. The high peaks, perpetually covered by snow, are joined by the rolling, fertile pastures and steep canyons of the high plateau, rich in trees, shrubs, and grasses. Even from earliest times herding existed here along with simple land cultivation—the two kinds of rural economy (57).

In the Alai district and in the Alaiku river basin pastoralism prevailed, requiring an abundance of grazing land (58). The scenic Alai Valley, situated between 3000 and 3200 meters above sea level between the Alai and Zaalai ranges with its abundant plant growth, from time immemorial has attracted nomads. Today, this is important for the local as well as for the export/import economy. Land cultivation in the Alai district is of secondary importance, however, and flour for bread is mostly brought from the outside (59). In the Kara-Kul and Tar river basins, where the natural conditions are equally congenial to both agriculture and animal herding, land cultivation emerged.

In other areas of cultivated land—the valleys along the Kok-Su, Isfara, Sokh, and Lyailyak rivers—dry-farming methods are employed. But, at the same time, the mountainous parts of these regions are amenable to animal herding (60). Typically, of the land available for cultivation, two thirds is used for dry-farming and one-third is irrigated (61).

Although by the beginning of the twentieth century land cultivation occupied a primary position in the rural Kirghiz economy, transition to this type of agricultural did not always involve the abandonment of animal herding. Even as the centuries-old nomadic customs were gradually displaced by settled land cultivation, deep traditions continued.

With nomadism, the driving of cattle to summer, fall and winter pasture, was based on socio-familial principals. In the most important of the commonly-herded pastures, each settled group occupied a customary site in the mountain villages (62).

The Kirghiz herded goats, camels, horses, sheep, and horned cattle. The leading form of animal tending was sheep herding. Although their wool was rough and inferior, sheep, having great hardiness and endurance and provided a significant amount of meat, and were important. In the territories of the southwestern districts (Lyailyak, Batken, Frunze) a type of sheep known as *ysar koi* was bred. Here, also, was the notable development of goat herding.

The camels were two-humped. By 1913, they were reduced to only a few in number (63), but some were still used by prosperous households. Traditions persisted longer in the east. But where change occurred more rapidly, as in the western regions, there were fewer camels.

All settlements had goats and goat-milk products were kept for family consumption. In land cultivation, oxen served as beasts of burden. In Alai and the eastern Pamir yaks were used (64). Yaks were valued not only for their high quality dairy products, but also for their strength as pack animals and their endurance at high altitude.

Horses were mainly Kirghiz bred, and they were widely used not only as pack animals, but also for making *kümuss* (fermented mare's milk). In western areas, donkeys were also used.

Among the settled farming cultures, spring wheat and barley were widely cultivated. (These crops grow well at higher altitudes.) In the past millet was grown, but, according to the tales of elders, it did poorly. Corn and rice were grown principally in the north and, in the west, the Kirghiz grew a type of sorghum called *jugaru*.

By the beginning of the twentieth century, the southern Kirghiz through technical advances were able to introduce cotton and melons.

Under the influence of neighboring settled agricultural populations, the Kirghiz (especially in the southwestern regions), developed market-gardens, in which they grew onions, carrots, and spices. The planting of fruit trees and grape vines in some garden plots, began in the twentieth century. Wealthy landowners planted large orchards of apricot trees (*uryuk*).

Despite the introduction of new plant cultures, land cultivation continued with the most primitive of devices. The mattock or hoe (*ketmen*) was universal. A wooden plough (*omack*) with a cast iron blade turned the soil. The modern plough, introduced under Russian influence, appeared only in isolated places in the northeastern part of the region. Crops were gathered using a sickle (*orok*). They sowed the soil with help of horses and oxen. For transporting harvests in dry-farming and mountainous areas a cart (*chiine*) was used. In western parts of the Alai Valley they also used sledges (*chigina*) adopted from the Tajiks.

As with other Kirghiz, hunting wild animals using flintlock guns occupied a crucial place in the economy.

The second half of the nineteenth and first part of the twentieth centuries were marked by critical historical events (65), The Kirghiz population periodically revolted against the yoke of the Kokand Khan. After his fall, the territory of Southern Kirghizia became a part of Russia (1876). Feudal-patriarchal relations began to break down, and capitalism appeared. Cotton, which demanded large acreage, was introduced. Trade strengthened and industrial enterprises such as coal mining appeared.

The penetration of capitalist relations, the decline of animal herding and the parcelling of agricultural lands led to deep stratification among the peasantry, bringing the necessity of new forms of subsistence. Poor peasants were taken over by the landowners, for whom they then tended herds, harvested crops and worked the land. The landowners exploited them, particularly those who used patrimonial holdovers. The Kirghiz went into the coal mines. (This work took on a seasonal character.) The means of earning money in mining was by hauling and reselling coal, carried from the mines on camels, horses, and donkeys. Others of the Kirghiz were occupied with chopping and selling firewood, and with firing and selling charcoal.

The Great October Socialist Revolution brought profound changes for the living conditions of the population. It became the boundary dividing the mass of people from their arduous past: manual labor, primitive technology, general poverty and illiteracy.

New life was achieved in the south after vicious class struggle. The post-revolutionary recovery was interrupted by the actions (insurrections against Soviet rule) of the Basmachi movement which continued to antagonize the people even after the end of the Civil War. Therefore, land reforms in the south of Kirghizia were conducted later (1927-28) than in the north. Land reforms played a great role in the rise of agriculture.

The far-reaching and radical transformations of socialist agriculture followed the victory of collectivization, bringing many major achievements. The unwavering conduct of the party with the guidance of Leninist national politics enabled them to bring this to life.

Today the south of Kirgizia is a region of varied and productive agriculture, whose development and growth is based on the achievements of modern science (66). Particular emphasis is placed on technical cultivation, in which cotton growing leads. Cotton planting is the major occupation for sixty percent of the collective farm regions (67). Cotton plantations occupy the mountain plains, which are an area of intensive farming. The development of cotton as a crop coincides with silkworm breeding and grape growing. This zone has a landscape characteristic of the entire Fergana Valley.

The Soviet era has seen the introduction of tobacco in the Naukat district. Grain (wheat and corn), fruits, and vegetables are now harvested. These include potatoes, tomatoes, and other produce—new plants previously unknown to the Kirghiz.

Animal herding occurs not only in the broad pastures of the mountain regions, but also in the lowland plains. Cattle raising today combines the knowledge of centuries along with contemporary zoo technology. Although new animals are introduced, sheep continue to be the most important.

Technology has changed before our eyes. In agriculture today, powerful new machines are everywhere. In the Soviet era we have been able to build engineered irrigation equipment, and to construct new reservoirs.

The development of the rural economy with new production conditions has entirely transformed the peasantry, has improved life, and has raised the cultural level. As a result of cooperative labor as a way of life in the multinational cooperative farms, an intensive process of mutual cultural exchange is underway, which is attested to in the more rational elements of culture.

The rapid development of productive forces has brought Soviet industry to life. For the first time we are finally able to employ the natural wealth of the region. In addition to coal mining, metallurgical and petrochemical industries have emerged. Cotton processing and textile factories have experienced corresponding growth.

At the present time, the construction of powerful energy sources is being completed. The Uch-Kurgan hydroelectric station, for one, will provide energy for the agriculture of Kirghizia but also for that of Uzbekistan.

With appearance of industry in the south of Kyrgyzstan, new cities are being built. At present nine cities and fourteen settlements of this type exist in Osh region. The oldest of these cities, Osh and Uzgen, are among five located in the south. Urban population is growing quickly. In accordance with the 1959 survey, there were 278,726 residents in the cities of Southern Kirgizia. The urban dwellers were sixteen percent of the Kirghiz population in 1939, but by 1959 it had doubled to thirty two percent (68). Along with the growth of cities the cultural ties between city and village have been strengthened.

In this manner, the south of socialist Kirghizia has been transformed into an industrial-agrarian region with great prospects for the future.

Notes

Osobennosti Materialnoi Kultury I Prikladnogo Iskusstva Iuzhnykh Kirgizov (Distinctive Features of the Material Culture and Applied Art of the Southern Kirghiz), Frunze, 1962, pp. 3-15; the footnotes (end notes) are numbered as in the original text. This edited translation is by Nathan Hodge and Sharon Weinberger.

1. Chokan Valikanov [sic]. *Collected Works.* Alma-Ata, 1958.
2. M. Venyukov [sic]. "Sketches of the Zailinsky kray and the Prichuis land," *Annals of The Russian Geographic Society,* 1861, Book 4.
3. L. F. Kostenko. *Central Asia and Its Settlement by Russian Citizenry.* St. Petersburg, 1870.
4. G. S. Zagryazhsky. *Sketches from Tokman District.* 1873, Nos. 9 & 10. *The Way of Life of the Kochevoj population of Chüy Valley and Syr-Darya.* 1874, No. 25, 27, 30. *The Kara-Kirghiz (An Ethnographic Sketch).* 1874, Nos. 41-42, 44-45
5. G. Bardashev [sic]. *Notes on the Stone-Age Kirghiz. Statistical Materials on the Turkestan Region.* St. Petersburg, 1874.
6. A. P. Khoroshkin [sic]. *Collected Articles on the Turkestan Region.* St. Petersburg, 1876.
7. N. L. Seeland. "The Kirghiz. An Ethnographic Sketch," West Siberian Dept., *Russian Geographic Society,* Book VI, Vol. II. 1885.
8. W. Radloff [sic]. *Aus Siberien.* Leipzig, 1893.
9. A. P. Fedchenko. *Journey to Turkestan,* Vol. I. St. Petersburg, 1875.
10. G. E. Grum-Grzhimailo. "Sketches of Pripamir Land," *Transactions of the Russian Geographic Society,* Vol XXII, 1886.
11. B. Ya. Grombchevsky. *Report on Journeys to Pamir, Raskem, South Kashgaria and the Northwest Border of Tibet.* Transactions of the Russian Geographic Society, Vol XXVII, 1891.
12. V. I. Kushelevsky. *Materials for a Medical Geography and a Sanitary Description of Ferghana Oblast.* Novyi Margelan, 1904.
13. V. A. Parfetiev [sic]. *The Population of Vuadil (Statistical Report). Annual of the Fergana Region,* Vol. III. Novyi Margelan, 1904.
14. N. S. Lykoshin [sic]. "Chapkullskaya volost [the smallest geographic administrative unit in tsarist Russia] of Kojent District. The Results of a Study of Economic and Living Conditions Among The Local Population," *Information booklet for Samarkand Oblast.* Samarkand, 1906.
15. N. L. Korzhenevsky. Journey to Pamiry, Wakan and Shugnai, 1903. St. Petersburg, 1906
16. G. V. Pokrovsky and N. I. Stogov [sic]. *Alai Mountain Village Societies in Margelan District,* 1909. *A Statistical-Economical Study. Introduction to the Statistical Survey of the Ferghana Oblast for 1911.* Skobelev, 1914.

17. A. A. Kushakevich "Information About the Khojent District," *Annals of the Russian Geographic Society,* Vol. IV, St. Petersburg, 1871.
18. A. Uspensky. *The Fergana Valley. A Brief Sketch.* Okraina, 1890, No. 279.
19. F. A. Fielstrup. *Ethnographic Studies Among the Kara-Kyrgyz. Ethnographic expeditions 1924-25.* Leningrad, 1926. *Dwelling of the Turkic Peoples, Material for an Ethnography.* Vol III, Leningrad, 1926.
20. Collections relating to the Kirghiz can be found in many of our country's museums. The most valuable of these are located in the Historical Museum of the Kirghiz SSR, in the Museum of Anthropology and Ethnography of the USSR Academy of Sciences, and in the Museum of Uzbek History.
21. S. M. Abramson. "The Works of the Kirghiz People," *Almanac of Soviet Ethnography,* 1940, III; "A Sketch of the Culture of the Kirghiz People," Frunze, 1946; "Tien-Shan Ethnographic Expeditions," *Abstracts of the Institute of Ethnography of the USSR Academy of Sciences,* IV, 1948; "Ethnographic Expeditions in the Kirghiz SSR, 1946-47," *Journal of All-Soviet Geography,* 80, No. 4, 1948; "In the Kirghiz Collective Farms of the Tien-Shan*," Soviet Ethnography* 4, 1949. "The Ethnographic Album of P. M. Kosharov (1857)," *Almanac of The Museum of Anthropology and Ethnography of the USSR Academy of Sciences Almanac,* Vol XIV, Leningrad, 1953; "Results of Monograph Studies on the Kirghiz Collective Farm. Kirghiz Miners of Kyzyl-Kul, Past and Present," *Soviet Ethnography* No. 4, 1954.
22. Almanac: *Science in Kirghizia: 20 Years,* Frunze, 1946, p. 182.
23. *Ibid.*
24. M. T. Aitbaev. *Historic-Cultural Connections Between the Kirghiz and Russian Peoples (Based on materials from the Issyk-Kul region of the Kirghiz SSR),* Frunze, 1957.
25. E. I. Makhova. Chapter entitled *Material Culture* and section entitled *Decorative Folk Art* as well as her descriptions of domestic craftwork (pp. 23-25 and 121-128) in *The Way of Life of the Collective Farmers of the Kirghiz Villages of Darkhan and Chechkan,* by Abramson, Antipina, Vaslievna, Makhova, and Suleimanov. Ethnographic Publishers USSR, New Series, Vol. XXXVII, Moscow 1958.
26. P. I. Kushner. *The Mountain Kirghiz. A Sociological Report.* Moscow, 1929.
27. A. F. Burkovsky. *On the History of the Woodworking Technology of the Kirghiz.* History Department of the Kirghiz State University, Ed. 3, Frunze, 1954; *Towards a Study of the Use of Animal Resources by the Kirghiz.* Kirghiz Women's Pedagogical University, Frunze, 1957; *On the History of Metallurgical Production Among the Kirghiz.* History Department of Kirghiz State University, V, Frunze, 1958.
28. M. R. Ryskulbekova. *On the History of Domestic Craft Production in Prerevolutionary Kirghizia.* Kirghiz State Pedagogical Institute, Ed. 2, 1958.
29. S. Ilyasov. *Cooperative-Collective Structures in Kirghizia (1918-1922),* Frunze, 1959, pp. 107-117.
30. G. Almasy [sic]. *Der Karakirgisen Ornamentik.* Anzeiger der Ethnographischen Abteilung das Ungarischer Nationalmuseum. Budapest, 1907.
31. A. Felkerzam. "Traditional Rugs of Central Asia," *Years of Old ("Starye gody"),* 1914, October-December; 1915, June.
32. S. M. Dudin. "Kirghiz Ornament," *Almanac of the East,* Leningrad, 1925. "Rug Making in Central Asia," *Almanac of the Museum of Anthropology and Ethnography of the USSR Academy of Sciences,* Vol VII, Leningrad, 1929.
33. V. Chepelev. *Kirghiz Folk Art.* Art No. 5, 1939.
34. A. Romm. *Sketch of the History of Decorative Art in the Kirghiz SSR.* Moscow/Leningrad, 1941.
35. M. S. Andreev. *Ornamental Art of the Mountain Tajiks of Amu Darya and the Kirghiz of Pamir.* Tashkent, 1928.
36. M. F. Gavrilov. *Ornamental Art of the Kirghiz of Susamyr.* Tashkent, 1929.
37. *Kirghiz National Design.* Leningrad-Frunze, 1948. Also in M. V. Rundin, "Kirghiz Design*," Studies of the Kirghiz Branch of the USSR Academy of Sciences,* 1st Ed., 1943, pp. 143-46.
38. S. M. Abramson. "Kirghiz National Design*," Soviet Ethnography,* 1950, No. 1, pp. 221-226. See also S. V. Ivanov. "National Ornament as a Historical Source," *Soviet Ethnography,* No. 2, 1958, pp. 14-16.

PART FOUR — WRITINGS

39. Kirghiz Archeological-Ethnographic Museum. *Moscow*, 1956, Vol. I. *Moscow*, 1959, Vol. II. *Moscow*, 1959, Vol. III. *Moscow*, 1960, Vol. IV.
40. Overview of work by ethnological teams in articles by the team leader, S. M. Abramson. "Field Ethnographic Research in the Kirghiz SSR, 1953," *Soviet Ethnography No. 2 (Chronicle)*, 1954: "Summary Data on Field Ethnographic Research in Kirghiz SSR, 1954," *KSIE*, ed. XXV, 1956.
41. E. I. Makhova. "The Material Culture of the Kirghiz as a source for the Study of Ethnogenesis," *The Kirghiz Archeological Ethnographic Expeditions*, Vol. III.
42. S. V. Ivanov. *Kirghiz Ornament as an Ethnographic Source*, loc. cit.
43. Here and in the passages to follow under the designation "southern Kirghiz" we mainly are referring to those Kirghiz who live in the southern part of Osh region, although in ethnographic literature the provisional term "Southern Kirghiz" is applied to the entire Kirghiz population of the whole Osh oblast. The designation "Northern Kirghiz", then, is understood to mean those Kirghiz who reside in the Issyk-Kul, Tien-Shan, and Chui valleys.
44. Among our many valuable informants we must thank personally Ukubai Abilov (Director of the Osh Regional Museum); Joldosh Busurov (born 1903 in the village of Kara-Bulak, Batken district); Taaji Imarov (born 1895 in the village of Okhna, Frunze district); Saltanat Kaipova (born 1898, village of Erkin, Kara-sui district); Pazydat Koldosheva (born 1885 in the village of Kok-Dzhatyk, Naukat district); Zuleika Ismailova (born 1879 in the village of Kok-Kochkor, Uzghen district); Altyn Kojogeldieva (born 1898, in the dzhailoo of Shumkar, Alai district); Sara Mambetova (born 1880, village of Sary Bulak, Uzghen district); Kalbya Ramonkulova (born 1890 in the village of Uluu Katyn, Aravan district); Amrakul Rakmangulaev (born 1897 in the village of Kara-Bulak, Batken district); Asel Samatova (born 1902 in the village of Dzhanalak, Osh district); Aijan Samadyarova (born 1875 in the village of Kara Teyit, Alai district); Nasbya Sartalova (born 1884, village of Ak-Terek, Uzghen district); Gulsun Toichieva (born 1879, village of Palal, Batken district); Cholponai Topchubaeva (born 1879, dzhailoo of Kuugandy, Alai district); Koshobai Turdubaev (born 1890, village of Kyzyl-Dzhol, Soviet district); Uulbya Cholponbaeva (born 1896, village of Tersk, Alai district); Bedenie Cholponkulova (born 1895, village of Oruktuu, Alai district); and Samar Shergazieva (born 1888, village of Kara-Taryk, Uzghen district).

    Of notably great help to us were the reports of the older folk artisans. Their names appear in the text in accordance with the appropriate chapter.

45. Some of the photographs taken during the expedition appear in our book. They are, of course, taken between the years 1955-58. In addition to these, the book is illustrated with photographs by S. M. Dudin, whose negatives have been preserved in the State Museum of Ethnography (as the signatures at the bottom of the photos attest). They show much of the material characteristic of the culture of the Southern Kirghiz at the end of the nineteenth and the beginning of the twentieth centuries.
46. This work, in particular, does not examine a major aspect of the material culture: food. A separate publication will be devoted to this topic.
47. Ya. R. Vinnikov. "Native Composition and Settlement of Kirghiz in the Territory of Southern Kirghizia," *Works of the Kirghiz-Archeological-Ethnographic Expedition*. Moscow, 1956, Vol. I, pp. 180-181.
48. Up until the nineteenth century there continued to exist ethnographic groups of Kirghiz who remained from ancient and medieval tribal groups. Today they no longer exist. Ethnographic groups are named in the text of the book in accordance with their customary group identity; where local parlance allows, it is necessary to understand that they are the descendants of former tribes.
49. Ya. R. Vinnikov. *op. cit*, 152.
50. S. M. Abramson. Questions on the Ethnogenesis of the Kirghiz based on Ethnographic Data. *Works* Vol. II, Frunze, 1959, p. 37.

51. S. M. Abramson. *op. cit.,* Concluding Remarks on the Report *Questions on the Ethnogenesis of the Kirghiz based on Ethnographic Data,* p. 223.
52. Reports on the settlement of Kirghiz clan groups in migrations through the Osh region are collected in the work by Ya. R. Vinnikov cited above.
53. Ya. R. Vinnikov. *op. cit.,* pp. 157-159; S. M. Abramson, *Questions on the Ethnogenesis,* pp. 34-35, 42-43.
54. *Mojamu-at-tavarik (Gathering of History),* prepared for publication by A. T. Tagirjanov. Department of Iranian Philology, Leningrad University, 1960.
55. Materials on land usage by the nomadic Kirghiz population of the southern part of the Fergana region (Osh, Skobelev, and Kokand Districts). 1915, pp. 104-107, 118-124.
56. See also S. I. Ryazantsev, V. D. Pavlenko. Kirghiz SSR, 1960, pp. 397-477.
57. A. I. Bernshtam. *Ancient Fergana.* Tashkent, 1959, pp. 4, 5, 11.
58. Materials on land usage, pp. 120-122.
59. Stokasimov. *Military-statistical Description of the Turkestan Military District. Fergana district.* Tashkent, 1912, p. 114.
60. Materials on land usage, pp. 106-107, 122-124.
61. *Ibid.,* p. 116.
62. *Ibid.,* p.113.
63. Stokasimov. *op. cit.,* tables 4 and 5.
64. In the Settlements of Palal, Raut, and Dara (Batken district), as was related to us by the chair of Lenin Collective Farm. Yaks were also herded.
65. On the history of southern Kirghizia, see K. Usenbaev: *The Union of Southern Kirghizia with Russia.* Frunze, 1960; and *Socioeconomic relations among the Kirghiz during the reign of the Kokand Khanate.* Frunze, 1961.
66. For information about the contemporary situation in rural agriculture in the region, the work of K. Otorbaev was consulted, *Osh Oblast* (Osh, 1961).
67. V. V. Grechko. *Rural Economy* in Osh Oblast. Frunze, 1962, p. 31.
68. *On the population, level of education, and national composition of the inhabitants of the Kirghiz SSR (in accordance with 1959 population survey),* Frunze, 1960.

PART FOUR   WRITINGS

Figure 4.1 (Fig. 32 in the original)
Preparation for weaving a large rug, 1903
Fergana Valley
(Photograph by A. Felkerzam, GME No. 114-1)

Figure 4.2 (Fig. 33 in the original)
Pile woven *chavadan*
Naukat region

Figure 4.3 (Fig. 34 in the original)
Pile woven *chavadan*
Frunzen region

Figure 4.4 (Fig. 35 in the original)
Pile woven *bashtyk*
Alay region

PART FOURWRITINGS

Figure 4.5 (Fig. 36 in the original)
Pile woven suspended shelf *(ayak koychuk)*
Soviet region

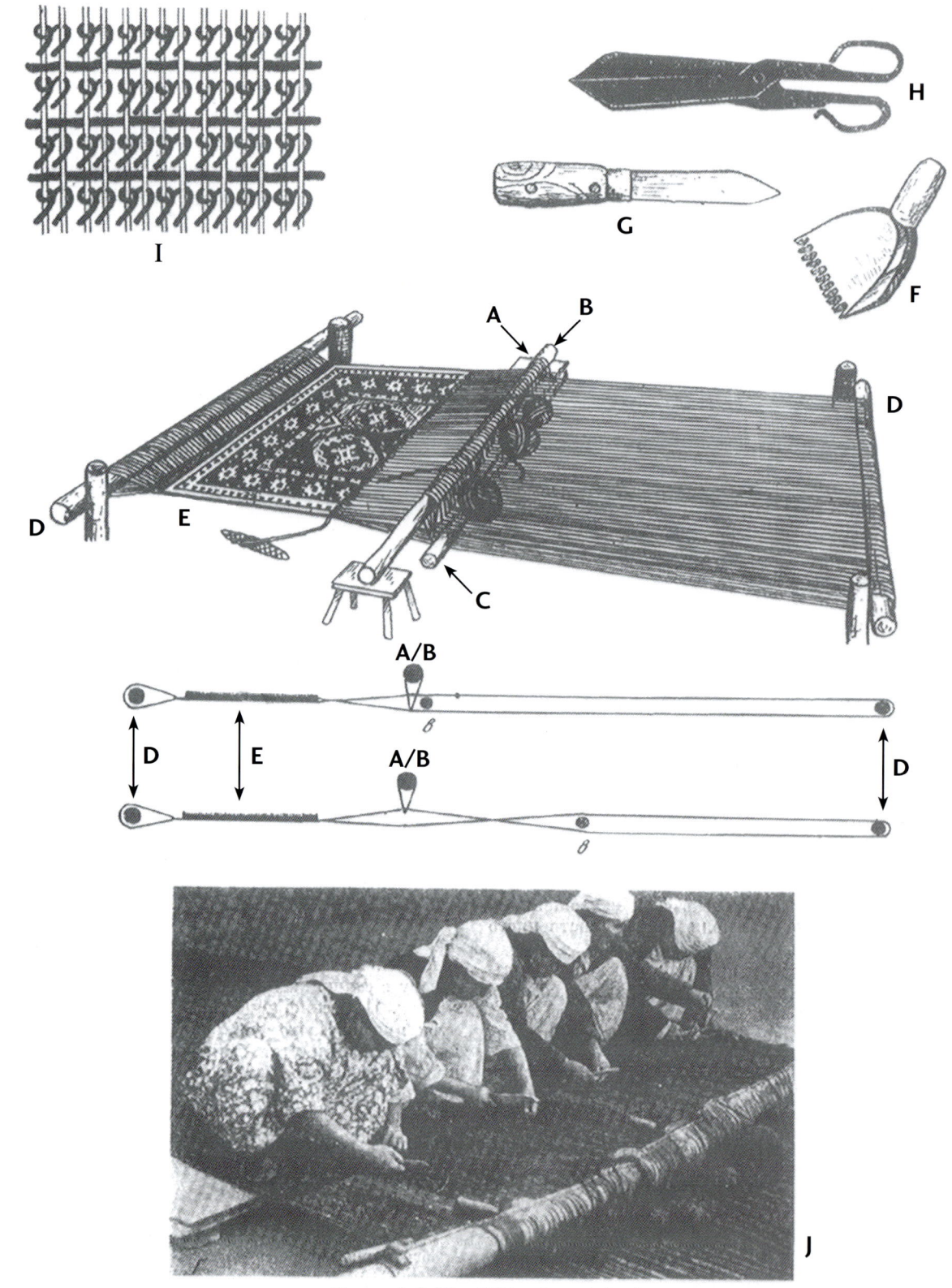

Figure 4.6 (Fig. 37 in the original)
Rug loom, Batken region
A. Heddle *(remiz kuzuk)*, B. Heddle rod *(remiz kotorchu)*, C. Shed rod *(chalysh aluu saboo)*,
D. Foundation poles *(jigach)*, E. Completed portion of weaving, F. Weft beater *(tokmok)*, G. Knife *(pychak)*,
H. Scissors *(kaichi)*, I. Diagram of the asymmetric knot ("open to the right"), J. Weavers *(Kara-Bulak Village, 1955)*

PART FOUR

WRITINGS

Figure 4.7 (Fig. 38 in the original)
Detail of pile woven rug showing *Orus Kochot* design
Osh region

Figure 4.8 (Fig. 39 in the original)
Pile woven rug
The field design is divided longitudinally.
Frunzen region

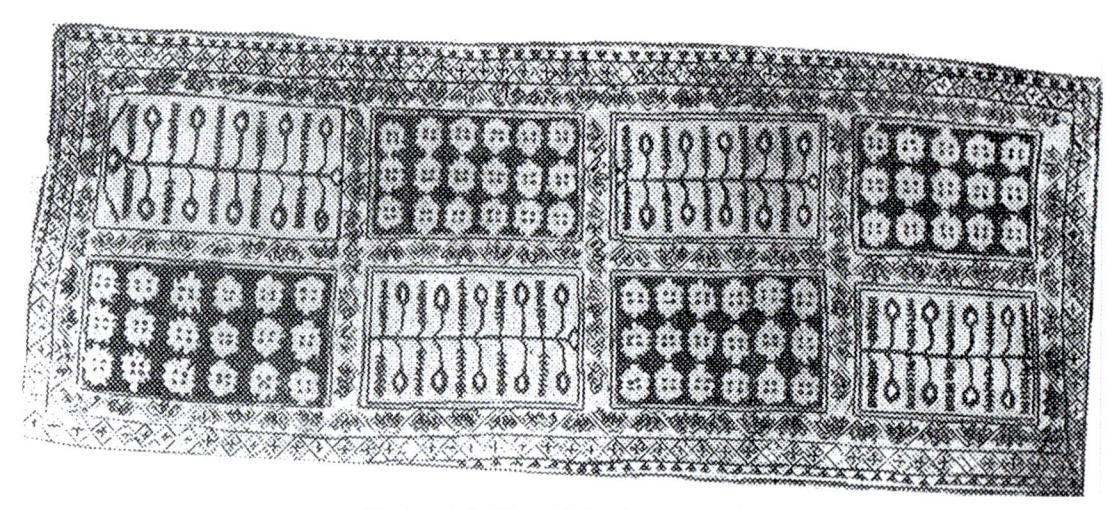

Figure 4.9 (Fig. 40 in the original)
Pile woven rug with *kytay shak* and *mashaty* designs
Frunzen region

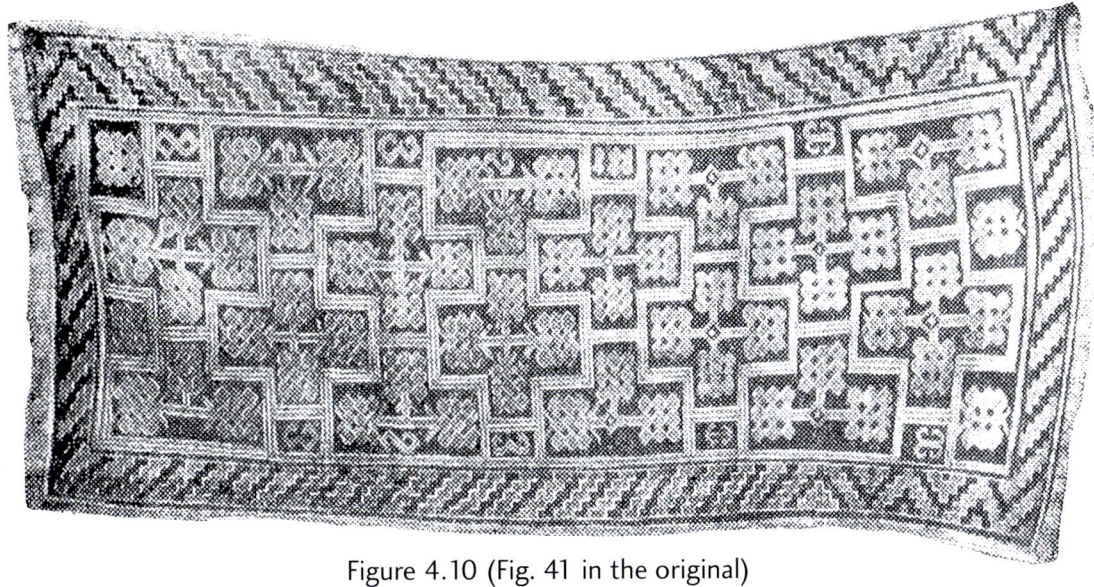

Figure 4.10 (Fig. 41 in the original)
Pile woven rug
Cruciform ornaments in field
Naukat region

Figure 4.11 (Fig. 42 in the original)
Pile woven rug
Arranged tile design
Batken region

Figure 4.12 (Fig. 43 in the original)
Pile woven suspended shelf *(ayak koychuk)* with *mashaty* design
Uzgen region

Figure 4.13 (Fig. 44 in the original)
Two tent bands *(tegirich)* sewn together
Frunzen region

KLAVDIYA ANTIPINA

Figure 4.14 (Fig. 45 in the original)
Designs in rug fields
1-6: *gaz ayak, karga tyrmak*; 2-5: *kochkor muyuz; Kockorok, kaykala*;
7, 8-10: *kosh muyuz, kaykalak*; 11-14: *kochkor muyuz, kaykalak*; 15, 24: *ilmek, kaykalak*;
16: *omurtka*; 17-19: *kekilik kash*; 18, 23: *dzhyldyz*; 20: *taytuyak*; 21: *toguz dobo*;
22: *pashayy kochot*; 25: *taylak taman*; 26: *alma gul*; 27: *kurakcha*; 28: *bali-bali*

PART FOUR — WRITINGS

Figure 4.15 (Fig. 46 in the original)
Designs in fields of pile weavings
1: *chit kochot*; 2: *orus kochot*; 3: *kynyr moyun*; 4, 5: *pashayy kochot*; 6: *kalkan*; 7: *chayan kuyruk*; 8: *chayan*; 9: *tutkuch*; 10: *omurtka*; 11: *kytay shak*; 12, 26: *gul keshte*; 13-15, 19: *mashaty*; 16-18, 22: *karakalpak kochot*; 21, 23: *kosh muyuz*; 25: *kyygach kochot*; 24, 27, 28: *kaykalak*

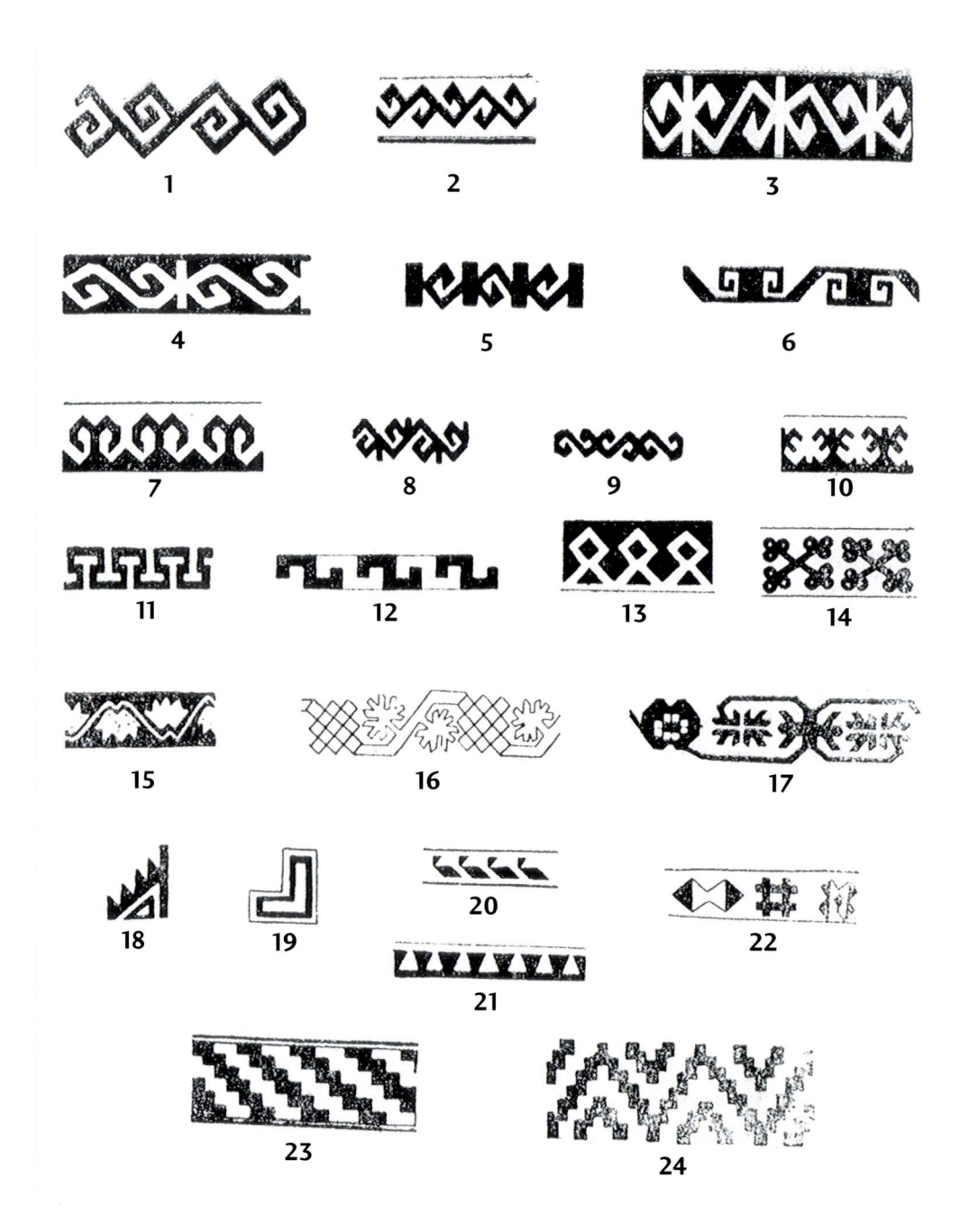

Figure 4.16 (Fig. 47 in the original)
Rug border designs
1: *synar muyuz*; 2, 5, 8: *ilmek*; 3: *kosh ilmek*; 4, 6, 9, 12: *it kayruk*; 7: *kaykalak, kosh muyuz*;
10: *bagdzhagay*; 11: *kalit*; 13: *bash kerege*; 14: *bali-bali*; 15-17: *gul keshte*; 18-19: *pychak uchu*;
20: *kynyr moyun*; 21: *tumarcha*; 22: *it taman, kopolok kanat*; 23-24: *kavyrga*

Figure 4.17 (Fig. 48 in the original)
Pile woven bag with *chaydosh* design
(Photograph by S.M. Dudin, GME, No. 14-77)

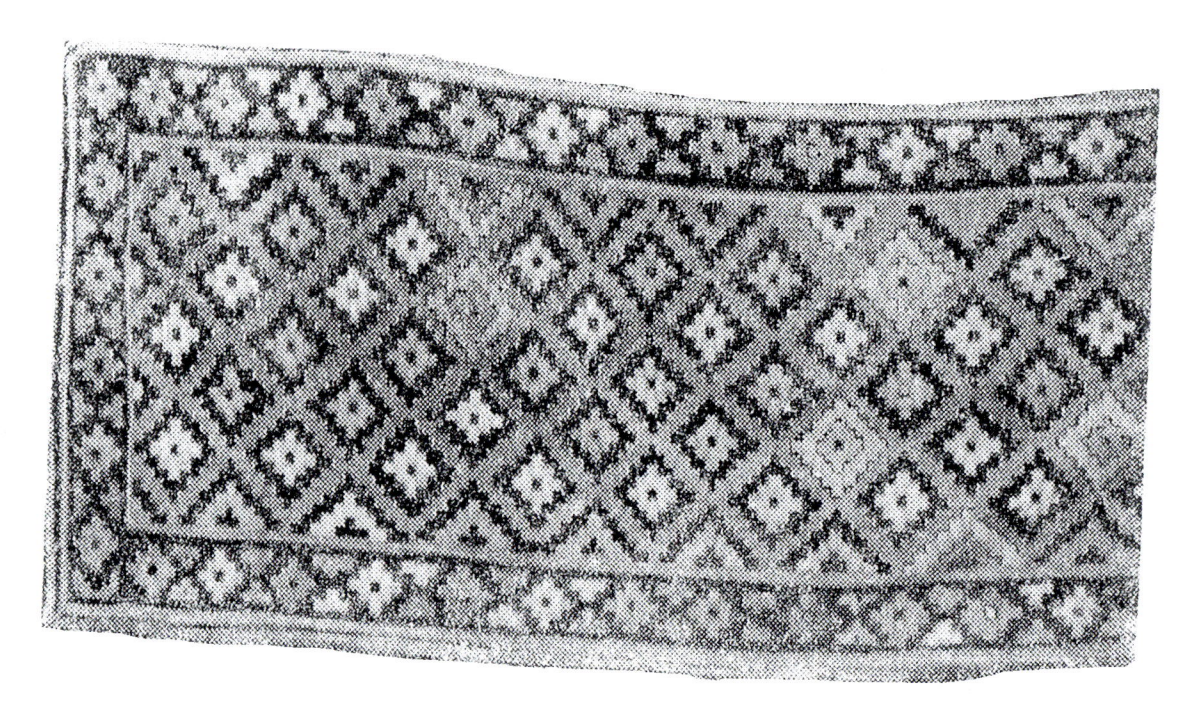

Figure 4.18 (Fig. 49 in the original)
Flat woven Palas (*arabi kilem*)
Batken region

PART FOUR   WRITINGS

Osobennosti Materialnoi Kultury I Prikladnogo Iskusstva Iuzhnykh Kirgizov (Distinctive Features of the Material Culture and Applied At of the Southern Kirghiz), Frunze, 1962 pp.3-15

This edited translation is by Nathan Hodge and Sharon Weinberger.

The best studies of Central Asian applied arts from the first decade of this century have indicated the particular importance of pile weaving. At the turn of the century, there developed an enthusiasm for Central Asian rugs; and this, in turn, led to a new respect and renown for Kirghiz pile woven rugs.

A. A. Bogolubov's albums, published in connection with a handicraft exhibition (181), are regarded as the first serious work on this subject. Bogolubov had the opportunity to make an extensive collection of central Asian rugs, the basis for his research. This was the first attempt at classification of these rugs. His attention was mainly devoted to Turkmen weavings.

In Bogolubov's second album, Kirghiz rugs are represented in two plates, XLII and XLIII; in plate XLII there are depictions of rugs which, according to the author, belong to the Andizhan Kirghiz. Plate XLIII depicts four pile-woven rugs and one felt rug (*shyrdak*) produced by the Kirghiz of the Kydyrsha, Tyuyakhos (182) and Kypchak tribes.

The next research dedicated to Central Asian rugs was the work of A. Felkerzam (183). The author gave thorough descriptions of Central Asian rugs and, through his acquaintance with the tribes of Ichkilik, Kydyrsha and Tir (184), it is evident that he was familiar with Kirghiz rug making. He believed that the Andizhan and Osh regions in the Fergana district were the main centers of rug weaving. With regard to rug weaving in East Turkestan, he concluded that the so-called Kashgar rugs were woven by the Kirghiz living in that region, and that they were, in the full sense of the word, artists of rug weaving, their work being among the best of Central Asia (185). For him, the question about who made Khotan rugs remained open, the style and technique being rarely distinguishable from Kashgar rugs. He cites only the view of S. M. Dudin, who ascribed these rugs to one of the Uzbek tribes (186).

Important knowledge about Kirghiz rug-weaving is presented in A. A. Semenov's thorough work (187). He gives an objective evaluation of A. A. Bogolyubov's albums. Yet, there are ambiguities. For example, he states that "the Kirghiz are involved with rug weaving in almost all the districts" (187).

Articles by foreign authors are of interest. Le Coq acquired several large Kirghiz pile-woven rugs during an expedition in Turfan in 1911-1914. He gives a description with supplementary tables (188). The Swedish scientist, Gunnar Jarring, gives a detailed description of the Kirghiz rugs made in Kashgar (189).

Generally speaking, the descriptions, the mentioned designs, and the authors' conclusions are based on small amounts of actual material. Their arguments are created with imprecise information received secondhand from persons "familiar with the people and with rug weaving."

S. M. Dudin made a valuable contribution to the study of Central Asian rug weaving (190). He developed his work on the basis of material he collected in Central Asia, as well as on the basis of a critical reworking of research done by A. A. Bogolyubov, A. Felkerzam, Neugebauer, Orendi, and Hasenbalg (191). In this manner

S. M. Dudin systematized all the information of the period concerning Central Asian rugs. It is a shame that this work is not illustrated. However, since his tables contain ornamental patterns of Central Asian rugs (including Kirghiz), they provide valuable comparative material. Table VII, for example, contains Kirghiz ornamental rug motifs that may serve to supplement our own data.

Dudin assigned all Central Asian rugs to one category. He found in them "something" common which clearly distinguished them from Persian or Caucasian rugs.

Dudin regarded the Kydyrsha and Mangit as the best examples of Kirghiz rugs. These rugs, which are from the Fergana District, he mistakenly attributed to the Semireche district.

In a short sketch, which appeared as a guidebook for an ethnographic exhibition in the Russian Museum, A. A. Miller wrote a characterization of rugs from Turkestan and other regions. In some editions of this guidebook, Miller presents Kirghiz pile woven rugs as traceable to a Persian influence (192). It is difficult to agree with this.

More scientific interest in Kirghiz rug weaving was shown by the Soviet scientist V. G. Moshkova, who collected valuable material and wrote a few studies about the Turkmen (193), Uzbek (194) and Kirghiz rug weaving. Her study and materials, which deal with Kirghiz rug weaving in a scientific manner, are held in the Museum of Fine Art, Uzbekistan, USSR (195).

Other authors also gave important attention to Kirghiz rugs. (196).

Questions are linked to the study of rugs. Speaking about the value of rugs, researchers mention two aspects: First, the rug as a historical remnant, a source of knowledge about national history, its character, its being, and its ties to other peoples; and, second, the rug as a product of national art, with a potential for further development and evolution.

From these points of view, we will try to explain the Kirghiz rug.

Pile weaving has long been known to the Kirghiz of the current Osh district. Moreover, pile weaving exists everywhere in the south. Even the Kirghiz who live in the northern part of this region—the former Jalal-abad district situated close to the Fergana Valley—weave pile-woven rugs.

By contrast, in other Kirghiz regions, not a single Kirghiz ancestral tribal group produced pile weaving (197).

The Kirghiz living beyond the borders of Kirghizia, however, are familiar with pile weaving. These locations include the Mugrab (198) and Jirgatal (199) regions of Tajikistan; the Andizhan, Namangan, and Gergana districts of Uzbekistan (200); the Xinjiang-Uighur region of China (201), and Afghanistan.

A. A. Semenov notes the manufacturing of Kirghiz-Uzbek rugs by members of the "Katagan" tribe, who live along the banks of the Amu-Darya and Baksha (202).

Kirghiz pile weaving disseminated to areas far beyond Kirghizia. Moreover, in Tajikistan, Uzbekistan and in the People's Republic of China, all of the Kirghiz who know how to make pile woven rugs are descendants of the Ichkilik. In the Osh region, in addition to the Ichkilik pile weaving is also practiced by the neighbors of the latter, the ancestral tribal groups of the Adigin, the Mungush, the Basiz, the Munduz, the Kutchu and the Bagysh.

Collections of Kirghiz pile weavings are kept in government museums. In the State Museum of Ethnography of the Peoples of the USSR some rugs obtained by Dudin are kept as part of a collection of Central Asian rugs. He had collected these rugs from the southern Kirghiz, and from the Kirghiz in Eastern Turkestan and

Uzbekistan. Smaller pile-woven items in these collections were acquired for the museum by B. K. Balakin and E. I. Makhova during a museum-sponsored expedition to southern Kirghizia in 1941.

Two Kirghiz rugs, acquired in 1910 and in 1920, are kept in the archives of the Museum of Anthropology and Ethnography, Academy of Sciences of the USSR.

Kirghiz pile-woven pieces are housed in the Historical Museum, Academy and Sciences, Kirghizia. Most are smaller woven pieces. There are no large Kirghiz rugs in the museum (203). A few examples of smaller pile-woven rugs are kept in the Museum of Decorative Art in Kirghizia.

Valuable pile weavings, made primarily by the Kirghiz living in Uzbekistan and belonging to the Kydyrsha and Kypchak groups, are kept in the archives of the Museum of Fine Art in Uzbekistan. V. G. Moshkova dates the majority of these weavings to the end of the nineteenth century.

The oldest pile weavings we encountered in the Osh district, were made not more than a hundred years ago.

In the second half of the nineteenth century, rug weaving in the southern part of Kirghizia was widespread and exclusively the work of women. Arising out of the needs of the nomadic life style and the semi-settled agricultural conditions, rug weaving bore the character of home production since it was intended for the nomadic family. However, at that time, rugs were being acquired by the highest levels of society—the Kirghiz aristocracy.

Kirghiz rug-making emerged, over the centuries, in close relation to the development of commercial production in the Fergana district and other Central Asian rug centers. Eventually, rugs were being made for sale (204). With the penetration of capitalist relations to Central Asia, Kirghiz rugs also began to enter the market. At the turn of the century when the market for rugs was revived in the cities of the Fergana Valley, the Kirghiz began to make rugs with the intention of selling them. In this manner, rug production developed into a trade. Thus, among the Kirghiz there appeared an overt class of entrepreneurs who profited from the production of rugs. These were members of the advantaged strata of wealthy landowners. With their help, there were more and more handicraft peddlers, among whom were Tatars and Armenians.

Joro Tashtanov (born in 1877) lived in the Jalpalak state farm in the Osh region. He was a former farm laborer on the estate of Asana-Minbashi (205). He told how the person who commissioned a rug would assemble eight to ten women, and that "without even straightening their backs", these women worked at making the rugs. Among them, were "even younger wives of the land-owning class."

Tashtanov estimates that in the area of Japalak there were 17 estates, which acquired a great deal of money from rug weaving. Satymbay Ishiyev (born 1887), a worker at that same state farm, told of being shocked when, for not paying taxes, he was brought to the house of the Absatarova-Kaz and then to another estate, on seeing the furnishings of the rooms. The floors and walls were covered and hung with beautiful Kirghiz rugs.

Exploitation of labor was based on the use of the national village custom of mutual aid, *ashar*. Those invited to weave were fed. This was their only pay—paltry compensation for intensive rug weaving.

Upon the order of the Khanate nobles, often superior weavers made rugs for the Khan's estate. In particular, according to various sources (206), particularly large rug enterprises were located on the Solton estate. The Khan's wife, Alima, gathered women to weave larger rugs. Among them, there was a division of the labor, some spinning, some dyeing and some preparing the loom and weaving. Other women prepared food for the workers.

Kirghiz workers made rugs to order for the rich Kirghiz. The customers provided the workers with raw materials. In southern Kirghizia, the diffusion of this system developed into the giving of rugs as presents (*tartuu*) to prominent persons.

The Kirghiz produced rugs during the summer. In the fall, they took them to market in the cities of Uzbekistan such as Andijon, Margelan, Kokand, Skobelev. (207) In large numbers, rugs came not only from these localities, but also from eastern Turkestan, from the Transcaspian area and from northern Afghanistan. Undoubtedly, this "encouraged the penetration of new designs and patterns into the local rugs, as well as the creation of new and original ideas in the rug crafts." (208) Uniformly our informants emphatically assured us that the chief consumers of Kirghiz rugs were the Uzbeks and the Tajiks.

According to A. A. Semenov, the rugs did not enjoy particular success among Europeans. "They were not often seen in the bazaars in Andijon," he wrote, "since the usual buyers of these rugs were almost always local natives." (209) The rugs were of high quality and relatively cheap. Not only did the local Kirghiz acquire the rugs, but also those coming from northern and central Kirghizia. The usual method of payment was barter, the exchange of livestock for goods.

As mentioned, the production of pile-woven rugs among the Kirghiz was geared to the requirements of nomadism. Every item was adapted to the practical and to the aesthetic needs of this lifestyle. Pile weaving gradually replaced some of the felt production, despite the latter being simpler and quicker.

The rug (*kilem*) (210) gained special popularity even in the context of nomadism. Such rugs were spread in the place of honor (tor) in the yurt. They were placed atop other rugs of fabric or fur.

Both the felt and the woven Kirghiz rugs were rectangular. The most common size was 150cm by 300cm (211), but these dimensions could vary by as much as 20cm (212).

Later, when Kirghiz women began to weave rugs for sale to the wealthy, measurements became larger, for example, 200cm x 600cm (6ft 7in x 19ft 8in). The increase in size of the rugs was an adaptation to the demands of the market, the buyers being prosperous Uzbeks and Tajiks who lived in big houses. A. Felkerzam wrote that, in size, rugs made by the Kirghiz, "surpassed other rugs of Central Asia" (213).

Large rugs were given special names by the Kirghiz. Weavers in the western regions of the Osh region and in the Alan Valley, named the larger rug *ordo kilem* (214). In the central part of the regions (215), such rugs were named *kali kilem* (216). This name was understood to mean not only a larger rug size, but also a better quality of rug, a more luxurious rug. It is possible that the Kirghiz name became established because the majority of rugs for the Khan's estate and for the wealthy were supplied by the Kirghiz weavers.

In addition to the two names given above, the larger rugs have a second name, not always used: *zor kilem* ("larger rug") and *jailoo kilem* ("summer rug").

Smaller rugs were also made, for example the *jai namaz*, especially intended for Islamic prayers. These were widespread in the western regions where the influence of Islam is greater than in the east.

The Osh Kirghiz rugs appeared to be necessary furnishings in yurts at wakes, at weddings and during holidays. Also, this was the case in wealthy dwellings on normal days. Such pile rugs not only adorned the yurt on festive occasions, but also, for example, paved a pathway between close-standing yurts at a funeral (*ash*) arranged by wealthy Kirghiz.

In families of moderate means, the number of rugs in a dowry was a part of the marriage agreement. Wealthy families would include the traditional "nine" rugs.

The prosperity of the yurt's owner was easily determined by the appearance of the *juk*. Similarly, prosperity could be judged according to where the extra rugs were placed. When there was a large number of rugs, the *juk* was higher and wider than usual.

Pile-woven rugs not only adorned the household, but also were used during migration. Rugs covered the camels, onto which were loaded the household goods. (The Kyrgyz gave particular attention to camels.) The young camel would be specially decorated with a pile-woven carpet, called a *tailak kilem*. (217)

Of the pile items woven in the Osh district, the narrow, long sack, *chavadan* (218), for storing various items is interesting. Its front consists of a pile strip, and the back is of homemade material. The edges of the fabric and the carpet strips are sewn together. The remaining opening is 20-25 cm. Items such as harness, jewelry and personal items could be put into the bag. The width of the *chavadan* varies from 35cm to 42cm and the length varies from 80cm to 120cm. The *chavadan* in the *juk* has a defined place. It is placed at the very bottom, the decorated (pile) side visible. (In the house (as opposed to the yurt), the *juk* is arranged in a special wall niche, made especially for protecting things. Among the southern Kirghiz, *chavadans* exist up to the present day. Earlier, it was only in exceptional cases that they were absent from the Kirghiz dwelling. The *chavadan* was a necessary part of the dowry, customary for weddings even in poorer families. They were made by the bride's mother, not the bride. (219)

There also existed sacks among the previously nomadic people of Central Asia, and also among the partially-nomadic Uzbek tribes of Tajikistan and Uzbekistan, and the Turkmen Karakalpaks. One of the utilitarian intentions was storing valuable items in a defined place in the *juk*, always at the very bottom of the stack. The sacks have various forms and designations. The Lokai had the *mapramach*, which resembled the form of a trunk (220). Another form occurs among the Turkmen. (221) This sort of rug craft seems to be equally widespread among the Karakalpaks. This item, which is similar to the Kirghiz *chavadan* has the name *karchin*. (222)

Elderly women reported that in the past the *chavadan* was made from felt, the front side being decorated with colored wool stitchery (223). In the southwestern portion of the Osh district the front side of the *chavadan* is made with a patterned cloth.

Various leather and felt bags for protecting household articles, previously made by the Osh Kirghiz, gradually changed to being pile-woven. Suspended shelves made of pile weaving (*ayak koichu* and *kosh jabik*) added a special decoration to the appearance of the inside of the yurt as did bags (*bashtyk*) for small, everyday things, and smaller bags for such things as the storage of scissors (*kaichi kap*).

Adaptations for protecting teapots and kettles were also made from pile-woven material.

The interior surfaces of the yurt are covered with richly ornamented decorative pile-woven bands, *tegerich*, 35cm to 45cm wide. The *tegerich* found more extensive use among the Kirghiz who lived in the southern part of the Osh district. A similar decoration was used widely in Eastern Turkestan and among the Uzbeks in the Samarkand district. The Kazak also made this decoration.

The Kirghiz made pile-woven door rugs, *eshik tysh*, which were hung outside covering the door of the yurt.

The pile-woven saddle-girth, *basmayil*, the saddle bags, *kurjun*, (224) and the saddle cover, *kopchuk*, were used widely in saddle and pack transport. The size of the saddle cover, *kopchuk*, was 35cm by 45cm. During migration, the ends of roof poles were placed in a pile-woven covering as were the ends of the wall lattices. Among the southern Kirghiz pile-woven crafts came to be used in these ways.

Since there are few young weavers, older women now preserve the traditions of rug making learned in childhood. The better weavers who can tastefully reproduce rug designs and teach others this art, enjoy a sincere and wide respect. People will travel long distances to obtain the help of such experts in weaving their rugs.

Such rug weavers, themselves, traveled extensively, from village to village, *kishlak* to *kishlak*, following such calls for their expert services. Often outstanding specialists, such migrant craftswomen did not weave for themselves nor did they have looms of their own (225). Such experts were put in charge of the rug weaving, to organize the work and to manage all of its stages. Poems (*koshaks*) about them have been preserved. Here is a *koshak* about a mother (*enye*):

> In my *juk* I don't have the best carpets,
> Because my respected *enye* is no more.
> She wove the best carpets for the *juk*
> She decorated the yurts of others.
> Her carpets reached from the door to the *tor*
>   and to the *kapshit*.
> Her loom is no more, my dearest *enye*.
> [Translation by Ovadan Amanova]

The best rug weavers were also skilled in other crafts, such as stitchery and felt-making. Many were well known also for their virtuosic skill in painstakingly making patterned reed screens:

> Raising her little finger,
>   She wound the reed screen from *chiy*,
>   Kind *enye*,
> She pressed her middle finger
>   And made the pattern,
>   Kind *enye*,
> You, who hang a lamp on the *jabyk*
>   Cut a pattern for the *jabyk bash*
> You, who hang a lamp on the door
>   Cut a pattern for the *eshik tysh*.
> [Edited translation by Ovadan Amanova]

A number of deeply-held traditions guided Kirghiz rug weaving in the Osh district. For example, certain days were auspicious for the beginning of a project. Usually weaving a rug would begin on a Sunday or a Monday. These were particularly good days, and, if weaving were begun then—especially on a Monday—the enterprise would be blessed with good fortune.

Collective help, called *kilem ashar*, was widely used in rug weaving. Every day, over a period of twenty to thirty days, five to eight invited relatives or close friends would weave the rug. Over the course of these days, the weavers collectively arrange two or three breaks during which there was entertainment arranged by the owner of the rug. This is called *kudayi* in the Alay Valley (226). The invited women would take food, a flat cake, *boorsok* (227), *kattama* (228), meat, sugar, raisins and, sometimes, prepared hot dishes—*pilaf*, for example. These foods, arranged on a large tray, tavak, were wrapped in a cloth, *dastarkhan* (229). No one went home with an empty *dastarkhan*; the hostess always filled it with something to eat.

In the past there existed the widespread custom of giving expensive gifts, such as fruit or goats, to the rug owner. Nowadays, the gift is usually money .

Of interest, we recorded a legend of the existence of a rug-making paton, Pir Aiyym (230):

> Three sisters, Byubyu Aiyym, Byubyu Adzhar and Byubyu Aysha wove rugs and hung them up. Byubyu Aiyym made a very big rug, on which she sewed designs of flowers and leaves. Their rugs were so good that everyone came to admire them. After that, Kirghiz Women took up rug making and Byubyu Aiyym became their embroideress. At the start of weaving, they turned toward the rug and prayed for help, the oldest person turning toward their patron, Pir Ayym. At the conclusion of the weaving, they uttered a prayer of thanks.

This legend speaks of the more archaic type of rugs filled with stitchery in floral design. They were not "woven."

In the Suzak region, we know from the outstanding crafts woman, Dzhumakyz Mambetaliyeva (born in 1833 in the Frunze State Farm) about the existence among rug weavers of another patron of rug making, Jaysan Juvan. No work was begun on a rug without first invoking his blessing. The existence of such legends may be construed as evidence for the antiquity of rug weaving.

During the years of the imperial and civil war and during the Basmachi Rebellion, rugs were not woven in southern Kirghizia. Only following these difficulties did the weavers resume producing rugs. In the new conditions, smaller "throw" rugs had lost their value and room-size rugs became the basic type.

The Soviet government, in the 1930's, undertook a number of measures to develop Kirghiz rug weaving. Manufacturing cooperatives were organized. The first Soviet efforts to produce rugs in southern Kirghizia were the cooperative associations "The Red Soil" (1927) (231) and "Gayrat" (1928) (232). In the following years, other cooperatives developed the system of the Osh industrial cooperative society, notably in northern Kirghizia. These, however, were not widely developed.

Recently, industrial rug weaving was organized in Frunze. The products are still made by hand, but on vertical looms. However, this sort of rug production does not fit the national taste in art because authentic national weavers are not accustomed to this type of production and the artists, who create the drafts, have not assimilated Kirghiz rug weaving traditions.

Rug weaving in the home showed the greatest development in the Lailak and Batken regions. Rug weavers made rugs not only for their own needs, but also for sale. They would take their rugs to the markets in Isfara, Tajikistan. On Sundays, the bazaar was filled with rugs hung in doorways, on posts, on duvals, or spread on the ground. Crowds admired Kirghiz women's artistry. The colorful Kirghiz rugs received great attention and they were quickly sold to buyers, mostly Tajiks and Uzbeks. As soon as rugs were sold, they were replaced with other rugs, which also did not remain for long.

Such intense market place activity speaks, on the one hand, of the growing need of settled populations for good quality decorative rugs, and, on the other hand, of the degree to which the neighboring nations valued the art of the Kirghiz rug weavers.

The basic stages of rug weaving consist of preparation of the yarn for the weft and pile, the preparation of the rug's warp, and the process of weaving at the loom. Rug weaving is labor intensive. Traditionally and since antiquity, all tasks have been done by hand.

The Kirghiz wove rugs primarily of wool but with a cotton warp, although rug weaving using a cotton weft, also existed. According to the weavers it was customary to purchase cotton yarn in the market for the warp. A. A. Semenov mentioned the presence of rugs made on a cotton warp with a wool weft among the Kydyrsha Kirghiz group, who live in Uzbekistan (233). In eastern Turkestan, Khotan rugs were woven, as a rule, on a cotton warp (234).

Sheep wool, goat hair and camel hair were used by the Kirghiz for making rugs. It appears that camel hair, because of it durability, has always been preferred. In the Lailak and Batken regions, however, we did not encounter rugs of camel hair.

Other than camel hair, goat hair is also widely used for the warp. Goat hair is strong, but it is thick, as are the products made with it. In recent time, goat hair has been used in the rugs in the Lailak, Batken and southern Alay regions. For the pile (*tuk*), white goat fleece is occasionally used. Commonly, however, in the Osh district natural brown sheep wool was used for the warp, the weft, and the pile.

Sheep wool from the spring shearing is preferred,. (Wool from the fall shearing is also used.) Thicker wool is used for the warp and the weft of the rug, and softer wool—as from the Spring shearing—for the pile. The sheared wool is washed in cold water and dried. (235).

Usually, the wool is separated by hand. The weavers spin the wool into yarn, which, for the warp, is treated differently from that for the weft and the pile.

The warp yarn is spun tightly, then plied to a uniform thickness. Any unevenness of the warps adversely affects the weaving process. The warp is then subjected to further processing. The yarn is wound on two pegs and the resulting skein is boiled in salted water for an hour and then plunged into cold water. The wool, now cold and wet, is wound onto two pegs standing a distance of six to eight meters apart. Twice daily over the next three days, hot water is poured over the yarn and each time this is done, the yarn is tightly stretched. In this way, the yarn becomes more durable and elastic. This entire process of preparation of the warp yarns has the name *chynoo* or strengthening. Finally the warp yarn is wound into balls convenient for later use.

The wool of the warp significantly defines the quality of the Kirghiz rug. It is durable, coarse and thick. These qualities distinguish it from the warp made by the Turkmen, which is better known for its refinement. (In this regard, the Kirghiz antique "throw" rugs differ from other rugs that have a thinner warp.)

The uniqueness of the Kirghiz rug can be seen in the fringe, which is 20 to 25 cm in length and is plaited from the warp yarns.

Preparation of the weft yarn is less complex. The weft yarn is spun loosely and later plied with another, loosely. This allows the weft yarns to be soft and somewhat downy. For weaving, the weft yarn is wound on a shuttle 20 to 25cm long.

The selvage of the Kirghiz rug is usually set with narrow stripes called *joorop*. For this, doubled warps are plaited with colorful wefts of brown, green, red or blue, like the braid *chirmama*.

For the pile, better quality wool with longer strands is used. The wool of the pile always defines the quality of the rug. This wool is also spun loosely. It is not plied. The spun wool, usually white, is dyed.

The loom for making pile rugs in southern Kirghizia has no special name. It is called, only, the loom, *dukon*. Its simple structure is analogous to that of the Uzbek and Turkmen loom (236). It stands horizontally about 25 to 30cm off the ground.

In photographs (Figure 32) it is possible to see the structure. The frame of the loom is fastened to four posts anchored in the ground. In the past, Kirghiz used such looms for making rugs to sell. They made looms in this primitive fashion and they continue in this same manner. Prepared warp yarns are wound onto two beams, *jigach*, situated opposite each other at a distance greater than the length of the proposed rug (237).

Two to four, sometimes even six, women take part in placing the warp yarn onto the loom. Some of them begin winding the thread from the middle, the others from the ends of the beam. This process is called *jip juguru*. After the warp yarns are wound, they are made even and tightened. The beams are smeared regularly with clay to stabilize the warps where they wrap around the beams. The Turkmen follow the same procedure.

An important part of the loom is the heddle or *remizka* ("*kuzuk*"). A *remiz* stick (*kuzuk kotorchu*) is used. It has a diameter of 6 to 8 cm and a length somewhat greater than the width of the proposed rug. The ends of this heddle stick are supported on bricks or stones to a height of 30 to 35cm. A small *remiz* stick, the string heddle, is tied with cotton threads passing through loops to the *remiz*. The loose cotton thread on this string heddle, loops around alternate yarns of the warp. When tension is exerted on the alternate warp threads by this string heddle, a "shed" is formed (Figure 37).

The shed is maintained with the aid of the shed stick, *chalysh aluu saboo*, located behind the *remiz* sticks. (The shed stick has a diameter of 10 to 15cm.) Moving it closer or further away regulates the shed.

Work at the loom begins with the weaving of a simple flatwoven strip, *jabayy*, with a width of from 7 to 10cm. The color of the Kirghiz warp is usually gray or brown. The material is thick.

Following this initial flatwoven strip, the weaving of the patterned pile part of the rug using dyed yarns begins. The head weaver positions the other weavers at the loom. The difficult parts of the central area of the rug are entrusted to the better weavers, and the less difficult areas closer to the edge to the less experienced.

The knots in Kirghiz rugs are "one and a half", i.e., asymmetric. They are tied in the following manner: The weaver takes a pair of warp threads with the index fingers of both hands, one from the top and one from the bottom. Then, holding the pair of warps with the left hand, the right hand passes the pile yarn between the two warp yarns and one end is wrapped around a warp, the other is passed under the second warp and brought forward toward the weaver. The warp yarn is cut using a sharp knife. The process is called *bayloo*.

After every row of knots, the weft is passed, *arkak atkorot*. This is a difficult process on a horizontal broadloom and significantly more complicated than on a narrow-beamed loom. The weft in Kirghiz rugs is passed once or twice. The weft, following insertion, is pounded into place using a hammer or weft-beater, *tokmok*, which is made of a strong wood, usually of apricot. The *tokmok* resembles a wooden block (10-12cm by 16-18cm) with a handle (Figure 37). The Noygut Kirghiz group use a hammer of distinct form. The hammer resembles a human leg with its handle arranged at almost a right angle. The hammer has teeth, 1.5 to 2.0cm in length, which strike through the warp yarns. Positioned atop the completed portion of the rug, the weaver directs the hammer strikes toward herself rhythmically several times. The weft yarn is thus securely seated along with the "knots."

Afterward, when two to three rows of bound knots are completed, the pile thread is trimmed using a scissors. The height of the pile is about 6 to 8mm.

Certain technical characteristics define the quality of a rug. Evenness, the thickness of the warp yarns, the density of the warps, the character of the weft and the quality of the pile knots. The knot density is measured as "knots per square decimeter." The greater the knot density, the better the quality of the rug. The denser the rug, the more precisely visible the design, and the more clearly its details stand out.

Kirghiz rugs can be classified as "medium quality" according to their pile density. The vertical linear knot count and the horizontal linear knot count are almost identical, yielding a square format in which symmetrical designs can be nicely executed. The knot density fluctuates between 80 and 90 thousand knots per square meter. In smaller pieces, such as the *bashtik* and the *chavadan*, the knot density is higher: 100 to 110 thousand knots per square meter.

Antique Kirghiz rugs distinguish themselves by their highly artistic quality. This, however, does not exceed the bounds of modesty or of refined simplicity. A high diversity of dyes and ornamentation is alien to these rugs. The organic design is tied to the background and creates a single whole. In rugs made 70 to 80 years ago, we noticed that the colors were limited to two: red and blue, both muted.

Vegetal dyes played a greater role in the artistic design of antique rugs. S. M. Dudin noted that the rugs with limited numbers of basic colors "show the traits of greater antiquity" (238). It is impossible to disagree with this. This is even supported by archaeological evidence. During excavations at the ancient Hun burial site of Noin-Ula there were "found a series of large and small rugs, identical in material, technique, composition, and use of colors." The basic colors found were red, blue and yellow. (239)

Other than red and blue, colors of limited quantity were used in Kirghiz rug weaving. These colors were yellow, orange, pink, green, white and brown. They were used to fill in details of the rugs.

In the smaller pile-woven pieces, such as the *chavadan*, *bashtyk* and *tegirich*, these colors are used more abundantly than in rugs. In these you may find bright-red, crimson, raspberry, and sometimes violet. Such items are particularly differentiated by their polychromatic decorative stripes.

The use of black yarns in rugs was not widespread, although we did notice this in the Batken region.

White is one of the oldest "colors" used in rugs. White was widely used for pile-woven items that were either hung on the doors of yurts, or used as prayer rugs (240). In both rugs and smaller pile-woven items we can see borders created with a white ground, filled with colorful ornamentation. (Rugs with a central white background filled in with blue and red designs are made by the Noygut Kirghiz.)

As a rule, rug patterns have a narrow outline of knots of a contrasting color, which is subdued by the common background. A red pattern is usually outlined in the same color but in a brighter shade, or in brown. A brown design is outlined in blue, and vice versa.

Kirghiz rug designs contain features typical of the Kirghiz decorative arts. This is seen in the alternation of background and design colors—a pattern on a red background adjacent to (or surrounded by) a pattern on a blue background and vice versa—as well as in the balance of the main colors, blue and red. At the same time, the creation of a common impression of peaceful, subdued red dominates in Kirghiz rugs.

A characteristic of Kirghiz rug design is a border framing a central field. End borders and side borders are identical, the only deviations being caused by weaving technique.

Usually, two or three stripes of varying width constitute the framing border, which is also filled with various designs. The design of the border is distinct from that of the field. Borders are clear but do not dominate. Attention is focused principally on the central field of the rug.

The ratio of the width of the framing border to the width of the central field varies in Kirghiz rugs. We have noticed several variations: 1:3, 1:3.5, 1:4.5.

Above all, the design of the central field is marked by the rhythmic arrangement of the ornamental motifs. The Kirghiz rug is not overloaded with diverse designs, as, for example, is typically seen in Caucasian rugs. Uniformity of the pattern, with two or three repetitions, gives Kirghiz rugs a distinctive appearance. There are several types of compositions for the central area:

1. The field is divided into two, three, six or ten lengthwise stripes in which the designs are placed. There are two variants of this composition:

    a. The color of the background panels alternate, the designs changing colors accordingly.

    b. The color changes only within the design, the background color remaining the same throughout.

    The presence of stripes in the composition, as V. G. Moshkova noted (241), allows us to suggest, that the more antique forms of rugs were made of pile-woven strips, sewn together, the strips having been woven on a narrow-beamed loom.

    Ornaments are different. Mostly they are rounded rosettes or diamonds with offshoots. The Kirghiz of the Kydyrsha group in the past had preferred patterns of flowers, branches, and leaves (242).

2. On a monochrome central field, the composition is a grid or lattice with patterns of a uniform size and color. The designs are small colorful rosettes, squares, four "C's" coupled together, or other shapes.

    Given this sort of rug decoration, we can describe all patterns of solid or of broken lines variants, called *chatyshma* by the weavers.

3. The entire field is divided into squares of right angled triangles, 2 to 4 along the width and 4 to 8 along the length, separated from one another by patterned bands. Every right triangle is filled with designs on a blue or red background. The right triangles or squares are arranged in a diagonal direction by color and pattern. Every separate part creates an impression of a small rug of the *ayak koychu* and *bashtyk* types.

    A similar composition is seen on reed screens (*chiy*). Rugs of this type are seen in the western parts of the Osh region.

4. The entire field is covered with cruciform shapes outlined in a color distinct from that of the background. There are usually two types of designs in this composition: *karakalpak kochot* and *mashaty* (243); each of these has many variations.

    Variations of this design may be seen in the use of two patterns, different in form and color and with a diagonal composition.

The use of cruciform patterns of the *karakalpak kochot* type is seen in Andijon rugs (244), and also among the Karakalpaks. An analogous pattern is seen in Kirghiz reed screens (chiy).

5. The field is covered with hexagons, pentagons or polygons in a "tile" arrangement. The most characteristic is a rhombus or a stepped polygon with hooks. The spaces between polygons are either empty or filled with designs. These rugs are seen in the western part of the Osh region where the weavers call this composition *kalkan* (shield) or *kal* (birth mark). An analogous layout of the field as well as the name of the pattern of the rug, is noted in Samarkand rugs. (245)

    A tiled arrangement of medallions with patterns is seen in the reed screens made from *chiy* grass.

6. There are zig-zag lines that run along the central axis of the rug. These form closed squares or rhombuses containing uniform patterns. The remaining space is filled with patterns either related or different. This composition, called *Kunava*, is considered difficult to weave. Rugs of this pattern are seen in the western part of the Osh region. An analogous design exists in Andijon rugs. (246) Another typical design, characteristic of this type of decoration, is the *mashaty* design. This distinctive pattern is seen in Beshir rugs. Kirghiz rug motifs of this pattern are usually placed inside cruciforms, rhombuses or squares.

    It is important to be attentive to the mashaty design, which is usually combined with patterned stripes filled in with small figures which resemble birds, but which are called *kynyr moyun* (crooked neck). An analogous pattern is noted among the Kydyrsha Kirghiz. (247) A similar pattern is used on Kirghiz reed screens made from *chiy* grass.

7. The field contains, on the horizontal axis, two or three large medallions in the shape of polygons, rhombuses, squares or enlarged right triangles. The free area is occupied by the repeating motif called *karakalpak kochot*. Rugs of this design are called *ashkana kilem* by the Kirghiz weavers and are seen in the Batken and in the Lailak districts.

8. The entire field is covered in an arrangement of identical large patterns connected in a unified design. There are many variations of a design called *rogov* that spreads out from a central rhombus. These rugs are characteristic of the Kirghiz and can be seen in all parts of southern Kirghizia.

9. The field is filled with distinctive designs derived by weavers from the patterns of Uzbek hand-woven silk cloth. A similar innovation in rugs is noted in the western area of the Osh district. Analogous motifs also appear on reed screens (*chiy*). The appearance of these motifs on rugs and on reed screens occurred simultaneously.

A. Felkerzam noted seven types of eastern Turkestan rugs (248). Two of them are analogous to Kirghiz weavings: rugs with the *reshetchat* pattern (four coupled "C's") and those with a tiled arrangement of the pattern. We classify rugs with the *reshetchat* pattern as the second type. This design became popular among the southern Kirghiz and those living in the Pamir (Afghanistan). Rugs with a tiled arrangement, according to our typology, are ascribed to the fifth type. The remaining five types are not native to the Kirghiz. However, in all probability, the Kirghiz adapted many ornamental patterns—meanders, interlacing lines and the image of a tree—to their own rugs.

Each arrangement of patterns on smaller woven pieces, such as the *tegerich*, was distinctive.

The pile bag *chavadan* has the following design variants:

1. The entire piece is divided into three or four squares, separated by crossing bands containing identical patterns.
2. Three to four adjacent medallions, without the crossing bands.
3. A pattern analogous to the sixth type, called kunava.
4. The field, filled with cruciform motifs, is divided by a cruciform medallion.

There are two variations in the arrangement of the *chavadan* borders: 1) borders on the ends only, and 2) borders on all sides, including the ends.

An invariable characteristic feature of pile-woven bags and sacks is that the corners are filled with triangles or with sharply-notched projections (Illustrations 47: 18, 19). This resembles the design on the rugs of western Turkmenistan in which corners are filled with patterns of meandering and interlacing lines (249). This is seen on antique Turkmen rugs. (250)

Pile-woven bags, *kosh jabyk* and *bashtyk*, and suspended shelves (*ayak koychu*) also have a defined design composition. In these, there are always two or three borders one of which is wider. In recent years, a single border is usual.

In the older pile-woven bags, a triangular closure flap was woven, reproducing in this manner the felt bag that resembles an envelope. Later, it became common to weave a false flap. Antique bags were distinguished by the presence of pile weaving on both the front and the back. Later, the back was made of plain flatwoven material.

Pile-woven articles such as the *kopchuk* and the *kurjun* are designed in much the same way as the pile bags and the suspended shelves.

It is impossible not to mention the pile curtain on the yurt door, the *eshik tysh*. We observed them primarily among the Ichkilik. The Kesek Kirghiz in the Lailak region also have these door rugs, primarily in red and blue. These have primitive patterns with hook shapes (251).

In the Batken region, we saw door rugs (*eshik tysh*) with white backgrounds decorated with small rosettes, stepped polygons and flourishes. Within the polygons were eight-pointed stars or crosses.

M. S. Andreyev (252) wrote about the yurt door rugs among the Kirghiz in the Pamir plateau , which repeat a pattern seen on a reed screen (*chiy*), discovered in the Frunze region among the Jookesek Kirghiz group. The pattern is copied, in all probability, from Uzbek hand-woven silks.

On *tegerich* pile tent bands the arrangement of the patterns is especially distinct. Most often the composition is a continuous chain of changing pattern, separated by narrow bands or a change in background color (Figure 44). One design variation is the alternation of two (or three) motifs or groups of motifs. Another, the simplest, is the repetition of the same motif. There is a border, often the same, on each side. Usually this is brown. (The pattern *bagjagay* shows up clearly. It is a standard pattern on the flatwoven fabric known as *kajari*.) The basic designs on the *tegerich* are the sum of those ornamental motifs the Kirghiz used in rug weaving at the turn of the century.

The patterns on Kirghiz rugs are distinctive and sometimes complex. Their origins have been little studied.

Many Kirghiz rugs patterns are similar to those of other areas of Central Asia, such as Kazakstan, The Caucasus and Xinjiang. This similarity says much about the common origins of these peoples. Some Kirghiz rug patterns are clear. Probably, they reflect, figuratively, some actual object. Countless individual variations, impossible to overlook, led to a greater variation in the patterns over time. Weavers maintain that rug patterns and motifs are either handed down to them from their mothers or borrowed from antique rugs or fabrics.

Based on semantic information from rug weavers, it is possible to decipher the origins of some patterns. Sometimes, however, the weavers made completely contradictory statements, interpreting some designs differently, as becomes evident in some of the following descriptions.

Proceeding from a name, several groups of rug motifs can be studied. This is the case with rugs of the southern Kirghiz. Motifs reflect the real world surrounding the Kirghiz nomads. These motifs depict many things: the plant and animal world, concrete objects, material objects, art of another people and representations of the divine world. We will consider, in brief, the characteristics of the basic rug patterns.

With the exception of one design that resembles an amulet, there are no Kirghiz rug patterns that can be tied to religious images.

Often the names of patterns come from the animal world. First among these is the horn-shaped motif, *Kochkorok* (*kaykalak*). This motif is woven by all weavers. On smaller antique rugs, it is the principal motif. Sometimes there is a problem in understanding complex patterns. The horn motif appears as a branch off the side or the corners of a rhombus or a square. It is sometimes placed inside the rhombus or it branches off a wavy line, as in border patterns. Among the many variations of the horn-shaped motif, we note the arrangement of four or nine "Russian F"-shaped figures, reminiscent of the ornament on eastern Turkestan rugs of the nineteenth century. (253)

The *kochkorok* pattern is typical for the Kirghiz rug weavers who live in the Pamir and in Uzbekistan. (254) An analogous pattern is known to the Uzbeks. (255)

In rug patterns, the *kekilik kash* (eye brows of the stone partridge) is a stepped medallion with a geometric center and hooked projections on the sides. This is used by the karakalpak weavers (256) and by the Lokai in weaving *mapramachs*. (257)

The following widespread patterns the so-called tracks of distinct animals: *it taman* and *mishyk taman* (cat's paw), *taylak taman* (camel track) and *ulbars taman* (tiger track). However, the majority of these also take the form of rosettes, weavers using them as floral ornaments, and many weavers call them *toguz dobo*. The first two patterns are commonly seen on borders, the following two usually in the field in cruciform arrangement, noted earlier in the rug design of the second type. Analogous patterns of this design are found on Andizhan rugs. The patterns are seen less often on small rugs.

Among pattern names related to the animal world, we must mention *kavyrga* (rib, ribbed), *omurtka*, and *barmak*. These patterns, of differing origins, are popular for the decoration of rug borders. The *kavyrga* pattern is typically Chinese and was, apparently, borrowed. The *omurtka* and the *barmak* designs are related to the Iskon Kirghiz, the *omurtka* being seen in embroidery and woven fabric, and *barmak* in the ornamentation of "mosaic" felt rugs (*shyrdaks*) in which the field is separated from the border by a design in the shape of a projection.

The *it kuyruk* pattern, an S-shaped figure, is often seen in the borders of *ala kiyiz* rugs (felt rugs with "imbedded" patterns), pile bags and embroidery.

The weavers copied the "Turkish cucumber", which is widespread in Central Asia and beyond. The Kirghiz weavers call it *boto moyun* (camel's neck) or kynyr moyun (crooked neck). In the Andizhan Kirghiz rugs it is called *badam* (almonds) or *kalampir* (pepper). A similar pattern, similarly named, is typical in the embroideries of the Tajik and Uzbek people, as well as the Kirghiz. This pattern is also seen on reed screens (*chiy*).

The pattern called *koy koz* (the eye of the sheep) is a simple spot on the background.

Other pattern names tied to the animal world are *chayan kuyruk* (scorpion's tail) and *kopolok kanat* (butterfly wing). The scorpion theme is deeply imbedded in Uzbek national art and is popular also in Andijon rugs.

The image of a butterfly is a typical Chinese ornament. In Kirghiz rugs it is rarely used, and then usually only in borders.

The floral world is represented by distinct patterns with related names. First among these is the *togus dobo* pattern, which has many variations in the form of rosettes widely used by Kirghiz. The weavers, as noted earlier, also give the smooth-contoured rosette the name of animal footprints. In the western districts of the Osh region, there is parallel usage of another name, *segiz pista* (eight pistachios), borrowed from the Uzbeks.

The *kyrk shak* pattern is commonly used in the flatweave, *terme*. Pile weavings with this pattern are differentiated by the pattern's degree of completeness. The term *shak* is applied to border patterns in the shape of wavy lines with branches. *Kyrk shak toluk* means "forty whole branches, and *kyrk shak jarty* means "forty half branches." The Kirghiz weavers also use the term *kytay shak* (Chinese branch) for a pattern, which is seen in eastern Turkestan rugs.

The patterns *alma kochot* (apple pattern), *alma gul* (apple blossom) and *anar kochot* (pomegranate pattern) appear in the complex of rug patterns in eastern Turkestan. On Kirghiz rugs, however, *alma kochot* appears in the shape of a tree trunk with branches ending in small circles. This pattern is also called *kytay kochot*. We ascribe rugs with this pattern to the third type. The pattern *alma gul* resembles a rosette and is arranged on rugs of the first and second types. Weavers sometimes call this pattern *jolbors* taman.

Felkerzam gave special attention to the pattern called *anar kochot*, judging it to be characteristic of Kashgar Kirghiz weavings. We did not observe rugs with this pattern among the Osh Kirghiz, but weavers there remembered the pattern.

We encountered other names of rug pattern such as *jidy gul* (jidy blossom) and *tal berki* (willow leaf). (261)

Silk cloth patterns are especially interesting. Those with the names *pashayi kochot* and *kimkap kochot* were the more fashionable in Central Asia. Rugs with these patterns were made in the eastern regions, but recently-made rugs no longer exhibit this pattern.

The pattern in the shape of four interconnected "C's" has two names: *chit* (chintz or printed cloth) and *orus kochot* (Russian pattern). This pattern is on Chinese brocades (262) and it is in the Chinese character for happiness (263). Probably it was taken by the Kirghiz to eastern Turkestan. According to some weavers the pattern was copied from chintz from Russia. Possibly this was also the way in which eastern motifs had entered the patterns of Russian chintz.

There is a group of rug patterns evidently derived from antique patchwork technique known as *kurak* (264).

Pile weaving with the *karakalpak kochot*, *kytay kochot* and *kalmak kochot* patterns are of significance. These names occur as a result of the ties between the Kirghiz and their neighbors. *In the* karakalpak kochot pattern, there is a characteristic placement of elements. Often the pattern is put within a cruciform frame. This popular pattern adorns the fields of pile rugs, pile bags and reed screens (*chiy*). In some places this pattern is known as *ashkana kochot*. Sometimes it is known as the Kypchak pattern. The Kypchak Kirghiz of the Batken district now adorn their rugs primarily with this pattern.

Kirghiz weavers give the name *kytay kochot* to the *alma kochot* and *anor kochot* patterns mentioned above. Apart from this, the name *kytai kochot* is given to a set of patterns including geometrical lines, meanders and colorful rosettes.

Our observation is that the greatest similarity to Chinese patterns is seen in the rugs from the Lailak, Batken and Frunzen areas.

The group of patterns the weavers call *kydyrsha kochot* is distinctive. In the past they were typical of the *Kydyrsha* tribal group, but most of these patterns are no longer used.

The Kirghiz weavers give to some patterns the names of household utensils and other items of the nomad dwelling—the yurt. The *kazan kulak* (ear of the cauldron) is similar to the common *tumarcha* pattern.

The name of the *potnos kochot* pattern is tied to the Russian word for "tray" (*podnos*). Some weavers call this pattern *tegerek* (circle) or *chomuch bash* (spoon ladle). The *takta kochot* (bar, board) is usually put on narrow rug borders.

The completely original *chaydosh* (teapot) (265) pattern is of special interest. This is the name of the group of rhombuses with anchors and branches that resemble a human figure. From an outsider's point of view, the pattern has nothing to do with a teapot, either metal or ceramic. The pattern is seen on rugs of the first design type, on sacks and on door rugs (Figure 46, 28). The pattern is antique. In weavings and other crafts from the last few years, it has not been used. Kirghiz weavers now apply the name *chaydosh* to the design that reproduces ornamental motifs of Uzbek homemade cloth.

In the borders of rugs, we often encounter the *kerege bash* (the upper part of the latticed walls of the yurt) design, which resembles a rhombus with elongated lines from one side. The *kalit* (lock) design is closely tied to its origin in rugs from eastern Turkestan, where it is also used in the borders.

Weavers give the name *ala monchok* to any sort of pattern in which there are alternating colors. This pattern is used in the borders or within a medallion.

Patterns with the names *ay*, *ay nuska*, and *zhuldyz* (star) are also encountered. The latter is in the form of an eight-pointed rosette. These rug patterns fill the so-called "free space." The collections of The Museum of Art in Uzbekistan USSR preserves a rug made by Kirghiz of the Osh region from the end of the nineteenth century. A moon and star-filled sky are depicted on the rug, and the thematic composition is distinctive (266).

Geometric lines, as in all Kirghiz patterns, have a specific interpretation. The *karoo* and *korgon* patterns deserve attention. These patterns define the enclosure and outline the independent motif.

Kirghiz weavers call lined patterns with a rhythmic zigzag repetition, *kigach* (crooked) and *iyrek* (zigzag). Often these lines accompany hooked figures called *ilmek*.

Analysis of the Kirghiz rug data along with information of the rugs of other peoples (267) allows us to draw some conclusions.

The Ichkilik Kirghiz have the most developed rug-weaving. Their presence in eastern Turkestan enriched

Kyrgyz rugs with traditional Chinese patterns adapted partly from Khotan rugs and partly from Chinese textiles.

Small rugs display the more archaic features. They have the greatest similarity to the weaving of the Uzbek-Lokai and the Karakalpak.

According to the basic indicators—technique, pattern, colors and composition—Kirghiz rugs show either a partial or a complete similarity to rugs of the Andizhan type. It may even be suggested that the Kirghiz played a role in creating this type of rug. Among the various tribes, representatives of the Kypchak and Kydyrsha, presently living in the Andizhan district, were the most important in this.

Rugs of the Samarkand type are the most closely related to Kirghiz rugs, by both pattern and composition.

But even disregarding the commonality of many techniques and artistic styles with the rugs of other peoples, there is a great deal that is original in Kirghiz pile weaving. It is as if the artistic taste of the Kirghiz became concentrated on creating its own stylistic features. The Kirghiz created a particular harmony of motifs and a distinctive color composition. Kirghiz rugs are not difficult to identify.

In a broader sense, Kirghiz rugs have had a large role in the development of national art. The study of rug weaving art is not just of academic value, but has a larger practical meaning as well.

Kirghiz rug weaving will develop further on the basis of these powerful and centuries-old traditions, which are the art of a people.

The Production Of Palases

In Southern Kirghizia, in addition to the weaving of pile rugs, there is the weaving of rugs *without* pile. These flat-woven rugs are the type of wide "palases" known as *arabi kilem*. Similar flat-woven rugs are made by the Karshin Arabs (268).

Such palases became a major production among the Kypchak Kirghiz in the Batken district. They were also made in the Lailak district and, less often, in the Frunzen district (269). In the past, this type of rug was intended for the same purposes as pile woven rugs. They were used in nomadic transport and hung in the yurt on a pole. The *arabi kilem* was made with the same dimensions and patterns.

The Kirghiz in the Batken district were convinced that the palas was as ancient for them as the pile rug. However, the limited territorial diffusion of palases, the complete unfamiliarity of many Kirghiz in the Osh district with such rugs, and the absence of other crafts made with the same technique, allow us to conclude that the *arabi kilem* came to the Kirghiz in the recent past. Probably it came from the west, possibly from the region of *Kashka Dari*, Uzbekistan. In Uzbekistan there is mention of the making of palases.

Kirghiz weavers produce these rugs on the horizontal looms, the same as those used for making pile rugs. They create the warp in the same way, but usually goat hair is used, rather than sheep wool. The rug patterns are created with the weft, the yarns dyed blue, red or green. Brown and black are also used.

The pattern yarns are wool. The weft yarns in the main portion of the carpet cover the warp, but the *final rows* of weft yarns are not visible. To weave the rug, the weaver takes a few skeins of the weft yarn. By hand, she inserts the weft yarn between the warps and passes it not across the entire width of the palas, but only to the edge of the pattern color. From here the weft yarn is returned again to the other edge of the color in accordance with the pattern. The weft yarn is laid tightly with the help of the same hammer (*tokmok*), which is adapted from the weaving of pile-woven rugs. From the opposite side, as well, the weft is inserted consistent with the design. The "*arabi*" rug is tight, thick and durable, but also quite coarse.

At the present time, palas decoration has one style, and, according to the weavers, it is unchanged from earlier times. The character of the pattern is from ancient Syria. (270) The field is adorned with geometric figures with checkered drawings and stepped contours. The border design, usually smaller, is completed in the same style.

At the end of the nineteenth century, the Kirghiz also made the "*arabi kilem*" for sale.

Thus, the tradition of rug making, which is tied to the making of materials and to the organization of work, is also observed in the production of palases.

Notes

Osobennosti Materialnoe Kulturi I Prikladnogo Iskusstva Iuzhnykh Kirgizov (Distinctive Features of the Material Culture and Applied Art of the Southern Kyrgyz), Frunze, 1962, pp. 65-97; the footnotes are numbered as in the original text. This edited translation is by Nathan Hodge and Sharon Weinberger.

181. A. A. Bogolyubov. *Rug Crafts of Central Asia from the Collection Assembled by A. A. Bogolyubov*, Editions 1-2, St. Petersburg, 1908-1909.
182. A distortion of the name of the Toolos group.
183. A. Felkerzam. *Antique rugs of Central Asia, Years of Old,* 1914, October-December; 1915 June.
184. Probably, a distortion of the name of the Teyit group.
185. A. Felkerzam. *Antique Rugs of Central Asia,* "Years of Old", 1915, June, pages 19, 23.
186. Ibid., page 26
187. A. A. Semenov. *Rugs of Russian Turkestan. (Regarding the publication of "Rug Crafts of Central Asia from the Collection Assembled by A. A. Bogolyubov.")*, Ethnographic Survey, 1911, No. 1-2.
188. A.V. Le Coq. *Teppiche der Kara-kirgizen aus der Gegend des Terek-Passes in Russisch Turkistan,* Ostslavische [sic] Zeitschrift, Berlin 1929, pp. 15-17.
189. Jarring, Gunnar. *A Kara-Kirgize Rug from Eastern Turkistan* [sic]. Etnos, 1936, No. 4, pp. 103-104.
190. S. M. Dudin. *Rug crafts of Central Asia.*
191. R. Neugebauer u. G. Orendi. *Handbuch der orientalischen Teppichkunde.* Leipzig, K. Hierseman 1900; Werner Grote Hasenbalg. *Der Orientteppich seine geschichte und seine Kultur.* Berlin. Scarabäus-Verlag. 1922, Volumes I-III.
192. A. A. Miller. *Rug works of the East.* L. 1924, page 24.
193. V. G. Moshkova. *Tribal Guls in Turkmeni Rugs.* Soviet Ethnography, No. 1, 1946.
194. V. G. Moshkova. *Two unique Uzbek rugs from the Historical Collection of the Museum of History Academy of Sciences Uzbekistan.* USSR. First Edition, Tashkent, 1951; Rugs, pp. 65-98.
195. On the basis of collected material. Institute of Art Studies of the Academy of Sciences, Uzbekistan, USSR. A collection prepared for publication, *"Rugs of Central Asia."*
196. S. M. Abramson. *Sketch of Kirghiz National Culture.* Frunze., 1946, pg. 60. Ya. K. Machenko. *Rug Production in Central Asia.* National Economy in Central Asia. 1910, No. 10.

PART FOUR — WRITINGS

197. In Priissykkule, in the Dzety-Oguz district, we encountered rugs with a pile, put the technique used for making these had nothing in common with weaving. The rugs were sewn with a needle in the wool material using multi-colored thread, using feather stitches attached to the material. The pile is formed by cutting the drawn-out feather stitch loops. The technique was uncommon. It is interesting that the existence of an analogous technique is used by the south-western Kazaks (Adayevts), noted by V. V. Vostrov (*New Materials on the Ethnography of Kazak-Adayevts,* page 169.)

198. Yu. A. Shibayeva. *Materials on the Mugrab Kirghiz Dwellings,* page 108.

199. B. K. Karmysheva. *The 1954 Visit to the Jirgatal Kirghiz.* PROCEEDINGS OF THE SOCIAL SCIENCES DIVISION OF THE ACADEMY OF SCIENCES OF THE TADZHIK SSR, *10-11 (1956), 28.*

200. V. G. Moshkova, *Rugs,* page 66.

201. C. M. Abramson. *Kirghiz Population in the Xinjian-Uiguir Autonomous Region…* pages 348, 363-4.

202. A. A. Semenov. Previously cited work, pg. 141.

203. There is a very original rug (*kilche*), made in the village of Toguz-Torou, Tien Shan Region. It is held in the collection OF THE MUSEUM OF HISTORY [and] THE ACADEMY OF SCIENCES of the Kirghiz SSR (collection No. 658). The rug is made with a technique using combined material: it is flat-woven with a length of 30 cm. A similar technique is widespread among the Kazaks, Karakalpaks and Turkmen. Unfortunately, there is very limited information about this sort of rug. According to an expert, it was bought in Southern Kirghizia.

204. V. G. Moshkova. *Rugs.* Pp. 66-7.

205. "*Minibashi*"—Thousand. The literal translation: "*min*"—one thousand, "*bash*"—head.

206. This information was received from the Japalak village in the Osh region from Abdykadyr Berdygulova (Born 1873), Kokul Dosova (born 1898), Joro Tashtanova (born 1877), Akburul Telembayeva (born 1872), and others.

207. A Russian traveler gave information on the Autumn rug sales: "To our great despair, we learned that the Kirghiz bring the rugs for sale only in the fall." (Yu. D. Golovnina. *In the Pamirs.* M. 1902, page 195.)

208. V. G. Moshkova . *Rugs,* pg. 66-67.

209. A. A. Semenov. Previously cited work, pg. 153-4.
In the western part of the Osh Oblast, Kirghiz pronounce this word "gilem" (similar to the Karakalpaks and Uzbeks), in the eastern part, it is pronounced "kilem". From here on, we will refer to it as "kilem".

211. Typically, the older weavers use the same words in determining rug size measurement: *kulach* and *karysh*. The "*kulach*" is a measure of a length equivalent to the arms stretched out; the "*karysh*" to the space between the ends of the extended thumb and fifth finger.

212. According to weavers from the Alay Valley (Aysha Ormonova, Altyn Abdrakmanova) in the past, Kirghiz rugs of a smaller size, almost square (70 by 95 cm), were woven exclusively for dowries.

213. A. Felkerzam. Previously cited work. 1915. June, page 19.

214. *Ordo*—A Khanate House, a rich yurt of a well-known person. See K. K. Yudakhin. Previously cited work, page 327.

215. It is difficult to determine the limits of the diffusion of various names. We noted both names in regions close to the Kirghiz in the Osh Oblast.

216. K. K. Yudakhin. Previously cited work, page 357.

217. Erich von Salzmann. *In Sattel durch Zentralasien 600 km in 176 Tagen.* Berlin. 1903, page 294.

218. In the Lailak region (the Kesek group) the bag is called *naprach*.

219. S. M. Dudin (*Rug Works of Central Asia*, pg. 83) notes that the production of rugs for the dowry was the obligation of women. We did not encounter this among the Kirghiz.

220. B. K. Karmysheva. The Lokai "*mapramach*" and "*ilgich*". Information from *The Republic Historical Museum of Regional Studies, 2nd Edition, History and Ethnography* 1955, pg. 122-145.

221. C. M. Dudin. *Rug Works of Central Asia*, pp. 88-89.
222. T. A. Zhdanko. *National Ornamental Art of the Karakalpaks*, pages 389-390.
223. V. V. Vostrov notes the existence of knapsacks (*ten*) of the felt and pile-woven type among the Kazaks-Adayevts and the felt bag *"shabadan"* among the Aktyubin Kazaks (*New Material on the Ethnography of Kazaks-Adayevts,* pages 169-170.)
224. The pile-woven "*kurjun*" from the south of Kirghizia was not made everywhere. Even in regions where rug weaving was the most developed, it was made from patterned or striped material.
225. We do not have the possibility to speak about all the rug-weavers known to us. Their mastery and love for their work is a large subject. Thus we limit ourselves to introducing a list of a few of the best weavers: Aysha Ormanova (Born 1882 in the village of Kara-Shivak in the Alay Region; Toktokhan Baymurzayeva (Born in 1893 in the village of Kara-Shivak) in the Alay region); Altyn Abdrakmanova (Born in 1887 in the village of Chak in the Alay region); Saliya Isailova (born in 1888 in the village of Baul in the Lailak region); Aysha Matkarimova (born in 1898 in the village of Batken); Tomonay Ismanova (born in 1899 in the village of Batken); Zuleykan Koshoyeva (born in 1899 in the village of Kara-Bulak in the Batken region); Arzygul Chotanova (born in the village of Kara-Bulak in the Batken region); Tuurdu Suranchiyeva (born in 1884 in the village of Kara-Bulak in the Batken region); Nusi Mamyrjanova (born in 1905 in the village of Nichke in the Naukat region); Syra Eshinbayeva (born in 1872 in the village of Merkit in the Naukat region); Tajigul Dyusheyeva (born in 1877 in the village of Orto-Mechit in the Naukat region); Zeyne Beribayeva (born in 1886 in the village of Erke-Kashka in the Ararvan region); Sadyk Karaulov (born in 1885 in the village of Ak-Terek in the Uzgen region). Jamal Dyuysheyeva (born in 1896 in the village of Tengizbay in the Uzgen region); Ajar Moldokeeva (born in 1883 in the village of Tald-Bulak in the Alay region); Kurbubu Ismankulov (born in 1889 in the village of Shumkar in the Alay region); Akburul Telembayeva (born in 1972 in the village of Dzapalak in the Osh region.)
226. *Kudayi* is "an offering with a charitable intention." (K. K. Yudakhin, Previously cited work, page 394).
227. Slices of cut pastry, fried in ram fat.
228. *Kattama* is a rich layered flat-cake, fried in a cauldron with butter.
229. The word *dastarkhan* is also used for the offering, which is given to the guests.
230. This legend was written down from the weavers Toktokan Baymurzayeva and Tajigul Duysheeva.
231. Osh region (oblast) government archives of Kirghizia, USSR, Collection 105, d. No. 1, Description. 1, L.1
232. Ibid., collection 19 d. No. 61, description 1, L. 4.
233. A. A. Semenov. Previously cited work, page 152.
234. See the collection in the STATE MUSEUM OF ETHNOGRAPHY OF THE PEOPLES OF THE USSR, No. 1432-2.
235. The wool is combed on special flax combs. This is written about by S. M. Dudin (*Rug works of Central Asia*, page 84.) The Kirghiz also use this method.
236. S. M. Dudin. *Rug works of Central Asia*, page 85.
237. Recently, steel pipes with a diameter of 10-12 cm have replaced these wooden beams.
238. S. M. Dudin. *Rug works of Central Asia*, page 72.
239. Restoration of original rug dyes from Noin-Ula. Moscow-Leningrad., 1937, THE ACADEMY OF SCIENCES USSR AND GOVERNMENT HERMITAGE.
240. These Kirghiz articles are also made from white felt, brightened with appliques.
241. V. G. Moshkova. *Rugs*. Page 82. This scientifically grounded theory was shown by V. G. Moshkova in connection with rugs.
242. These rugs are held in the collections of the Museum of Art, Uzbekistan, USSR: book. No. 8552, inventory No. 8-3 (beginning of the twentieth century); book No. 8635, inventory No. 8-6 beginning of the twentieth century). See also pile-woven bags, book No. 8717, inventory No.

8-150 (end of the nineteenth century).
243. The names of the "*mashit*" design and "*mashadi*" are mentioned by A. Felkerzam in Kirghiz (Kazak) rugs. In these rugs the design is associated with the notion of a background (see previously cited work, "Old Years" 1915, pages 21-2).
244. V. G. Moshkova. *Rugs*, page 86.
245. V. G. Moshkova. Rugs, pages 89-90.
246. Ibid., page 82.
247. See the collection at the Museum of Art in Uzbekistan, USSR, book No. 8503, inventory No. 8-137.
248. A. A. Felkerkzam. Previously cited work., 1915, page 27.
249. F. V. Gogel. Previously cited work, page 174, illustration 84.
250. Ibid., page 116, illustration 24.
251. Reed screens in an analogous design are made in the Batken region among the Kirghiz group Noygut.
252. M. S. Andreyev, Previously cited work, page 34, Illustration 26.
253. F. V. Gogel. *Rugs*, illustration 36.
254. See the collection in the Museum of Art Uzbekistan, USSR, book 8447, inventory No. 8-61, book No. 8506, inventory No. 8-139, book p. No. 8451, inventory No. 8-162.
255. See the collection in the Museum of Art in Uzbekistan, USSR, book No. 8721, inventory 8-153.
256. T. A. Zhdanko. *National Ornamental Art of the Karakalpaks*, pg. 291, table IV.
257. B. Kh. Karmysheva. The Lokai *"mapramach"* and *"ilgich"*, page 137, illustration 5, 7, 8, page 142, illustration 16.
258. V. G. Moshkova, *Rugs*, page 85.
259. V. G. Moshkova, Rugs. Page 85.
260. See the collection in The Museum of Anthropology and Ethnography of USSR Academy of Sciences, No. 5676.
261. M. S. Andreyev. Previously cited work, page 31, 35.
262. See *Collection of National Designs of The Different Provinces of China.* Shanghai, 1953, pg. 4.
263. A. Felkerzam. Previously cited work, 1915, June, page 30.
264. "*kurak*"—made from separate pieces of scraps (K. K. Yudakhin. Previously cited work, pg. 401). Art composed of designs from colorful scraps is wide-spread among the Kirghiz for the making of pillowcases, curtains, and horse covers.
265. The design with the name "*chaydash*", "*chayjut*" is mentioned by A. Felkerzam (see the previously cited work, "The Years of Old", 1915, pg. 20.)
266. Collection in the Museum of Art, Uzbekistan, USSR, book No. 8554, inventory No. 8-141.
267. The question of the origin and time of the appearance of Kirghiz rugs is more interesting for future study, particularly interesting is the Alashan rug made by the Mongol Olots, who adopted rug-making from the Turkic Khotons, as noted by Grumm-Grzhimaylo (*Western Mongolia and Uryan-Kai Region, Vol. III, First Edition,* Leningrad, 1926, page 328).
268. A. A. Semenov. *Historical Outline of Artistic Handicrafts of Uzbekistan.* Literature and Art of Uzbekistan. Tashkent, 1937, No. 5, page 128; V. G. Moshkov. *Rugs*, page 72.
269. Flatwoven rugs of wider measurements were and are made by the Kazaks. See M. C. Mukhanov. *Rug production and its ornaments.* Institute of History, Archaeology and Ethnography, Academy of Sciences, Kazakstan, USSR, Volume 6, Alma-Ata, 1959.
270. V. Stasov. *The Slavic and Eastern Ornament in Ancient and Modern Manuscripts.* Saint Petersburg, 1884, Table CXXX. (Syrian ornament: 13th-15th centuries.)

Narodnoe Dekorativno Prikladnoe Iskusstvo Kirgizov (The Popular Applied Decorative Arts of the Kyrgyz) by S. V. Ivanov and K. I. Antipina. (The chapter on Pile Weaving was authored by Klavdiya Antipina.)

The footnotes are numbered as in the original text. This edited translation is by Nathan Hodge and Sharon Weinberger.

Pile-Woven Carpets

Among the rich and varied artistic traditions of the Kirghiz people, pile-woven carpets occupy a place of special importance. Among all forms of folk art, pile-woven carpets not only had their own artistic tradition but also they played a major role in the economic life of the Kirghiz at the end of the nineteenth and at the beginning of the twentieth century. It is not by chance that, of all the forms of Kirghiz decorative and applied arts, it is carpet weaving which received the earliest attention in ethnographic literature. Interest in Kirghiz carpet weaving began to develop at the end of the nineteenth and the beginning of the twentieth century, concurrent with a new and intense interest in Turkmen carpets at the time. These folk items were highly valued for their artistic merit. From that time on, museums began to collect artifacts of Kirghiz carpet weaving (1).

Pile carpet weaving in nineteenth-century Kirghizia was confined to a certain geographic area, the best known of which extended to the regions of the trans-Fergana (within the boundaries of the present-day Osh region (*oblast*). In this area, however, development was uneven. The broadest growth of carpet weaving occurred in the southwestern regions of Kirghizia, in places settled by those Kirghiz who in the past were united under the tribal union of the Ichkilik (2). As the first studies of Kirghiz carpet weaving attest, these carpet items were especially important among the Kydyrsh tribe (3). We can judge something of their artistry and high technical level by the number of examples which have been collected by the Museum of Art, Uzbek SSR (4). In addition to the Ichkilik people, pile woven carpets were vital to the Kirghiz living in their immediate vicinity, including those people who belonged to the clan/tribal groups of the Adigine, Mungush, Mongoldor (in the southeastern portions of Osh region (*oblast*) and of the Basyz, Munduz, and the Kutchu (in the northeastern parts) (5).

Under the conditions of primitive economy, for women pile weaving was a part of the everyday domestic production. They received the necessary raw materials as a by product of their main economic pursuit, animal herding. For their part, men aided chiefly by the construction of looms and the dyeing of yarn (6).

Kirghiz carpet weaving developed in close connection with the carpet weaving practices of the Fergana Valley and of other carpet-weaving centers of Central Asia, as well as those of Eastern Turkestan. Over the course of many years, they began to produce carpets specifically for sale. At the end of the nineteenth and the beginning of the twentieth centuries, when the markets of the Fergana Valley thrived on the carpet trade, the Kirghiz began not only making carpets to order, but also to sell at the market. They also began to obtain their necessary raw materials at the market. In this way, carpet production became a cottage industry and the job of selling the carpets fell to the men. Among the Kirghiz *bais* (wealthy landowners), enterprises sprang up that profited from weaving. Other kinds of entrepreneurs sprang up as well. On the orders of the feudal nobility the best masters were collected and put to work producing carpets. As an example, in the settlement of the Japalak, Osh region, seventeen *bais* had undertaken to organize carpet production at the end of the nineteenth century. Kirghiz carpet weavers, working without let-up, made these carpets.

The southern Kirghiz for many years continued to shoulder the burden of carpet production. They were also required to present carpets as tribute to the Kokand Khanate (7).

They wove during the summer, and in the autumn they carried their carpets off to the markets in Uzbekistan, Andizhan, Margelan, Kokand, Osh, and Uzgen as well. These markets not only featured local carpets (8), but also great numbers of the famous carpets of the Turkmen as well as carpets from Eastern Turkestan (9) and Northern Afghanistan (10). The concentration of carpets of different origin and the increasing familiarity with their styles of design further enabled local carpet producers to expand the variety of patterns as well as to create entirely new and unique forms of carpet weaving art.

The principal buyers of Kirghiz carpets were local Tajiks and Uzbeks, as well as the Kirghiz themselves (11). Not only did the locals buy the carpets; people arriving from the northern regions of Kirghizia did as well. In these instances, trade was often in the form of barter. They drove herds from northern Kirghizia and brought reed stalks or patterned reed screens and traded them for carpets (12). Weaving extended deeply into the lives of the southern Kirghiz. Each woven item was practical and utilitarian, necessary for the economy and way of life. At that time woven goods were also highly responsive to the aesthetic needs of the people, not only for decoration for one's dwelling but also for one's camel or horse during migration.

The pile-woven fabrics of the Kirghiz—both of small and large scale—had their own special purposes (13). The smaller items which functioned as bags and sacks of varied design and size, were used for storing household items and as saddle bags for pack animals. Small pile-woven articles are of early origin. Larger pieces were limited to the south of Kirghizia. Of particular interest is the storage bag known as the *chavadan* (Plate VIII, Nos. 3,4). It was sewn together with special strips of pile-woven carpet (which had the same name) and a piece of homemade felt. An opening (20 – 25 cm) which ran lengthwise was left unsewn as an opening for depositing household items in the bag. The *chavadan* had its place in the *juk* in the yurt, much as it continues to have today in the modern household. The decorative side is visible and at the bottom. The overall size of the *chavadan* varies, with an average width of 32 to 42 cm and an average length of 80 to 112 cm. In dwellings made of bricks of clay and straw (pise), where items are stored in a niche, the length of the *chavadan* corresponds to the size of the niche.

In the past, ownership of a pile-woven bag was considered a necessity for every Kirghiz family, and it constituted part of the dowry even in poor households (14). *Chavadans* still can be found in many homes, but all are antique. The *chavadan* is no longer made.

Among the semi-nomadic Uzbeks and the Karakalpaks, storage bags had the same significance they had among the Kirghiz. Serving exactly the same utilitarian function, they differed only in name and design. Thus, the storage bag (*mapramach*) of the Lokai tribe reminds us in its form of the *sunduk* (15).

The carpet bags (karshin), made of pile-woven strips and used by the Karkalpaks, are close in form to those used by the Kirghiz (16).

The small pile woven item used by the Kirghiz as hanging cases ("shelves") for storing linens inside the yurt were unique in design. One of the sides was attached to the upper part of the yurt wall trellis and the other to the roof poles of the yurt. They measured 85-90 x 75-80cm. Dependent upon the part of the Osh oblast, they had different names: *ayak koichu* (southeastern), *kosh jabik* (i. e., "covering from two sides", southern and southwestern) (17), *japsar* (northern). Hanging cases were strung from both sides of the *juk*. Beneath them, a bag called a *bashtyk* was attached. The *bashtyk* measured about 68 x 75 cm and frequently its edge would be decorated with a fringe.

In the Kirghiz domestic life there were different pile-woven bags for storage of all sorts of small household items, for example, the *kaichi kap* for a scissors, and the *kuzgu kap* for mirrors. Another small pile-woven item was the *tutkuch*, or potholder.

When discussing the extent to which pile woven articles played a role in everyday life it is important to note items which were used as saddle rugs. To this end they wove beautiful pack rugs known as *kupchuk*, which fit saddles of up to 34–40 cm; they also wove saddle girths for horses (*basmayil*) and saddle bags (*kurzhun*). For nomadic migration they employed special carpet covering cases, with which they covered the ends of the yurt roof poles (*uuk kap*) and also covered the end of the collapsed yurt wall lattice (*kerege kap*).

Among the larger items of pile-woven design were the unique tent band (*tegirich*), the entrance curtain-rugs of the yurt (*eshik tysh*) and the carpets (*kilem* or, sometimes, *gilam*) (18).

The *tegirich* is a long, narrow (35-40 cm) strip which decorated the interior of the yurt (Plate VIII-2, Plate VIII-6). It was attached to the outer wall lattice of the yurt and, anchored to each side of the door frame, served to constrict the wall lattice and to counter the downward and outward thrust of the roof and the roof poles. Visible as it encircled the interior space, the *tegirich* formed a unique frieze (19). With the decline of the yurt as the principle dwelling, the *tegirich* is no longer being woven. Older examples are cut into lengths, sewn together and used as carpets (illustration 3). The *tegirich* was most common in the southwestern parts of Osh oblast. A similar form of tent band (*tegerich*) was found among the Kirghiz of the Pamir, in Eastern Turkestan, and among the once-nomadic Uzbeks of the Samarkand region.

The *eshik tysh*, the pile-woven carpet used as an entrance hanging over the door of the yurt, also had a similar geographic range, and it gave the yurt elegance as well as national uniqueness.

Most valued of all pile woven articles are the carpets (20). Their measurements, as are those of the felt carpet, are approximately 150 x 300 cm. Within these boundaries there is a corresponding variation of form. Later, when the Kirghiz masters began to prepare carpets to order and for the market, the size of carpets increased. As A. Felkerzam relates, the carpets produced by the Kirghiz of the Fergana surpassed all the other carpets of Central Asia in size (21). The carpets were widely employed by the Kirghiz in everyday life.

During nomadic migrations, these carpets were used to cover pack camels. This accounts for how the nomadic caravan began to take on the appearance of a celebratory display. During weddings, feasts, and holidays, carpets decorated the earthen floor of the yurt when guests were entertained. Their appointed place (*tor*) was designated by felt mats and flatwoven rugs. Other carpets were stored in the juk. By the measurements of the *juk* one would be able to estimate the prosperity of the yurt's owner; by the presence of a large number of carpets a *juk* became larger and wider than ordinary. During funeral feasts (*ash*), carpets not only decorated the floor of the yurt, they formed paths between the yurts. In wealthy families and in families of middle means, carpets, traditionally nine in number, formed an obligatory part of the dowry (22).

The Kirghiz artisans also wove smaller carpets (*zhai namaz*) used during Muslim prayers. They were widely used through the western part of Osh region, where, unlike the eastern regions, there was a greater influence of

Islam.

The national traditions of carpet weaving are preserved by elder artisans (*chever* in the south), who practiced this art from childhood. Nowadays, unfortunately, young artisans are few in number. The best artisans—those who can produce almost any carpet design—enjoy deep respect among their people. They are invited to the preparation of a carpet and they will be sent for no matter the distance. They are the recipients of lavish thanks for their assistance There are still some carpet weavers alive today who ply their trade from one mountain village (*kishlak*) to the next. The life of a carpet weaver was not easy. Dedicating themselves to their beloved art, often they owned no carpet of their own.

The master artisans oversaw the production of the carpet, organizing and supervising all stages of the work, teaching the younger artisans. Each of these artisans began to practice her craft sometime between the ages of 9 and 12. The best of them knew not only pile weaving but all kinds of non-pile weaving. Many were praised both as capable weavers who could also make patterned felt rugs (*shyrdak*) and decorated reed screens (*chirmagan chiy*). They were genuine folk artists of great artistic sensitivity, who preserved and perfected the best traditions of the preceding generations. Not a few of them will serve a masters for forthcoming generations.

Just one example of a master artisan who possessed great artistic taste and made many marvelous carpets was Aisha Ormonova (23), who learned to make pile-woven articles under her mother, who was considered one of the best weavers in the mountainous regions of the Alai. The mother, Kumush Ormonova (24), had, in turn, gained her mastery from *her* mother, who, like Kumush herself, was considered one of the great artisans in her region (Figure 4). No small number of folk songs are devoted to these women artists. (The words *masteritsa* and *khudozhnitsa*, "master artisan" and "artist" are feminine nouns.)

Kirghiz carpets differ in the quality and complexity of their weave. They are made principally from wool (25). In the past, however, cotton had been used for both warp and the weft. According to the accounts of several master artisans, cotton yarn obtained at the market was used. Among the Kirghiz Kydyrsh peoples, who lived in Uzbekistan, A. A. Semenov found carpets with cotton warps and wool wefts (26).

For pile, the Kirghiz used wool from sheep, goats, or camels. Camel hair was found to be especially durable. It was not, however, used everywhere. For example, among the nineteenth-century pile-woven articles which we found in the Lailak, Batken and Alai regions, we found none that used camel wool. In these areas the basic material for carpets was goat wool.

The material which found the broadest use among the Osh Kirghiz in the manufacture of carpets was sheep wool, most often gray, less often brown. It was used for the warp, the weft, and the pile. They set aside the sheep wool from the spring shearings. The rougher wool went to the warp and the weft of the carpet, and the softer wool was used for the pile. They also used white goat wool.

The yarns for the pile, weft, and warp were spun differently. The warp yarns were twisted and spun tightly and evenly, but not thinly. After this, the warp yarns were specially processed for extra durability (27). As a result the warp base of a Kirghiz carpet was durable, but thick and somewhat coarse. (The warps for smaller articles of early Kyrgyz pile weaving were thinner.) The weft was loosely spun and softer. Often the master artisans would make a double pass-through (double "shot") of the weft. For the pile, they used the best white or gray wool which, when dyed ,would give the best colors.

The loom for weaving of pile carpets is simple. It is horizontal in type and is placed directly on the ground. It is similar to the Turkmen loom. It is universally known in southern Kirghiz as the *dukon* (i. e., workbench).

In earlier times the loom was fashioned out of four squared beams. Such looms were employed everywhere for the manufacturing of large carpets to be sold at market or to be displayed in the kahn's palace. Today, looms are made of two poles (or iron pipes) fastened to stakes and placed horizontally and parallel, their length slightly exceeding the width of the carpet. The warp yarns are looped around the poles and are divided into two levels, an upper and lower level (Figure 5).

Work on the loom begins and ends with the weaving of a coarse, flatwoven section for a distance of 7 to 10 cm, running the width of the carpet. Usually this is a grey or brown weave. The majority of antique carpets have a long braided fringe, extensions of the warp yarns. Characteristic of the weaving in the valley settlements was framing of the carpet by a colored flatweave (2.5-3 cm), the *zhorop*, fashioned of warp and weft. The weft threads alternating colors every 2 to 3 centimeters.

The tools for carpet weaving are simple. They include the weft beater which is a heavy but fine-toothed comb (*tokmok*) made of wood for compacting the weft and the pile; a knife (*pychak*), for cutting the pile yarn after a "knot" is "tied"; and a scissors (*kaichi*), for uniformly trimming the pile after two or three rows of "knots" have been placed.

The knots in Kirghiz carpets are one-and-a-half knots—that is, they are asymmetrical. The pile is from 6 to 8 mm in length. The density is from 80 to 90 thousand knots per square meter. In some of the smaller antique carpets the density is somewhat greater, ranging between 100 and 110 thousand knots per square meter.

The weaving of carpets among the Kirghiz involves deeply-maintained folk traditions. For example, the Kirghiz employ a form of collective, comradely labor called *kilem ashar*. During the weaving process, the carpet is woven on a daily basis, morning to evening, until it is completed. Depending upon the size of the carpet being woven, the woman of the household (the carpet's owner) is helped by a number of weavers who may be neighbors, relatives, or friends. The woman prepares food for all the participants, and all of those who arrive to take part in the *kilem ashar* bring a *dastarkhan* (28). On conclusion of the work, the participants usually receive gifts. The eldest master, under whose direction the work is conducted, is rewarded more generously.

The custom of presenting gifts to the hosts, widespread in the past, has been preserved. As soon as the neighbors would hear of the decision to weave a carpet, they would begin to make presents for the host. Sometimes the presents would be significant: sheep, goats, or money. While presenting gifts they would express a wish for the carpet to be completed successfully and before the time allotted.

In a few regions, particularly in the Alai Valley, there still exist some earlier customs, such as the gathering of elderly folk before beginning of work. Elderly persons would be seated on a carpet and treated to entertainment and refreshment. Before the work would begin, the oldest of the gathered elders would address the patron-protector of weaving (29) with a prayer for help in the work.

Kirghiz pile-woven items are of great artistry. They reflect an instinctive feel for beauty and measure which the masters bring along with their understanding of the decorative effect of the weaving. The carpets are a marvel of color and are, without exception, made distinctive by the pleasant contrasts.

The basic color scheme for carpet wares is the two colors, red and blue, a combination going back to earliest times (30). Both colors are rendered in muted tones.

It is well known what a great role plant dyes played in the carpet weaving arts; they gave the carpets their marvelous brilliance as well as a softness and richness. The Kirghiz masters used plant dyes, and the more antique pile weaves preserved the charm of these colors. In such carpets we encounter indigo's wealth of deep

PART FOUR   WRITINGS

blue and the fineness of madder-rose.

In addition to red and blue, a limited number of carpets display other colors—yellow, orange, rose, green, as well as the naturally-occurring white and brown. These colors make the carpets even more vivid, especially when the colors are interspersed, seemingly accidentally, with bright designs of simple ornamental motifs.

In such pieces as the *chavadan*, and *ayak koichu*, *bashtyk*, and *tegirich*, additional colors are employed more often than in carpets. (The *tegirich*—which can be thought of as a kind of "architectural textile"— becomes a decorative multi-colored frieze on the interior of the yurt.) We can find color variations: bright red, crimson, berry-red, sometimes even violet.

There are, to a limited extent, carpets with black yarn. At present, such carpets can be found only among the weaving arts of the Batken district (Plate VII-5). A few weavings can be found which have white thread, most frequently on door rugs (*eshik tysh*) or on prayer rugs (31). A white background is common as well for the *tegirich*. It is not uncommon to find a carpet or another woven article with a white border. In addition to this, white yarn is used for executing pattern detail. Also, many borders are made of brown yarn.

As a rule, the patterns of pile-woven articles are outlined. Accenting the form of the pattern, the color of the outline softens the general tone of the carpet. A pattern is usually outlined by the same color, but in a distinctly brighter tone, or by a brown thread. Brown patterns are outlined by blue, and blue patterns by brown. In some cases this is not a strict rule. The masters have a distinct feeling for color and without error incorporate an outline which makes the pattern distinct without disrupting the general harmony of the red and blue colors.

Several traditional aspects of the Kirghiz decorative art appear in weaving art, and they are expressed in the sequence of the colors in carpet backgrounds and pattern as well as in the interaction of the basic colors of blue and red. Along with this, it is the color red which creates the general color scheme.

The surface of most pile-woven articles is divided into a central part (field) and a border (*kaima*). Furthermore, each part of the weave maintains traditions of design, layout, and color combination. Simultaneously, the less expressive the *kaima*, the greater the attention to the field and to the overall background.

The designs of Kirghiz pile woven articles are extraordinarily diverse, with a limitless number of variations. The leading role in design belongs to the pattern. The pattern varies and is characterized by forms that are both large-scale yet detailed. Many motifs specific to carpet weaving art can be found. This testifies to the close cultural links in the lives of the Central Asian peoples: the Kirghiz, the Karakalpak, the once-nomadic Uzbeks, the Turkmen and the peoples of Kazakhstan, the Caucasus, and Eastern Turkestan. Although each group's style is unique, in each case we can find closely related forms. Despite the overall commonality of motifs found among other people, there is no doubt that the Kirghiz pattern stands apart and is entirely original.

Pile-woven patterns, much like any others, appear at first to be stable in form. But, they change persistently and visibly. Despite this, they nevertheless preserve some of the old forms while achieving new artistic images.

The creation of carpet designs and their structural composition, as our study has endeavored to show, is the product of collective labor on the part of several masters. Usually the eldest of the masters offers her suggestion first, and it is then discussed. After a decision is made, resolving the issue, the eldest master estimates the number of warps required, especially if a new design is to be employed or if new elements are to be added to a traditional design. The master strives to enrich traditional pattern with new forms. Sometimes these new forms incorporate patterns which are traditional for other forms of Kirghiz decorative art, particularly from weaving. As a result, a number of new elements have entered pile weaving: typical pattern weaves such as rhombs with characteristic extensions flanked with other rhombic or diamond-shaped outgrowths (Figure 6. No. 11); a diamond composed of interlocking hooks with contrasting colors (Figure 7, No. 19); a figure the masters call the *omurtka* (vertebra) (Figure 10, No. 3). Patterns characteristic of the pile weave in a *kajar* have also been introduced successfully. Some examples of these are: the *bagzhagai* (Figure 9, No. 8) which decorate the *kaima* in carpets and in the *tegirich*; patterns of wavy lines with extensions (Figure 9, No. 10) and with quadrants and echelons (Figure 9, No. 16); in narrow *kaimas*, the masters often incorporate a design called the *tarak* (comb) which is a typical *kajar* pattern.

The folk masters who created these ornamental motifs gave voice to nomadic way of thinking, expressing their interests and imaginations. The names of their designs call to mind the nomad's animal and plant world.

However, the meanings of the patterns often differ from the interpretations given them by other contemporary carpet weavers. This results in the patterns being given different names At the same time, we also find certain patterns which every master knows and to which they apply the predetermined motif. In most cases these are ancient patterns, found on some of the oldest artifacts and which still persist in the practice of Kyrgyz carpet weaving—designs such as the *toguz bobo*, the *kaikalak*, the *kochkor zhuyuz*, the *kochkoro, ut kuiruk, kyyal, kavyrga* and others. These names can be found in the pattern nomenclature of other applied arts.

Traditional pattern names—which are found among other peoples as well—have persisted in carpet weaving, particularly when they have some fixed significance. The naming of designs in some instances helps us to understand origins and historical development. For instance, we begin to understand the origin of Kirghiz patterns by their names: *karakalpak kochot* (32), *pashayi* (33), *orus* (which means "Russian"), and so on.

In pile-weaving, geometric forms prevail, but organic forms are also common and clearly expressed, particularly in stylized designs. Among the geometric forms, we encounter rectangles, rhombuses, triangles, star-shaped images, and sharp corners. The most common is the rhombus or diamond with tendrils, hooks or flourishes of varied design extending from the corners. This basic pattern allows for a multitude of variation. The rhombus pattern is one of the most ancient in weaving. Common among the Volga peoples of Russia, it is used by many of the peoples of Europe and Asia.

The motif of the tendril or hook is used in all the pile woven rugs of Central Asia and Kazakstan, but in each case it has its own individuality. In the art of the Kirghiz masters this pattern shows endless variation. (Figure 6, Nos. 1-21).

Sometimes a rectangle or an octagon can be found in place of the rhombus (Figure 6, No. 22). Often the extension ends in smaller rhombic forms which resemble an anchor (Figure 6, No. 12). At times a group of complex composition combines hook motifs to form a medallion (Figure 6, No. 21). The varied symmetry of the hook forms the remarkable contours of the design (Figure 8, Nos. 6, 12, 19). The design of the rhombus with offshoots sometimes creates a terraced form (Figure 6, No. 23; Plate VIII-4). The complex reworking of patterns in Kirghiz carpet weaving with hooks and tendrils can be further studied in the material collected by S. M. Dudin at the end of the nineteenth and the beginning of the twentieth centuries (34).

The name for the pattern which derives from the horns of a sheep—*kochkor, kochkorok,* and *kochkor zhyuiyuz* is commonly encountered. But, in the south (in the Alai Valley) and southwest, the name *kaikalak* also is used. (35).

It is not uncommon for the masters to elaborate on the composition of one single pattern—the *kochkorok*—as their sole decorative endeavor. It can be found often in the central field of smaller pile-woven articles such as the *bashtyk* (Plate VII-1), the *chavadan* (Plate VIII-3) as well as in large-scale rugs (Plate VII-2; Plate VII, No. 5) and in the *tegirich* (Plate VIII-2; Plate VIII, No. 6). The pattern designed around a rhombus with offshoots remains to this day one of the favorites of the Kirghiz carpet weavers. This most typical design of Kirghiz carpet art encompasses many deep folk traditions. It repeats the motifs and the cruciform placement which is employed in so many other forms of Kirghiz folk art: in embroidering, in weaving, in woodcarving, in jewelry making, and in reed screen making. The carpet pattern known as the *kochkorok* (*kaikalak*) is characteristic of the great artistry of Kirghiz national art.

The master weaver was impressive. Her imagination, her talent, her skillful execution of the design, combining the color combination between the pattern and the background and accenting the pattern of the central field by surrounding it with the bordering *kaima*—all this she called upon in her artistry.

Attention is also given to the internal execution of the rhombus. Motifs characteristic of weaving are placed within the rhombus (Figure 6, Nos. 13-20; Figure 7, Nos. 7, 10, 13, 16, 22). We can find a group of simple or terraced rectangles, rhombuses, zigzags, eight-pointed rosettes, cruciform figures, and triangles. Sometimes the rhombus is divided into triangular sections that are executed as individual patterns based on their colors alternating with the background. The appearance of applique work—typical for the earliest types of Kirghiz artwork—is also repeated (Figure 7, No. 15). Pile woven *bashtyks* and *ayak koichu,* which have patterns executed with designs characteristic of early Kirghiz needlepoint work (*ters kayik*), have also been preserved (Figure 6, No. 20).

The masters also achieve great artistic effect by intensifying the complexity of the pattern. Figure 8, Numbers 6 and 12, demonstrate original designs. They are the result of the creative imagination of the folk artists. In the vertical elements or rhombic device we find a system of lines branching out which remind us of a human figure with extended arms. In small, pile-woven articles this pattern appeared frequently at the turn of the century, as seen in the small rugs woven by the masters of the Kyrdysh people. The entire design carries the original local name of a teakettle (*chaidosh*) (36). In contemporary carpets, such designs no longer appear.

One of the most ancient designs, still commonly found, is known as *karakalpak kochot*. This pattern originates among the Karakalpak and the pattern is characterized by the cruciform layout of its elements. The design is enclosed in a cross-like frame. The masters of Batken district have reworked this pattern in a unique and new compositional form in contemporary carpets (Plate VII-5)., which does *not* have cruciform placement. Its motifs take the form of a multiterraced medallion, in the central field. An analogous design is used by the masters in the south of Kirghizia for decorating reed screens. It is for this reason that carpet weavers sometimes call the total composition *ashkana kochot* (37).

The Kirghiz pattern *mashaty* (38), which resembles a saw-toothed blade, is unique. It is usually arranged in a cruciform manner, but there are many variations (Figure 7, Nos. 7, 9, 10, 11, 12). In pile-woven articles, color variations are particularly beautiful; the masters introduce white and rose outlining which enlivens the pattern. The *mashaty* ornament is placed in the central field of the *bashtyk* and of the carpet (see table VII-3, VII-4) and has an analogue in the carpets of the Beshir (39).

Polygons of various forms are of importance in Kirghiz carpet design (Figure 7, Nos. 1-4, 13-17, 18, 20, 22, 25). One of the commonest is the multi tiered medallion with extensions in the form of hooks externally and with geometric indentations internally in the forms of rhombuses, triangles, and rectangles (Figure 7, No. 14). This design is one of the most pervasive among the pile-woven articles of the *Karakalpak* (40), appearing as well among the Lokai in their pile *mapramach* (41).

Medallions with indented edges (Figure 7, Nos. 3, 17) are found in early Kirghiz carpet work. They have something in common with patterns on thick antique pile carpets, the well-known *julkirs* which were woven in the Samarkand region (42).

The medallions which appear in Figure 7 (numbers 4, 15, and 18) were woven by Kirghiz masters on antique small items. They are characteristic in being divided into four parts, each sector of the design juxtaposed with diametrically opposed coloration, a common device found also in Turkmen carpets.

Turning to the organic forms of ornamentation, we will devote most of our attention to the flowering or rosette forms (Figure 8, Nos. 1-5, 7, 8, 10, 11, 22). As we can see from the drawings, they are of varying degrees of complexity. The expressive complex rosettes seen in pile-woven articles are enhanced by blossoming forms, which give contour to the composite parts of the rosette, are used to introduce other colors. The rosettes are situated rhythmically on the field of the carpet. Sometimes they are united by broken lines resembling birds in flight.

It is possible that some of these designs represent concrete objects. The countless variations, each the result of an individual handicraft, introduced great variation in the forms of ornament, each in accordance with individual taste, eventually leading to the stylization of the pattern. Earlier significance has been lost, and today they are simply decorative forms. In each case, the rosette design has a dual name. On the one had, the name *toguz bobo* (literally, "nine hills") is used (43). (This ancient folk appellation also refers to a plant which has round, serrated leaves, used for feeding cattle. Common in Kirghizia, this pattern is seen in all forms of decorative art.) Rosettes with a smooth contour, of the other hand, are called "paw prints" or "tracks" (*taman*) by the carpet weavers (44), and the names for these are reminiscent of the kinds of animal represented: *it taman* (dog tracks), *myshyk taman* (cat prints), *tailak taman* (camel tracks), etc.

It is important to note that similar flowering rosettes, known as stylized chrysanthemums, are characteristic of Khotan (45). In Kyrgyz pile weaves, they can be found on antique carpets, on the *tegirich*, and on the *eshik tysh*.

Tree-like ornaments are also of interest. The prototype is a vertical stalk, from which stylized branches extend on both sides. At the end of the branches, we have elaborations of varied form (Figure 8, Nos. 13, 17). This pattern is found on carpets as well as on door rugs, *eshik tysh*. A similar design can be found in Turkmen carpets (46).

There is an entire series of folk names for organic designs: *kytai kochot* ("Chinese branch"); *alma kochot* (apple pattern); *alma gul* (the apple blossom) (47), *anar kochot* (pomegranate). A. Felkerzam devoted particular attention to the pomegranate design, which he considered to be related to items made by the Kashgar Kirghiz. However, we were unable to find patterns with the pomegranate design among the southern Kirghiz. Although some masters had preserved some recollections about how such a design would be executed on a carpet. Designs names *jiyda gul* (jida flower), *tal berki* (willow leaf). The *kyrk shak* (forty hills) is also widespread, as is *kyrk shak zharty* (forty hills halved). These two designations are familiar terms in the pattern weaves of the south of Kirghizia.

In both the field and the border of a Kirghiz carpet, we find the trefoil. The masters consider this to be one of the most difficult to execute (Figure 7, No. 20; Figure 10, Nos. 7, 17). The very same pattern is found on Turkmen carpets (48).

Some pile designs have come from simple weaving. Many Kirghiz carpets feature a design in the shape of four interlocking C's—which the Kirghiz call *orus kochot* (Russian pattern) (Figure 8, No. 22; Plate VIII-1). We may presume that this design is copied from the patterns of brocade weaving (Figure 8. No. 18) (49), or from Russian calico (which is entirely possible, since in cotton weaves eastern themes commonly were added in the interests of commerce). Carpets with the *orus kochot* pattern are some of the most common throughout the Osh oblast. Thanks to its color combination, the carpet with the *orus kochot* design became fashionable (50).

A design well known in Asia and Russian ornamental weaving and embroidery as the "Turkish cucumber" (Figure 8, No. 16) also entered Kirghiz carpet art where it could be found as a design 80 or 90 years ago. The Kyrgyz masters call this the *boto moyun* (camel's neck) or the *kynyr moyun* (crooked neck).

In both the carpet and the *bashtyk* we find the scorpion (*chayan*) pattern (Figure 8, No. 15). This pattern gives a decorative effect with its undulating line.

A pattern, no longer woven, found on the *besh keshte* weave (Figure 8, No. 9) had the very same name as the carpet.

In their pile woven carpets, the masters often employed designs copied from patterns widely used and popular in Uzbek weaving. Such patterns were uniquely reworked (Figure 8, Nos. 19-21). This kind of pattern was used by the masters of the southwestern part of Osh oblast. They reproduced the patterns of Uzbek silk weavers and of carpet makers from other regions. Usually such designs were executed on a white background, using blue and red thread for the patterning. These patterns were called *pashayi kochot*, *kymkap kochot*, and reflect the names of those Uzbek handicrafts on which they were based.

The border plays an important role in the artistic elaboration of pile-woven articles. In Kyrgyz carpets, borders vary. They are composed of one, two, or three *kaimas* and a few thin, plain stripes which give distinction to color boundaries.

Borders have varying widths. The relationship between the measurement of the *kaima* and the scale of the central field varies from 1 to 1.5 to 1 to 4.6.

The spectrum of colors in the border usually is the same found in the field, but the border is often rendered in brighter tones as well as in brown. As noted above, the border is sometimes has a white background. The elegance of the *kaima* is enhanced by the pattern *"ala monchok"* (colorful dazzling beads). *"Ala monchok"* refers to the small-scale ornamental motifs and or lines which alternate color contrasts. Today, it is customary to find in the border indication of when and for whom the carpet was woven along with the name of the artist.

The border of a Kirghiz pile woven carpet is as important as the central field, and is enriched with expressive patterns (Figures 9 and 10). In this respect, folk custom provides the material. Of the ornamental motifs that recur on both the central field and the *kaima*, it is worth noting the motif of the branch or hook; in borders, this design does not have cruciform placement. Individual rosettes also serve as single ornaments on the border and *kaima* (Figure 10, Nos. 5, 7-11, 17).

One of the most typical of all the different types of Kirghiz pile-weave is the *kaima* pattern of an unbroken line with curves and with extensions of individual branches or hooks. (Figure 9, Nos. 1-10).

We find among these designs which outline the background and the ornaments, particularly those which are adapted from the most typical designs of Kirghiz decorative art such as felt rugs and reed screens. These patterns have the same names as the motifs for felt articles: *kochkorok, kochkorok myuyuz, synar myuyuz, kosh myuyuz*. Furthermore, in the east and north of the Osh region, wavy patterns with offshoots are called *kyyal*.

Included in this category is the S-shaped motif, the *it kuyruk* (dog's tail) (Figure 9, Nos. 10, 18). We find in pile-weaving deep resonance with other folk traditions.

Frequently we find an original *kaima* made of sloping lines with terracing. This design carries the name *kabyrga* (ribbing) (Figure 9, Nos. 13-15). Usually this is given a brighter color scheme.

The meandering pattern, quite characteristic of East Turkestan carpets, is often found in Kirghiz borderwork. It is found usually in the more complex configurations (Figure 9, No. 12), as well as in simpler variations (Figure 9, No. 11). The simpler form carries the name *kalit* (clasp or lock).

Some of the more ancient and pervasive designs are worth singling out: geometric patterns such as the triangle—*tumarcha* (amulet) (Figure 9, No. 20); rhomboid forms—*kerege bash* (top of the wall lattice) (Figure 9, No. 17); the design known as the *ut taman* (dog tracks); star-shaped designs—*zhyldyz umurtka* (vertebrae) (Figure 9, Nos. 16, 19); the *zholbors taman* (tiger tracks) (Figure 10, No. 12); *kerege kos*—(the yurt wall lattice openings) (Figure 10, Nos. 2, 10). Another ornamental name derived from the terminology of nomadic life is portrayed in Figure 10 (No. 14). The masters refer to it as the *tutkuch* (a device for pulling the cauldron from the hearth).

Garland or wreath patterns also lend elegance (Figure 10, Nos. 3-8; Plate VIII, No. 1). They are light, rhythmic and composed of a series of rosettes or palmettes, and are connected with each other by interlocked branches; they sometimes form a triangle in which the design is inlaid. Flowering motifs are expressive (Figure 10, Nos. 16, 18, 19; Plate VII, No. 3).

The compositional layout of the field varies depending on the clarity, precision, and rhythm with which the ornamental motifs are situated. It is characteristic to have one type of ornament in the layout or a mixture of two or three different types. There are no carpets where the ornament is overloaded, nor are there any empty spaces. The pattern is linked organically to the background, becoming one with it; this is characteristic of Kirghiz national art. While design is based on the rules of symmetry, it is not limited by such rules. The rhythmic construction of the pattern depends on the prescription and form of pile weaving. At the same time, each individual work is notable for a few compositional decisions. The design of the field can be divided into nine basic types (51):

Type One. The central field is divided into two, three, six or ten lengthwise strips, within which the patterns are laid out (Figure 11, Nos. 1-3). Within this scheme we may note two variations: a) the colors of the background alternate and the corresponding designs change in coloration; b) only the colors of the designs themselves alternate, and the background remains monochromatic. As V. G. Moshkova has observed, the existence of carpets with such composition allows us to suggest that the most ancient form involved the sewing together of a few strips of carpet, woven together on narrow-frame looms (52). The patterns for this type vary, but they often feature multi-petaled rosettes and rhomboid forms with offshoots. Among the Kirghiz, the Kydyrsh group in the past favored representations of organic ornaments—flowers and vines with leaves.

Type Two. In the field, a single pattern is elaborated on the linear and on the transverse axis (Figure 11, Nos. 4-6). These may be eight-petaled circular rosettes, rhomboid forms with offshoots, the interlocking of four S-shaped figures, and so on. One variation of this type is the joining of forms with straight or broken lines. In this instance it creates a straight or a diagonal network. The masters refer to this entwined composition as *chatyshma*.

The carpets of the first and second type are found throughout Southern Kirghizia. They are characteristic of items made in the nineteenth century as well as in contemporary times. Small items with this composition are rare.

Type Three. The field is divided into quadrants or rectangles (two to four along the width and four to eight along the length), separated from each other by patterned stripes (Figure 11, Nos. 7, 8). Each rectangle is filled with a pattern on a red or blue background. The patterns are laid out according to either color or pattern in a diagonal order. Each separate part or square creates the impression of being an individual rug of the *ayak koichu* or *bashtyk* type. The patterns are usually tree-like in appearance or are of the *mashaty* or *chayan* type in a *besh keshte* weave. Carpets of this type are widespread throughout the southwestern part of the Osh region. Kashgar carpets are well-known for a similar composition, which appears as well in the reed screens of northern Kirgizia.

Type Four. The field is formed by the boundaries of cruciform shapes within which patterns of similar shape are composed (Figure 11, No. 9). The patterns and lines of the boundaries are of a single color, distinct from the background. Two types of pattern are typical of this composition; *karakalpak kochot* and the *mashaty*, each having its own variation.

The diverse appearance of such a composition is due to the juxtaposition of two kinds of pattern, differing in form and color, and laid out in diagonal alternation (Figure 12, No. 1.).

The cruciform designs which are situated within these boundaries are a well-known feature of Andizhan carpets. A similar creative approach is found in Kirghiz reed screens.

Type Five. The field is occupied by six- or eight-sided medallions, which are joined in a linear network (Figure 12, Nos. 2, 3). Each medallion includes an identical ornament. The most characteristic designs are a rhombus with offshoots, the terraced polygon with hooks or other figures. The spaces between the polygons may be either free or occupied by other patterns. Carpets of this type are particularly common in the southwestern part of the Osh oblast and in the Alai Valley. The masters call this design the *kalkan* (shield) or the *kal* (birthmark). Similar renderings of the field pattern have been noted in Turkmen and Samarkand carpets. An analogous placement of the medallion pattern can be found in the reed screens of the northern Kirghiz.

Type Six. Perforated or broken stripes extend through the center of the field, as if forming enclosed quadrants or rhombuses (1-5 rows), each of which is filled with a single pattern in different variations. One of the most common variants is a column of wide rhombuses or rectangles which form a pair of broken lines. The remaining free space is filled with elements of the same pattern or with designs of a different shape (Figure 12, Nos. 4, 5). A composition of this type, complicated in execution, is called the *kunava*. Carpets of this type were commonly seen in the southwestern regions of the Osh oblast and in the Alai valley. A similar rendering is found in the field of the Andizhan carpet.

The patterns most characteristic of this sort of carpet are the rhombus with offshoots and the *mashaty* pattern. This is often mixed with ornamental stripes, which are filled with stylized bird figures. This pattern is called the *kyngyr moyun* (Plate VII-4). Carpets of a similar type can be found among the Kirghiz who once belonged to the Kydyrsh group.

Type Seven. The central field features two (or, more rarely, three) large-scale medallions along the horizontal axis; they are in the form of a terraced polygon, a rectangle, a rhombus, or a stretched-out polygon. The spaces between the figures are occupied by other ornamental motifs (Figure 12, no. 8). Such a composition is called the *ashkana kilem* (by analogy to a type of reed screen). This type of composition is found frequently in carpets from the southwest of Osh oblast.

Type Eight. The entire field is covered by uniform patterns which are connected to each other and which form, as it were, a unified whole. They are made of different variations on the rhombus pattern with a diverse array of offshoots extending from two sides of the rhombus (Figure 12, No. 6). Similar compositions are ubiquitous. It is a typical reed screen design and has broad application in the north of Kirghizia.

Type Nine. The field is occupied by a large pattern, individually adapted from Uzbek handcrafted silk weaves (Figure 12, Nos. 7, 9). Similar reworkings can be found on decorated reed screens.

Of particularly great interest are the patterns and compositional layouts for carpets which have an analogue in the patterns of decorated reed screen patterns.

Patterned red screens often repeat the patterns and composition of the carpet. But in the southwestern Osh region, the composition of the decorated reed screens is entirely different, there being a similarity here only with the carpets of type seven, eight, and nine.

The design of small pile articles and of the *tegirich* is unique. For example, in the patterning of the *chavadan* we may note the following variations:

1. The entire field is divided into 3-4 quadrants, each of which is marked off by crosswise stripes that form a unified design;
2. Three or four medallions extend into the field without crosswise partitions;
3. The design is rendered in the same way as carpets of type six, called *kunava*;
4. The field of the *chavadan* is occupied by cruciform borders and a cross-shaped pattern.

There are two variations for the placement of the *kaima*: along the two narrow sides, or along all four sides. The *kaima*, composed of ornamental strips 3-4 cm in width, is itself not particularly expressive.

The most characteristic pattern of the *chavadan*, and sometimes also of the carpets designated for use as bags, is the rendering of the corners which are distinct from the basic pattern, with designs in the shapes of triangles or saw-toothed lines (Figure 7, Nos. 21, 23, 24, 26). These are reminiscent of the Eastern Turkestan carpets, in which a fixed design such as a central rosette or medallion, is bounded on all sides by a meandering line (53). This device, found on the most ancient Turkmen carpets is clearly traditional in pile weaving (54).

The pattern on storage bags and hanging bags has its own composition. As opposed to the patterns of the *chavadan*, the field is usually surrounded by an expressive frame of two or three borders, one of which is wider than the others (Plate VII-1).

In some of the oldest pile bags, an additional triangular flap was woven, reminiscent of an envelope; felt bags were produced in the same manner. Later, it became practice to weave a false flap. Antique bags are marked by the presence of pile weaves on both sides. For some time, however, the back side of the bag has been made of a simple flatweave.

Saddle covers and saddle bags were designed in a fashion similar to storage bags and hanging bags.

Pile-woven door curtains for covering the entrance to the yurt (*eshik tysh*) have a broad border. Often the border demarcates the field from three sides, the topmost edge being left out. The compositional plan of the field varies depending on the character of the design. Often the designs are of antique appearance, and are composed of curls and tendrils or offshoots of varying shape. In these instances they occupy the field which is laid out in vertical rows along the entire length. The vertical rows can form a pattern of flowered rosettes. Rhomboid forms with offshoots are also interspersed on the field depending on its size. If the field is large, they are placed in the center, but if small, they are placed singly in a net-like arrangement.

Many of the pile-woven door curtains (*eshik tysh*) are also reminiscent in design and composition of the patterned reed screens. For example, an *eshik tysh* found among the Kirghiz of the Alai Valley and published by M. S. Andreev (55) repeats the design and composition of the reed screens which we found in the Frunze district. It is important to note that this pattern, found both on the reed screens as well as on the pile-woven door rugs, is a reworking of a pattern originating from handmade Uzbek silk weaves.

Worth noting is the design layout of the *tegirich*. In this case, the ornamental center is surrounded on two sides by a *kaima* border (Plate VIII-2, Plate VIII-6). In the execution of the field, we find variations. In the first variation, the field is composed of a broken chain of patterns, one new design laid on top of another, followed by thin stripes each different from the other and different from the background color. The second variation is the chain of two or three motifs which repeat in consecutive order. A third and simplest kind of pattern seen on the *tegirich* is the repetition of a single motif, one after another. As far as the basic design on the tegirich is concerned, it is a unique album of ancient pile-woven patterns. The *tegirich* collects and records all the motifs which the Kyrgyz brought to carpet weaving. The dominant motif is a variation on a rhombus with hooks extending off and rosettes.

* * * * * * *

The art of carpet weaving among the Kirghiz has continued to develop up to our own time. It received its greatest development, collectively, from the peasants of the south-western part of the Osh oblast. During the Soviet era, it changed and adopted new forms in accordance with the demands of the times. Production of small pile weavings ceased, as they lost their value in the conditions introduced by the new way of life (56). The basic pile woven article remains the carpet, however. At the same time, its function has changed. It not only covers the floor, it also decorates the walls of rooms. Many carpets, in this manner, have taken on a purely decorative meaning. Furthermore, the carpet has left the confines of the private dwelling and now decorates the interiors of public spaces; carpets can be found in the clubs and reception rooms of collective farm offices. In the south they cover the floors of tea rooms.

The organizational forms of carpet weaving have changed sharply. Beginning in the 1930's, both in the south and the north of the Republic, they began to organize carpet-weaving cartels (associations of independent laborers for collective work with division of profits). The artists who formally pursue decorative art began to take on a greater role. They have before them a great mission: using the best of folk traditions, they must enrich the artistic repertoire of pile-woven carpets and saturate them with new designs which reflect the current level of artistic culture and which respond to the new spiritual needs of the Soviet people. On the basis of the everyday needs and through the deep study of the Kirghiz design heritage, artists are at work on the creation of new carpets (Figure 13). New traditions are appearing: the execution of carpets with figurative designs (Figure 14). Based on a sketch by folk artist G. Aitiev, a carpet was woven which reflected the development of manufacturing and agriculture in the Kirghiz republic. Charming small mats with children's themes were created by the artist D. Umetov. Along with the artist M. Abdullaev, he also created a carpet based on the theme of friendship between the Russian and Kirghiz peoples.

Pile woven carpets remain the great pride of Kirghiz decorative folk art. They are displayed in national and in international exhibitions. Carpets are woven for presentation to visiting dignitaries, as well as for celebrations and holidays.

It is still unknown to us when the Kirghiz began to weave pile rugs. The chronological boundaries of our study do not go beyond the nineteenth century. Carpet weaving developed earlier among the Kirghiz of the Ichkilik tribe than among other groups. This is attested to by the strong identification of the Ichkilik descendants with the art of carpet weaving, especially by those who live within the bounds of the Republic.

Kirghiz weaving is enriched by Central Asian Karakalpak, Turkmen and Uzbek patterns, and therefore there are many analogous carpet patterns among these peoples. But for all the similarities that it displays, Kirghiz carpet art in its fundamental aspects—technology, ornament, coloration and composition—most closely resembles the carpets of the Adizhan type, a style which itself was reworked with the participation of Kirghiz masters from the Kypchak and Kydyrsh tribal groups.

At the same time, and despite the shared features of the technological and artistic devices of Kirghiz carpet art and that of other people, Kirghiz pile weaving is in many ways individualistic. We find in Kirghiz pile weaving art the synthesis of the artistic preferences of the Kirghiz; despite the great variety of patterns and compositional layouts, they managed to produce stylistic traits which created a particular harmony among the patterns and motifs and to develop unique color schemes. It is easy in this respect to distinguish Kirghiz carpets from any number of other carpets.

Kirghiz carpet weaving doubtless plays a great role in the formation and development of contemporary national styles in decorative art. Kirghiz carpet weaving should continue to develop its unique style into the distant future, grounded as it is in centuries of artistic traditions which are embedded in this folk art form.

Notes

1. Collections of Kirghiz pile woven articles are kept in several government museums. In the State Museum of Ethnography, St. Petersburg, some rugs collected by S. M. Dudin are kept as a part of the antique collection of Central Asian rugs. Dudin acquired these rugs from southern Kirghizia, East Turkestan, and Uzbekistan. The small pile items in this collection were collected by B. K. Balakin and E. I. Makhova on a museum expedition in 1941 to southern Kirghizia. Two Kirghiz rugs, acquired in 1910 and 1920, are kept in the archives of the Museum of Anthropology and Ethnography, Academy of Sciences. Kirghiz pile-woven articles are also kept in The Historical Museum, Academy of Sciences, Bishkek, Kirghizia. They consist primarily of small articles; large Kirghiz rugs are not found in this museum collection. A few examples of small items are kept in the Museum of Decorative Arts in Kirghizia. Valuable pile rugs, made primarily by Kirghiz living in Uzbekistan and belonging to the Kydyrsha and Kypchak groups, are kept in the archives of the Museum of Fine Art, Tashkent, Uzbekistan. Most of these rugs date to the end of the nineteenth and early twentieth century.
2. Outside of Khirghizia, pile weaving by the Kirghiz Ichkilik tribe is known in the Murgab and Jergatal areas in Tajikistan and in northern Afghanistan.
3. Felkerzam, A. A., *Antique Rugs of Central Asia*, BYGONE YEARS, June 1915, page 19; Dudin. S. M., *The Rugs of Central Asia*, MUSEUM OF ANTHROPOLOGY AND ETHNOGRAPHY REVIEW, Leningrad, 1929, Vol. 7, page 144; Semenov. A. A., *The Rugs of Russian Turkestan*, ETHNOGRAPHIC REVIEW, 911, No. 1, 2, page 153.

4. See the collection of the Museum of Fine Art, Tashkent, inventory book 8/171, vol. 8464; also see the collection of the Museum of the Peoples of the USSR, inventory no. 14-77.
5. The Kirghiz, who in the past belonged to the clan/tribal group of the Kutchu and occupied the Talas and Chatkal valleys did not produce pile weaving; this was also true of the clan/tribal groups of the Adizhan and Mongoldor, who live in the northern parts of Khirghizia.
6. Blue was an expensive imported dye. Usually the men took the wool to special dye workshops in town. Kirghiz craftswomen produced other colors at home.
7. Usenbaev, K., *Public and Economic Relationships of the Kirghiz During the Rule of Kokand Khanate*, Frunze, 1961, page 75.
8. Andizhan or Samarkand applies equally to the local group of carpets by name and quality. Andizhan carpets have been produced in the Fergana Valley by semi-nomadic groups of Kyrgyz and Uzbek populations. Pile items that were produced in the Samarkand area were woven by Uzbek, Arab, Karakalpak, Turkmen, and other nationalities who lived in the modern Samarkand and Bukhara regions. See Moshkova. V.G., *Rugs*, THE DECORATIVE FOLK ART OF SOVIET UZBEKISTAN, Tashkent, 1954, pages 78, 89.
9. The carpets of East Turkestan have not been studied, which is why we do not have a clear picture of Khotan and Kashgar carpets. Uighurs made the Khotan carpets on a vertical loom with cotton warps and wefts and a double weft shot. Kashgar carpets, most of which were made by Kirghiz on horizontal looms, were most often made with wool warps and wefts. Their techniques, patterns, and designs easily correlated with the carpets made by the Kirghiz from the Pamir-Alai Mountains and Fergana Valley.
10. In northern Afghanistan, mostly Turkmen, Kirghiz, Uzbek, and other nationalities did carpet weaving, Semenov. *op. cit.,* Page 152.
11. *Ibid.*, pages 153-154.
12. It should be noted that pile carpets had filtered into northern Kirghizia not only in the form of barter but also in dowries.
13. As mentioned previously, pile weaving was produced in the Osh and the Jalalabad regions. All weaving information presented in this article is based on analyses from the Osh region.
14. The mother of the bride made the *chavadan*, not the bride herself.
15. Karmysheva, B. Kh., *Lokai Mapramaches and Ilgiches*, REPORTS OF THE TAJIK SSR HISTORICAL-REGIONAL MUSEUM, Tajik SSR Academy of Sciences, Volume 2, History and Ethnography, 1955 Pages 122-125.
16. Zhdanko, T. A., The Decorative Folk Art of the Karakalpaks, Report of the Khorezm Archeological and Ethnographic Expedition, Moscow, 1958, Volume 3, pages 389-390.
17. In the same area of Kirghizia, hanging storage bags were made from felt and the front side was decorated with appliqued or brocaded fabric. These bags were called *sekichek* and *tekche*. See the chapter *Pattened Felt Items*.
18. The Kirghiz in the southwestern part of the Osh region pronounce this term as *gilam*, as do the Karakalpaks and Uzbeks, and in the eastern part as *kilem*. We prefer to stay with *kilem*.
19. The Kirghiz also made colorful flatwoven tent bands. Craftswomen in the southern area in addition to woven bands made them from embroidered cloth and velvet. See the chapter *Patterned Flatweave Techniques* of this publication.
20. Large rugs had different names given to them by the Kirghiz craftswomen. Weavers in the southwestern area of the Osh and Alai Valley called the large rug *ordo kilem* (khan palace, khan yurt, rich yurt). See Yudakhin, K. K., *Kirghiz-Russian Dictionary*, Moscow, 1965, page 557. In the central part of the Osh region, the same carpets were called *hali gilam*. This meant not only a large rug but also a better quality rug. It is also more difficult to design rugs of this type. It is possible this name arose in connection with the fact that the Kirghiz supplied many rugs for the Khanate estate and for noble people. Besides these names the large rugs have other rarely used names: *zor gilam* (large rug), *too'o gilam* (camel rug*), jailo gilam* (summer rug). In the southwestern part of the Osh region flatwoven rugs called *arabi gilam* were

woven. See Antipina, *Osobennosti Materialnoi Kultury I Prikladnogo Iskusstva Iuzhnykh Kirgizov [Distinctive Features of the Material Culture and Applied Art of the Southern Kirghiz]*, 1962, pages 95-96.
21. Felkerzam, *op. cit.,* page 19.
22. In wealthy families, the number of rugs that were agreed to for a dowry traditionally were in quantities of nine, such as nine rugs, nine blankets, nine sheep, etc.
23. Aisha Ormonova, born in 1882, in the Kara-Shivak village, Alai area.
24. Telman collective farm, Ala-Bukin area (field notes of E. I. Makhova).
25. Antipina, *op. cit.*, pages 76-80 for technical analyses.
26. Semenov., *op. cit.,* page 152.
27. Antipina, *op. cit.,* page 77.
28. *Dasterkhan* is a cloth that is spread on the floor; food is placed upon it.
29. *Some* elder craftswomen know the rituals associated with *gilam ashar* work.
30. *Restoration of Original Rug Dyes from Noin-Ula,* Moscow-Leningrad, 1937; Lubo-Lesichenko, E., *Ancient Chinese Silk and Embroideries,* Leningrad, 1961, pages 22-23; Dudin, *op.cit.,* Page 72.
31. The Kirghiz made not only pile items, but also light colored felt decorated with appliqued cloth.
32. *Kochot* means woven pattern.
33. *Pashayi* means Uzbek silk cloth.
34. Dudin, *op. cit.,* Table VI and pages 35, 37.
35. *Kaikalak* ("arch its back"), Yudakhin, *op. cit.,* page 318. The Pamir Kirghiz ascribe the same pattern differently. A cross pattern in the middle of a rhombus that represents a human figure with two raised hands is called *kaikalak*. Andreev, M. S., *Tajiks from the Khuf Valley,* Issue 1, Transactions of the Institute of History, Archeology and Ethnography, Academy of Sciences, Tajik SSR, Volume 7, Stalinabad, 1953, fn. 2. According to E. M. Peshereva, the Kirghiz pattern *kaikalak* is similar to the Central Asian pattern *khaikel* (icon, image, amulet). See Peshereva, E. M., *The Pottery Production of Central Asia,* Transactions of the Institute of Ethnography, New Series, Volume XLII, Moscow-Leningrad, 1959, page 112.
36. Felkerzam, *op.cit.,* page 20, mentions a pattern with the name *chaidish* in Kirghiz carpets.
37. Some craftswomen called this pattern *chomuch* (wooden spoon), one of the utilitarian utensils used by the Kirghiz in the past.
38. Felkerzam, op. cit., pages 21-22, mentioned that this ancient pattern was associated with a frame but, unfortunately, it was not described.
39. Dudin, *op.cit.,* plate V, Illustration 3.
40. Zhdanko, *op. cit.,* plate 4, page 391.
41. Karmysheva, *op. cit.,* page 137; plates V, VII, IX, Illustration 16, page 142.
42. Moshkova, *op. cit.,* page 93.
43. A parallel with the Kirghiz name *toguz dobo*, there is another name *sekiz pista* (eight pistachios) which is used in the western part of the Osh region and is borrowed from the Uzbeks.
44. The weavers also use the word *tapan* (print or trace).
45. Gogel, F. G., *Carpets,* Moscow, 1950, page 174, illustration 84.
46. Dudin, *op. cit.,* Plate I, 16; Plate III, 30; Plate IV.
47. *Gul* (flower) has the same meaning as *kochot.* The *gol* pattern is a standard feature in the pattern terminology of the Turkmens.
48. *Dudin,* op. cit., Plate IV.
49. This pattern applies equally to the Chinese symbol which is known as the symbol of happiness.
50. Jarring, G., *A Kara-Kirgize Rug from East Turkestan,* Ethnos, 1936, number 4, pages 103-104; Le Coq, A., *Teppiche der Kara-Kirgizen aus der Gegen des Terek-Passes in Russisch Turkistan* Ostslavische [sic] Zeitschrift, Berlin, 1929, pages 15-17.
51. Felkerzam noted seven types of East Turkestan rugs, *op. cit.,* page 27. Two of them are analogous to the Kyrgyz types: rugs with a lattice design (four coupled "C"s), and those with a tile arrangement. Rugs with

a lattice design according to our typology are ascribed to Group 2 and rugs with a tile design are Group 5. Felkerzam's remaining other five types of East Turkestan rugs are not traditional to the Kirghiz. However, in all probability, the Kyrgyz adapted many motifs (meander, tree of life) into their own rugs.

52. Moshkova, *op. cit.,* page 82. This scientifically grounded theory was shown in connection with the antique *julkirs* rugs. See Moshkova, V. G., *Julkirs*, Transactions of the Museum of History of the People of Uzbekistan, Tashkent, 1951.

53. Gogel, *op. cit.*, page 174, illustration 84.

54. *Ibid.*, page 116, illustration 24.

55. Andreev, M. S., *Decorative Art of the Tajik Mountains of the Upper Reaches of the Amu Darya and of the Pamir Kirghiz*, Tashkent, 1928, page 34, illustration 26.

56. Today in a modern Kirghiz family home, it is possible to see small pile items, sewn together and used as decorative objects of art hanging on the wall.

Figure 4.19 (Fig. 1 in the original)
Small pile carpet, *ayak kaochu*. Osh region, Uzgen district,
Ulgulu village, State Museum of Ethnography. Inventory #6371-8

PART FOUR

WRITINGS

Figure 4.20 (Fig. 2 in the original)
Pile woven door rug for yurt, *eshik tysh*.
Osh region, Batken district, Raut village, 1958

Figure 4.21 (Fig. 3 in the original)
Floor carpet. Pile woven tent bands (*tegirich*) stitched together.
Osh region, Frunze district, Okhna village, 1955

Figure 4.22 (Fig. 4 in the original)
Kumush Ormonova, a carpet weaver, demonstrates her work.
Jalalabad region, Ala-Bukinskii district, Telman Collective Farm, 1955

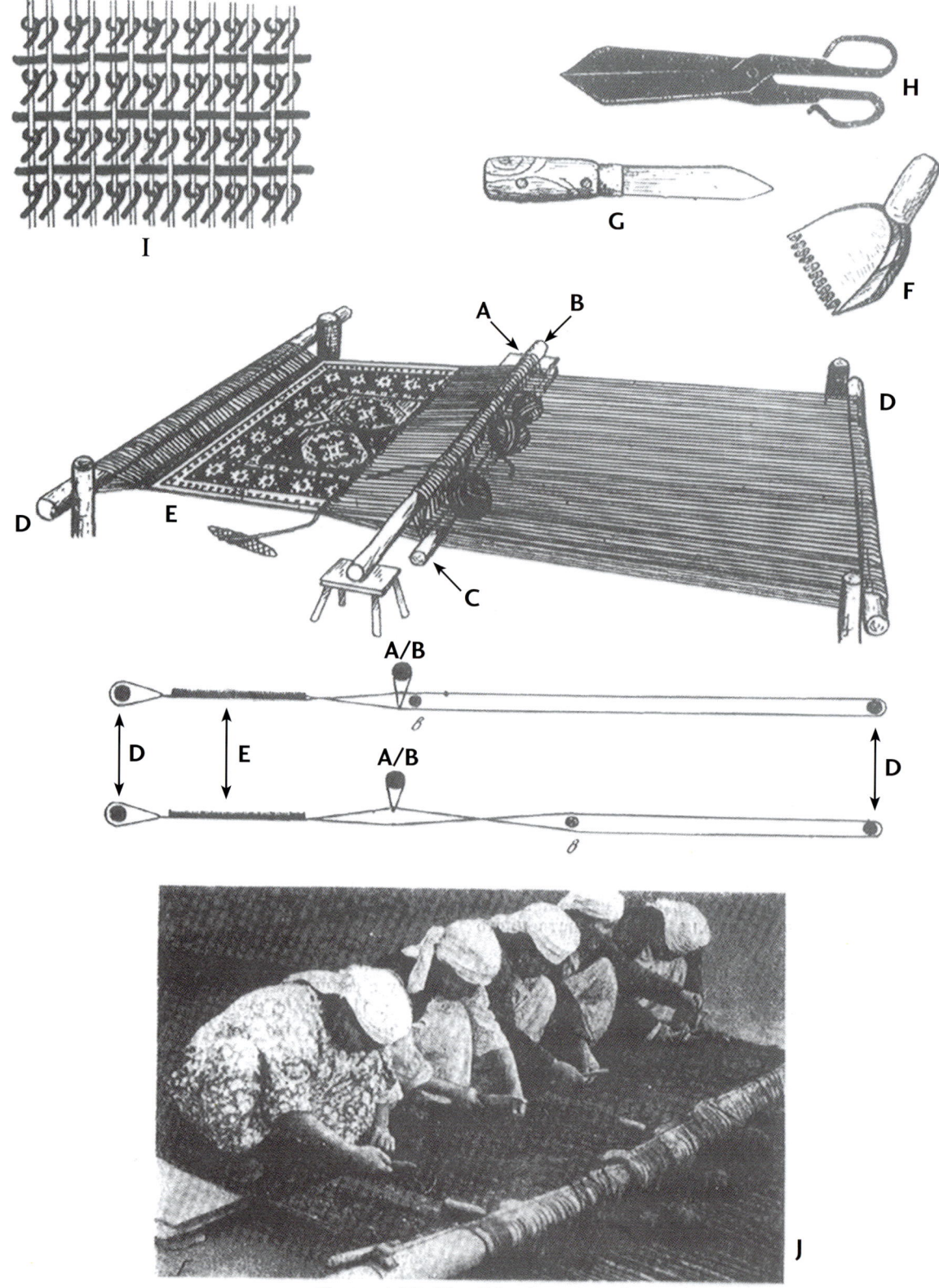

Figure 4.23 (Fig. 5 in the original)
Rug loom, Batken district
A. Heddle *(remiz kuzuk)*, B. Heddle rod *(remiz kotorchu)*, C. Shed rod *(chalysh aluu saboo)*,
D. Foundation poles *(jigach)*, E. Completed portion of weaving, F. Weft beater *(tokmok)*, G. Knife *(pychak)*,
H. Scissors *(kaichi)*, I. Diagram of the asymmetric knot ("open to the right"), J. Weavers *(Kara-Bulak Village, 1955)*

Figure 4.24 (Fig. 6 in the original)
Variations of Rhombic pattern with branches

KLAVDIYA ANTIPINA

Figure 4.25 (Fig. 7 in the original)
Examples of ornamental motifs for central field

Figure 4.26 (Fig. 8 in the original)
Examples of ornamental motifs for central field

Figure 4.27 (Fig. 9 in the original)
Examples of ornamental motifs for carpet borders

PART FOUR WRITINGS

Figure 4.28 (Fig. 10 in the original)
Examples of ornamental motifs for carpet borders

KLAVDIYA ANTIPINA

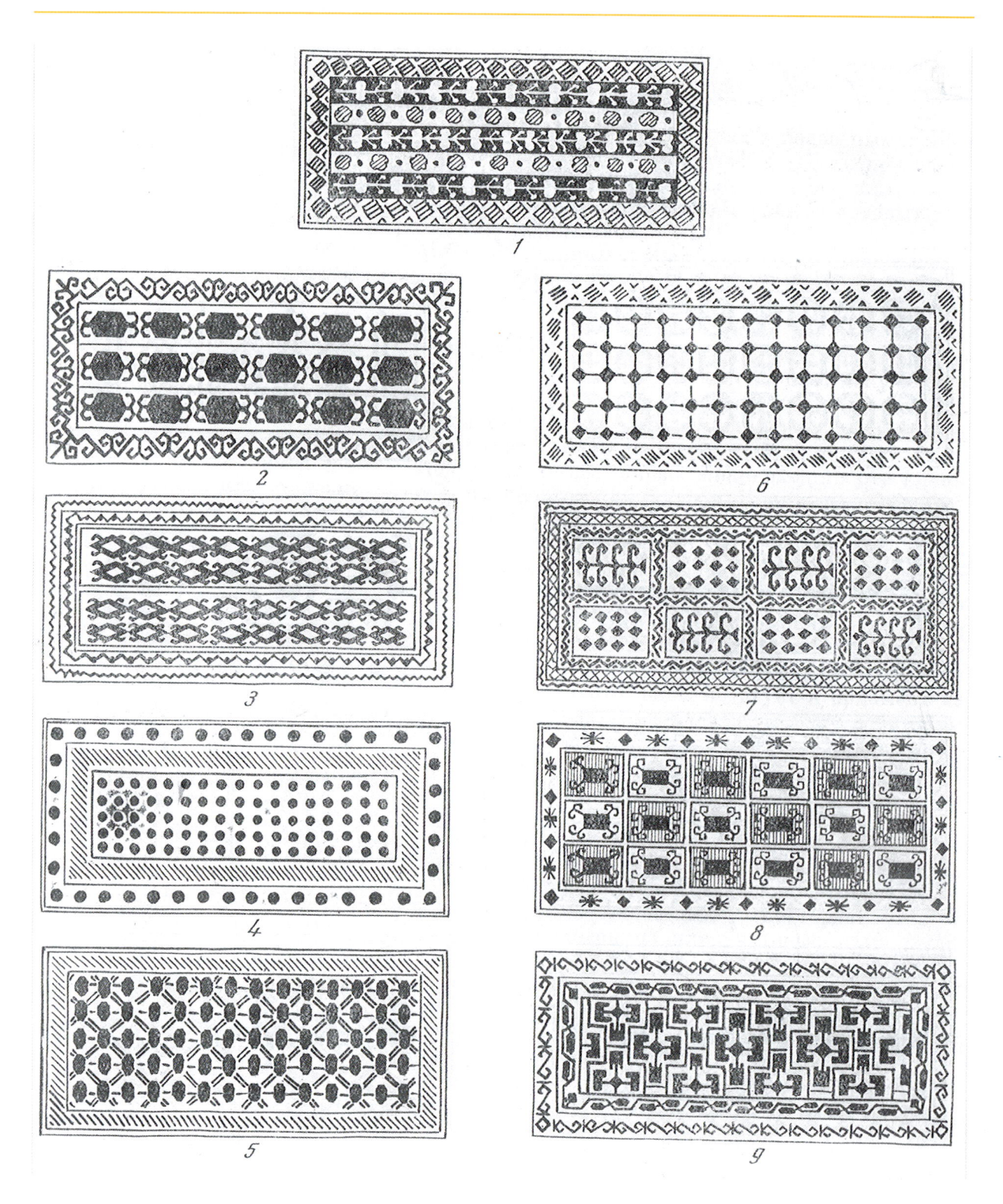

Figure 4.29 (Fig. 11 in the original)
Overall carpet designs

Figure 4.30 (Fig. 12 in the original)
Overall carpet designs

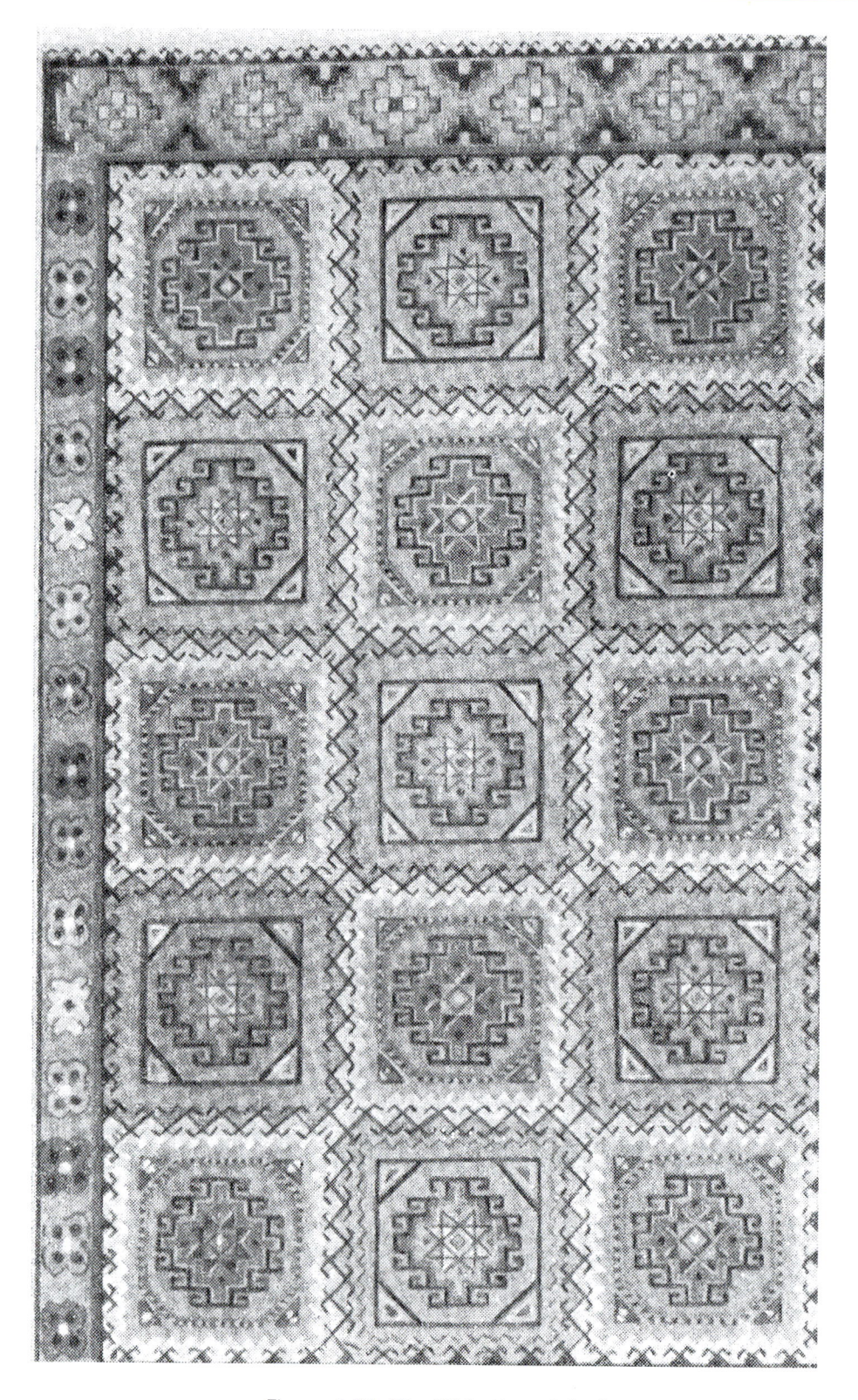

Figure 4.31 (Fig. 13 in the original)
Pile carpet woven in workshop at the State Artist Association of the Kyrgyz SSR.
Designed by M. A. Abdullaeva, Frunze, 1960

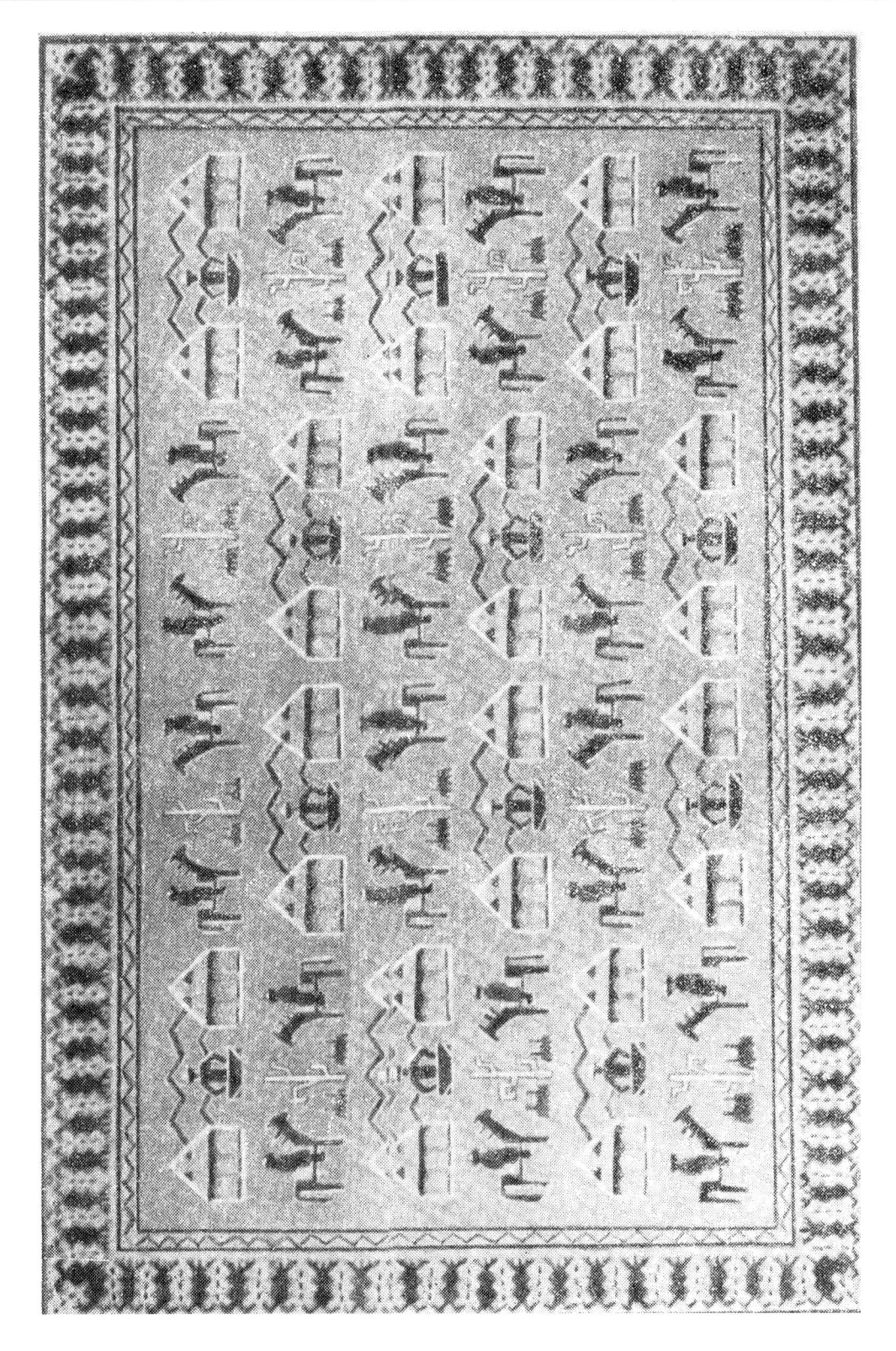

Figure 4.32 (Fig. 14 in the original)
Pile carpet woven in workshop at the State Artist Association of the Kyrgyz SSR.
Designed by D. Umetova, Frunze, 1962

Figure 4.33 (Plate VII-1 in the original)
Pile woven *bashtyk*. Dimensions 68 x 68 cm. Crafted in the early 20th century by a female weaver of the Kydyrsh tribe. Osh region, Kurshab district, the Ulgulu collective farm. State Museum of Ethnography, collection 6371-1.

Figure 4.34 (Plate VII-2 in the original)
Pile woven *kilem*. Dimensions 150 x 130 cm. Crafted in 1908 by the female weavers of the Noigut tribe. Osh region, Batken district, village of Gaz.
State Museum of Ethnography, 1955

Figure 4.35 (Plate VII-3 in the original)
Pile woven *kilem*. Dimensions 160 x 340 cm. Crafted in 1936; lead weaver
Adzhar Moldokeeva (Adigin). Osh region, Alai district, village of Taldy-Su.
State Museum of Ethnography, 1955

Figure 4.36 (Plate VII-4 in the original)
Pile woven *kilem*. Dimensions 345 x 150 cm. Crafted in 1934; lead weaver
Gulbu Bataeva (Mongoldor). Osh region, Societ district, village of Kolmo.
State Museum of Ethnography, 1955

Figure 4.37 (Plate VII-5 in the original)
Pile woven *kilem*. Dimensions 158 x 320 cm. Crafted in 1934; lead weaver
Tadzhi Karimova (Kypchak). Osh region, Batken district, village of Budzhum.
State Museum of Ethnography, 1955

Figure 4.38 (Plate VIII-1 in the original)
Pile woven *kilem*. Dimensions 145 x 300 cm. Crafted in the early 20th century; lead weaver Zuleikhan Koshoeva (Naiman). Osh region, Batken district, village of Kara-Bulak. State Museum of Ethnography, 1956

Figure 4.39 (Plate VIII-2 in the original)
A tent band for a wedding yurt, *tegirich*. Width: 50 cm. Crafted in the early 20th century.
Jalalabad region, Bazar-Kurgan district, village of Seitkazy. State Museum of Ethnography, 1955

Figure 4.40 (Plate VIII-3 in the original)
Pile woven *chavadan*. Dimensions 40 x 88 cm. Crafted in the early 20th century.
Osh region, Lailak district, village of Kurgan. State Museum of Ethnography, 1955

Figure 4.41 (Plate VIII-4 in the original)
Pile woven *chavadan*. Dimensions: 38 x 90 cm. Crafted in 1936; lead weaver
Adzhar Moldokeeva (Adigan), Osh region, Alai district, village of Kara-shyvak.
State Museum of Ethnography, 1955

Figure 4.42 (Plate VIII-5 in the original)
A pile woven *japsar* rug. Dimensions 77 x 77 cm. Crafted in the early 20th century by a weaver from the Basyz tribe. Osh region, Uzgen district, village of Zerger.
State Museum of Ethnography, 1955

Figure 4.43 (Plate VIII-6 in the original)
A pile woven tent band for a yurt (*tegirich*). Width: 48 cm. Crafted in 1915 by Topchu Baimurzaeva (Naiman). Osh region, Frunze district, village of Okhna.
State Museum of Ethnography, 1955

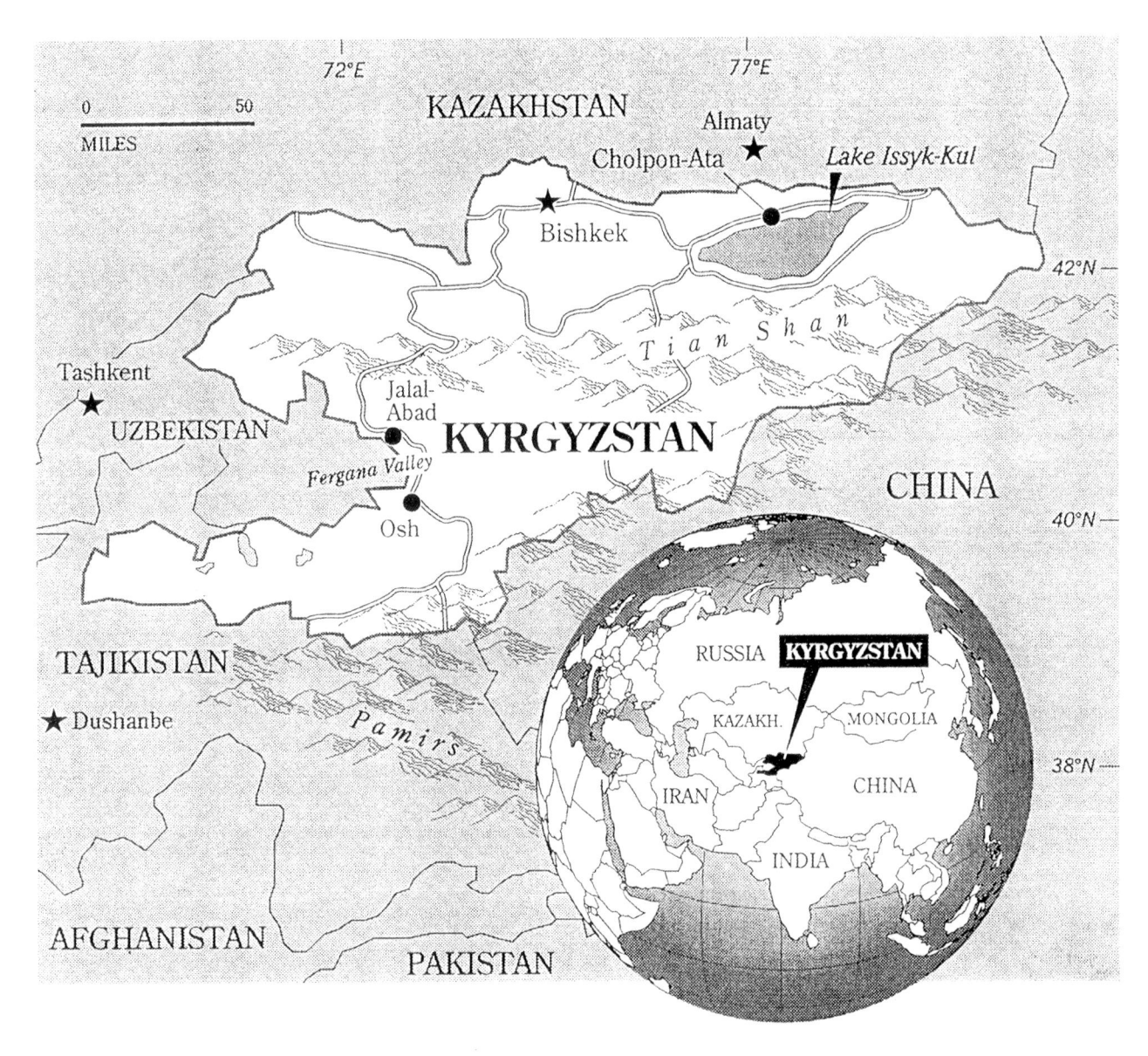

MAP 2

The Kyrgyz Republic

Map by Brad Wye

(Through the courtesy of Kenneth Rasmussen and Kathleen Kuehnast-Rasmussen)

MAP 3
The Kyrgyz Republic
Map showing the Oblasts (Regions)

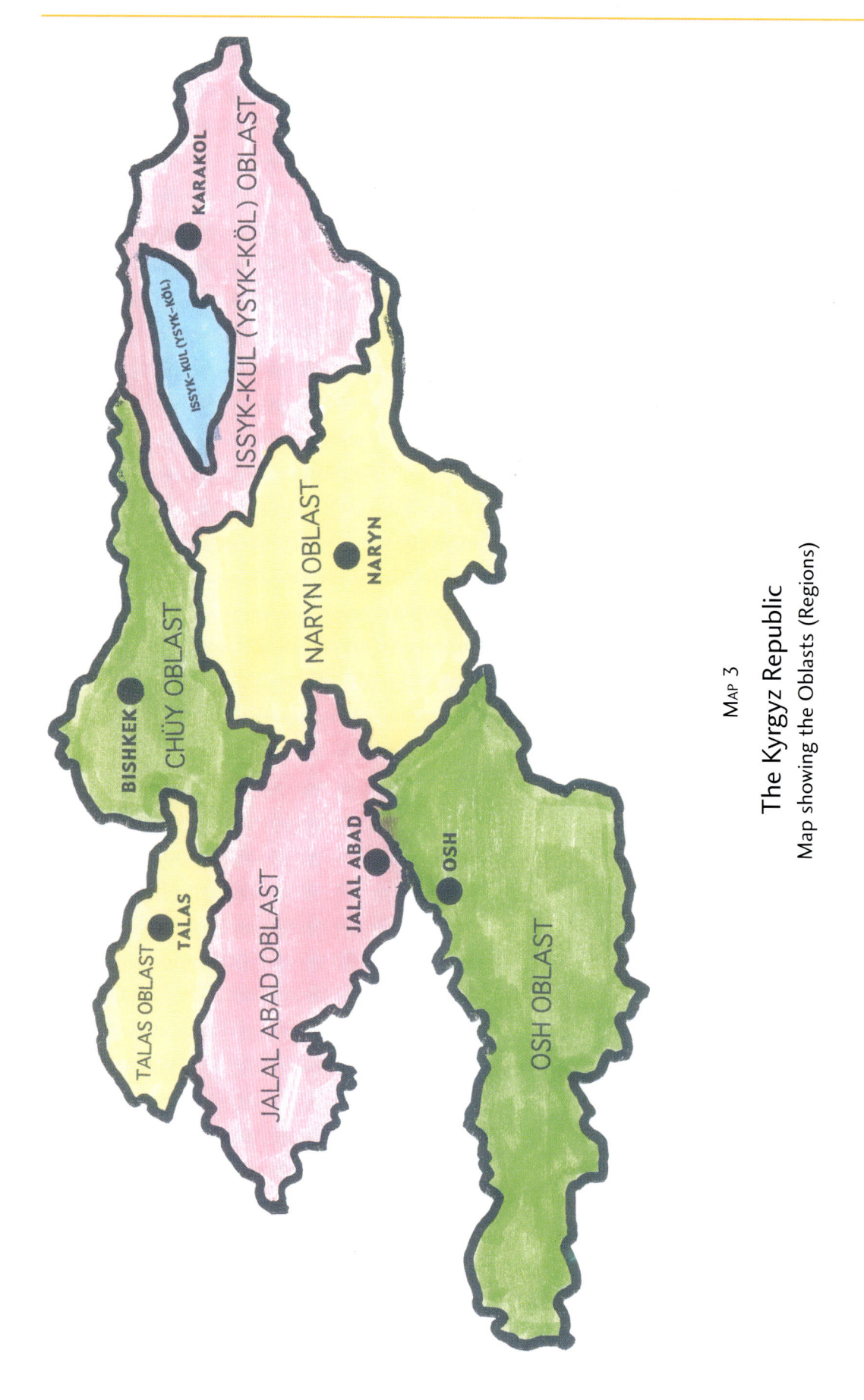

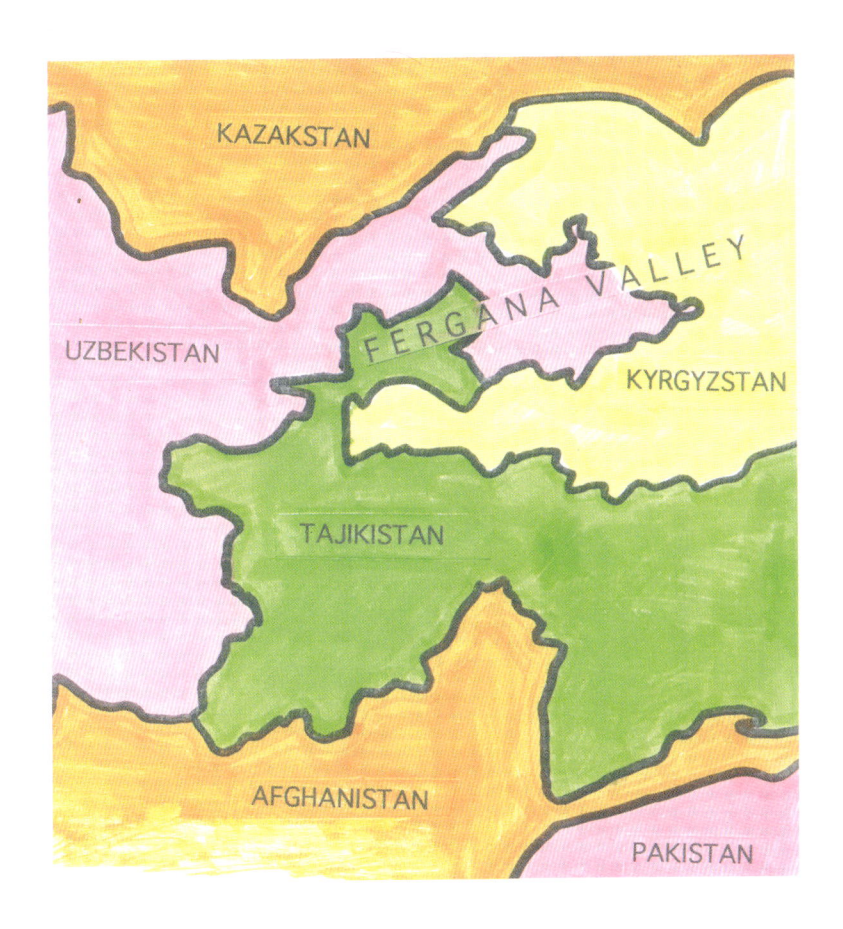

MAP 4

Fergana Valley Region
(Stalin divided it three ways, in an effort to suppress dissent)

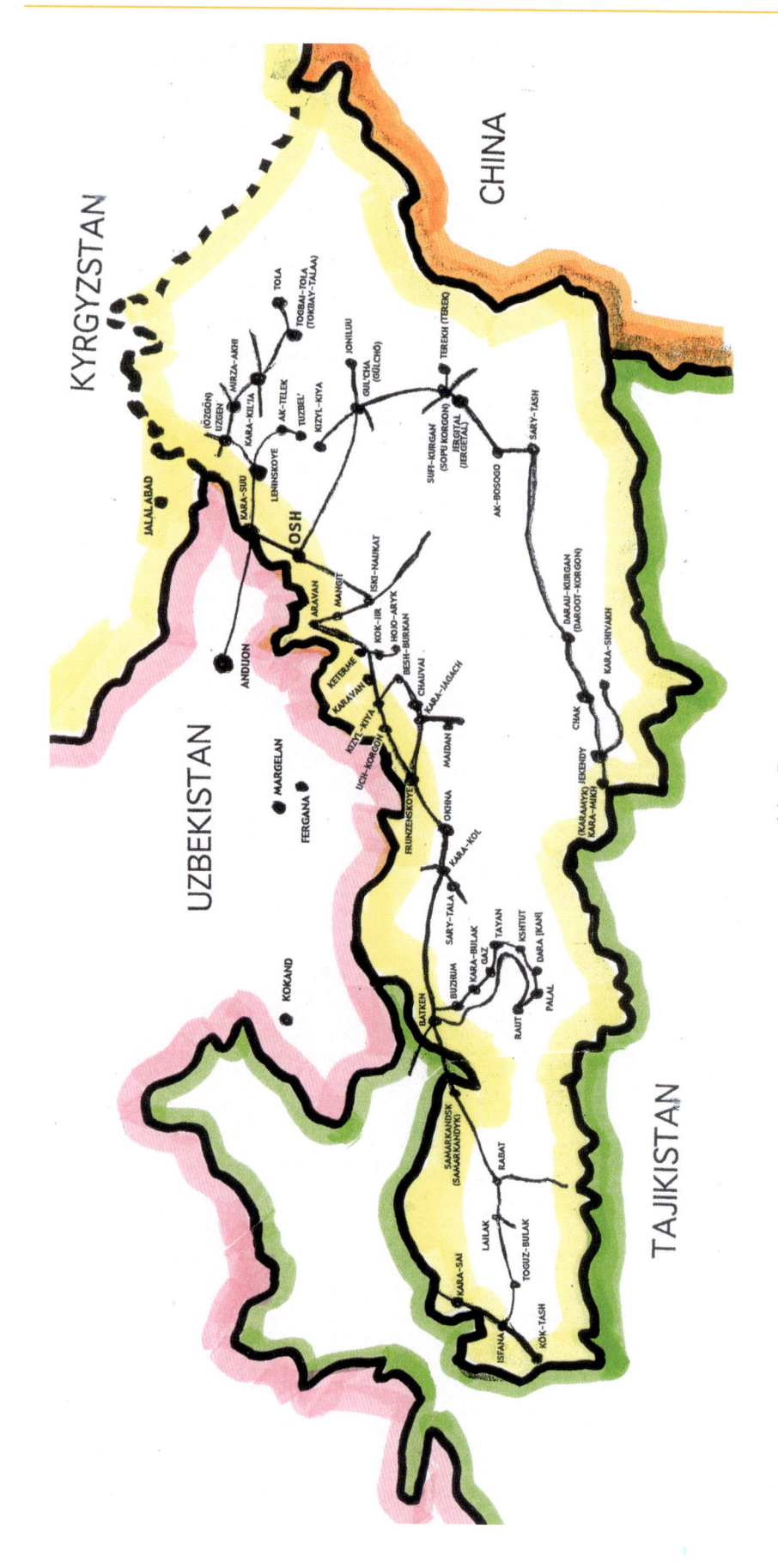

MAP 5
Routes of Klavdiya Antipina's 1955, 1956, 1958 ethnographic field work
Southern Kyrgystan, Osh Region (Oblast)

(Adapted by the authors from "Osobennosti Materialnoi Kultury I Prikladnogo Iskusstva Iuzhnykh Kirgizov" and other sources)

Afterword

Klavdiya Ivanovna Antipina had a deep interest in Kyrgyz costume. This was the subject of a book that she had written during the last three decades of her life—a book which has not been published and for which the manuscript's whereabouts is uncertain.

Not well known, however, is that she had produced a second book on the subject. For this book, she had dictated the text as well as the captions for the illustrations by the Kyrgyz artist, Temirbek Musakeev, and by the French photographer, Rolando Paiva. Recently, there has developed the very real prospect for the successful publication of this second book. We applaud.

Meanwhile the search for the whereabouts of the manuscript of Klavdiya Ivanovna Antipina's first book continues.

— Bibira Akmoldoeva and John Sommer

Glossary

arkak atkorot	The process of passing the weft in pile weaving.
alma gul	A rug design ("apple blossom")
anar kochut	A rug design ("pomegranate pattern")
arabi kilem	An "Arab rug." A rug without pile. A flatwoven rug.
aryk	Creek.
ash	Funeral.
ashar	Kyrgyz village custom of mutual aid.
ashkana chiy	The reed screen in the yurt that separates the central fire from the food storage and women's area.
ashkana kilem	A rug which resembles the size and the design of an ashkana chiy.
aul	A defined group of nomads from a specific small village location, migrating together, and who are usually related.
ayak koichu	"Suspended shelf" for use in a yurt. A kosh jabik (kosh jabyk).
baige	Horse race, as at a funeral or memorial.
balban	A tough wooden pole, literally "a strong man."
bashtyk	Storage bag for "small everyday things."
bai (bay, bey)	Wealthy Kyrgyz landowner.
bash bosogo	The upper edge of the door frame.
Basmachi Movement	Armed Kirghiz tribal resistance to Soviet changes in early twentieth century. Also, the Basmachi Rebellion.
basmayil	Saddle girth.
bayloo	In pile weaving, the process of "tying" and cutting a "knot."
besh parmak	In Turkic, literally "five fingers." That portion of a feast in which shredded mutton, noodles and broth are eaten using the "five fingers" of the right hand from a bowl held in the left hand. Also the feast itself, which includes the presentation to the honored guest of a cooked sheep's head.
Bishkek	A major city in the north, the capital of The Kyrgyz Republic. Frunze was the Soviet name.
boo	A woven strip, tape, or band.
boo chalgych	Woven band surrounding the lattice wall.
boorsok	Slices of cut pastry, fried in ram fat.
bordyur	Border.

bosogo	A yurt door frame.
boz ui	In northern Kyrgyzstan, the name for the yurt.
buila	A sharp stick fixed in a camel's nose cartilage.
chaban	Shepherd.
chamgarak	The wooden crossbars of the yurt dome wheel.
chalysh aluu saboo	Shed stick or shed rod.
chavadan	Long, narrow Kyrgyz storage bag. The front is pile-woven, the back flatwoven. [Note: in 1992, Klavdiya Antipina told us the chavadan was used as a pillow. Also, it was hung up as a talisman. She told us that the study or chavadans would lead to a knowledge of all Kyrgyz designs.]
chaydash	A rug design.
chayjut	A rug design.
chever (cheber)	A craftswoman skilled in a variety of applied arts—patterned felts, chiys, embroidery, the weaving of yurt bands, etc.
chigina	A sledge.
chiine	A cart.
chit	1) A rug pattern of four interconnected "C's." 2) Chintz. Printed cloth.
chiy	1) Kyrgyz reed screen. 2) The wild grass (Lasiagrostis splendens) of which reed screens are made.
chigdan (chygdan)	A term used in northern Kyrgyzstan for the "space divider" reed screen or ashkana chiy.
Chui (Chüy)	A region (oblast) in the north of The Kyrgyz Republic. 2) The Chui (Chüy) valley.
chyrak	A cast iron or ceramic lamp of ancient origin.
chyrmagan	"Wrapped" or decorated, as in chyrmagan chiy.
chyrmagan ashkana chiy	Decorated (patterned) reed screen of the type used as a space divider between the food storage and women's area and the cooking area at the central fire in the yurt.
chyrmagan chiy	A Kyrgyz decorated reed screen. (Individual chiy grass stems are differentially wrapped with unspun colored wool and bound together to make the pattern.)
chyrmagan eshik chiy	Term designating the yurt doorway reed screen. This decorated screen traditionally backs the felt door flap and extends upward toward the yurt dome wheel, resting on the roof struts and covered by the roof felts.
chyrmagan kanat chiy	Decorated red screens used around the yurt latticed wall (kanat).
dastarkhan, dastarhan	A cloth for wrapping food. A cloth spread on the floor under food. A "table cloth."

dikak	An embroidered Kyrgyz horse cloth placed on a young man's horse.
dukon	Loom. (Literally, a workbench.)
ergichek (or ergilchek)	A yurt door. Also eshik or kaalga.
eshik	A yurt door. Also kaalga, ergichek or ergilchek.
eshik boo	A woven tape or band, which fastens the door curtain and passes over the dome wheel and stretches back to the upper door frame to which it is again fastened.
eshik chiy	A yurt door reed screen. Usually it extends upward toward the dome wheel (smoke hole). See chyrmagan eshik chiy.
eshik tysh	"Door curtain" for special occasions. Sometimes pile-woven.
ethnology	The science that treats of the division of mankind into races, their origin, distribution, relations, and distinguishing features.
ethnography	Descriptive anthropology; sometimes, loosely, ethnology.
Fergana	The fertile valley in Kyrgyzstan's southwest. Political boundaries have been drawn so that parts of this prized area are Uzbekistan and parts Tajikistan.
flatweave	Textiles woven without supplementary threads or knots, thus without a pile, and thus "flat."
Frunze	The Soviet name of Bishkek, the capital of The Kyrgyz Republic.
Frunze, Mikhail	A hero of the communist revolution, from Kyrgyzstan. Because of his service to the Soviet state, the capital of Kirghiz SSR was named for him and a statue raised in his honor.
gilem	Pile-woven rug. (See: "Kilem.")
ilgich	Lokai pile-woven storage bag.
Issyk-Kul	A region (oblast) in the northeast of The Kyrgyz Republic. A large lake in the Issyk-Kul region
jabayy	Simple flatwoven strip with which a pile-woven rug begins on the loom.
jabyk bash	An ornamental felt for covering the front part of the yurt dome.
jailoo kilem	A large rug. (Literally, "summer rug.")
Jalalabad	A region (oblast) of The Kyrgyz Republic. A city in that region.
jel boo	Woven tapes or bands tied to the dome wheel inside the yurt for the purpose of strengthening the yurt as during windy weather. They are tied to stakes (or heavy stones).
jigach	The two beams of the loom around which the warp is wrapped.
jimolosty	A type of grass sometimes used instead of chiy for making doorway coverings.
jip juguru	The process of warping the loom.

jugaru	A type of sorghum.
juk, dzhuk	The place in a yurt for the storage of rugs, woven goods, and items of value. The relative richness of the juk was an index of the family's wealth. (In the modern dwelling, a special wall niche functions similarly.)
kaalga	A yurt door. Also eshik, ergichek, or ergilchek.
kaichi kap	Storage bag for scissors.
kalim, kalym	The bride price, bride money.
kali kilem	A large pile-woven rug of high quality. A luxurious rug.
kamush	A reed, which grows in clumps near water, and which is substituted for chiy grass when the latter is not available for making reed screens.
kanat	The manageable length, kanat, cut from the yurt lattice, kerege, and which means wing, an apt term for its folding and unfolding action.
kanat chiy	A reed screen for the wall of a yurt.
kapshit	As one enters the yurt, the left side, the men's part.
karakalpak kochot	A rug pattern. A reed screen pattern.
Karakol	A city in the Issyk-Kul region. Przwalski was it Soviet name.
karchin	A Karakalpak storage bag similar to the Kyrgyz chavadan.
karysh	A linear measure equivalent to "the space between the end of the extended thumb and of the fifth finger."
kattama	A rich, layered flat-cake. "Puff scones."
kaykalak	Design in the shape of ram's horn. Also, kochorok. In central Asia, this design is seen in many places.
Kazak	Also "Khazak." A tribal name. It can be used as a noun or an adjective. "The Kazak SSR" and "Kazakstan" are equivalent.
kerege	The latticed framework of the yurt wall made of shaped wooden sticks fastened together by rawhide strips passed through perforations at crossing points and knotted on each side. The kerege's full length is made of shorter manageable lengths each of which is named a kanat or wing.
kerege bash	1) A Kyrgyz rug design. (A rhombus with extended lines resembling the upper part of the yurt wall lattice.) 2) The forked projections along the circumferential lattice wall's upper edge.
Kerege kuz	The rhomb-shaped openings in the wall lattice kerege when opened. (Large openings: tor kuz; small openings: zhel kuz.)
kerege tanuu	The long stabilizing woven band passed around the yurt lattice wall, its ends tied to the doorway jambs at either side.
keregenin topchusu	The reinforcing knot made at both ends of the rawhide strip after it is pulled through the perforations in the wooden sticks of the kerege.

khan	A title of sovereignty applied to dignitaries of various rank in Central Asia.
khanate	Territory ruled by a Khan.
Khotan	A city in the Xin-jiang province of China.
KHP	The PRC. (The Peoples' Republic of China.)
kibitka	1) A nomad's tent. 2) A type of wheeled covered wagon. [Note: This term, which has two distinctly separate meanings, was common in the 19th century, but now is seldom used.]
kilem	Also, gilem. In The Kyrgyz Republic, a pile-woven carpet. [Note: This and similar terms have different meanings in different places. For example, in Turkey, the term "kilim" refers to the often colorful and boldly designed nomadic flatweaves, not to pile-woven items.]
kilomto	The yurt fireplace, a flat spot or a pit.
kimkap kochot	A Kyrgyz rug pattern resembling Uzbek silks.
Kosh jabyk (kosh jabik)	A suspended shelf for use in a yurt. See also ayak koichu.
Kirghiz	(See: "Kyrgyz.")
Kirghiz Archaeological-Ethnographical Expedition	The research projects (sometimes referred to in the singular) conducted variably in the 1950's by members from the Institute of Ethnography and the Institute of Archaeology of the USSR Academy of Sciences and from the Institute of History of The Kirghiz Branch of the USSR Academy of Sciences.
Kirghizia	(See: "Kyrgyz.")
Kitai	China, Chinese. Also: "Kytay."
knot density	The number of "knots" per unit of area, e.g., "one hundred thousand knots per square meter."
kochkorok	Also, kaykalak. A design in the shape of ram's horns.
koshogo	A curtain lowered over the place for a newly married couple to the left of the yurt entryway.
kopchuk	Saddle rug or cover.
koshak	Poem.
kudayi	An entertainment provided for rug weavers.
kuk	The kind of reinforcement made by knotted rawhide strips. (See: kereginin topchusu).
kulach	A linear measure equivalent to "the arms stretched out."
kumgan	Teapot.
kumuss, koumiss	Fermented mare's milk. A drink. Also: "kümuss", "koumuss."
kunava	A design seen in Kyrgyz rugs of type six.

kurak	A Kyrgyz pattern derived from kurak, a uniquely Kyrgyz patchwork or quilt technique.
kurjin	Saddlebag. (Also korjin, korchin, kurjun).
kushma	Felt.
kuzuk kotorchu	Heddle stick or heddle rod. See: "remiz ('kuzuk')."
kylakchyn	A special horse cloth, for a young unmarried woman, which covers all of the horse's head, neck, and back.
kynyr moyun	A rug pattern ("crooked neck"). (Also, kyngyr moyun). [Note: This design is also known as the "Turkish cucumber" and, in other places, as the "boteh."]
Kyrgyz	The current spelling of a tribal name, transliterated from the Kyrgyz language, not from Russian. "Kyrgyz" and "Kirghiz" are equivalent. Each can be an adjective or a noun. "Kirghizia", "The Kirghiz Soviet Socialist Republic", "Kyrgyzstan", and the current name, "The Kyrgyz Republic", are roughly equivalent terms.
Kyrgyzstan	See "Kyrgyz."
Lasiagrostis splendens	The botanical name of the slender, stiff tall grass, native to Kyrgyzstan, used in making reed screens (chiy). Both the grass and the reed screens are called chiy.
mapramach	Lokai storage sack in the form of a "trunk." See also: chavadan.
mashaty	A rug design. (Also: mashit, machadi, mashaty, etc.)
Naryn	A region (oblast) in the central part of The Kyrgyz Republic. A city in that region.
oblast	Region. A political territory with distinct borders. See also: rayon.
okrug	District, region.
omack	A wooden plow.
ordo	A rich yurt of a well-known person. A khanate house.
ordo kilem	A large rug.
orgoo ui	A wedding yurt.
orok	A sickle.
orus kochot	A Kyrgyz rug pattern of four interconnected "C's." Also, "Russian pattern."
Osh	A region (oblast) in the southwest of The Kyrgyz Republic. A city in that region.
pashayi kochot	A rug pattern resembling Uzbek silks. Also "pashayy kochot."
piala, pials	Porcelain teacups, small bowls, for serving tea or koumiss.
pile weave	Textiles woven with supplementary threads or knots, which impart a thick and textured surface, a pile. Originally this may have been a conscious imitation of animal skins.

Pir Ayyim	"Patron saint" of rug weaving to whom the prayers are directed requesting a blessing for the endeavor and the prayer of thanks at the end for such help.
rayon	District. A political territory with distinct borders. (Part of an oblast.)
reed screen	A western term, which refers, generally, to the various mats made of chiy grass.
remiz ("kuzuk")	Heddle.
Russian Turkestan	A province of the Russian empire that covered present-day Kyrgyzstan as well as Kazakstan, Uzbekistan, Turkmenistan and Tajikistan. (Alone, the term "Turkestan" referred to these regions along with portions of present-day Xinjiang province in China. In these areas, Turkic languages are spoken.)
saba	A large leather bag for processing kumuss.
sekichek	Shelf for furnishing the yurt, sometimes made of chiy. See also kosh jabyk (jabik) and ayak koichu.
shyrdak	A mosaic felt rug.
SSR	"Soviet Socialist Republic", as in "The Kirghiz SSR."
susmo	Cottage cheese.
tailak kilem	Pile-woven carpet, which decorates a young camel during migration.
Talas	A region (oblast) in the northwest of The Kyrgyz Republic. A city in that region.
tartuu	The giving of rugs as presents to prominent persons.
taval	Large tray.
tegerich	A tent band. An "architectural textile." Often more than forty feet long, its ends anchored to each side of the yurt entrance door, it supports and constricts the wall lattice, countering the downward and outward thrust of the roof. It was often made of pile. It was mounted on the outer side of the lattice wall, but within the outer felts. It was decorative as seen from within.
tekche	Shelf for furnishing the yurt; sometimes made of chiy. (See sekichek.)
ters kayik	A type of ancient embroidery in which can be seen oblique lattice patterns.
The Kyrgyz Republic	See "Kyrgyz."
tokmok	A weft beater or hammer.
tor	The place of honor in the yurt.
transhumance	The seasonal moving of livestock from or to the mountains.
tuk	Pile, as in pile weaving.
tunduk	The yurt dome wheel to which the roof poles are attached. It is located at the smoke hole.

tunduk jabuu	A square felt for covering the smoke hole.
Turkestan	The name once applied to a large part of Central Asia, which included modern Turkmenistan, Uzbekistan, Kazakstan, Kyrgyzstan, Tajikistan, and the Xinjiang Province of western China.
tuurduk	Felts which cover the yurt walls (In southern Kyrgyzstan, they are called tutuu.)
tuurduk boo	The woven patterned tapes fastened to the corners of the felts, which cover the yurt.
uryk	Apricot.
Uuk, ok	A yurt dome pole or strut.
Uukbash, okbash	Pile-woven bag for covering ends of roof pole (uuk, ok) bundles during transport.
volost	The smallest geographical administrative unit in tzarist Russia.
yak	A large wild or domesticated ox (Bos grunniens) of Tibet and adjacent elevated parts of Central Asia.
yurt	In English, the nomad's tent consisting of a wooden framework covered with panels of felt. ("Yurt" came into English from the Russian via French and German). In Turkic languages, however, yurt means location or place. (An English language analogy is house and home.)
zor kilem	A large rug.

Bibliography

Antipina, K. I. "Khranit I umnozhat traditsii narodnogo prikladnogo iskusstva [Treasuring and Multiplying the Traditions of the Folk Applied Arts]." In *Materialy Respublikanskoi nauchno-prakticheskoi konferentsii na temu: Sostoianie i problemy dal neishego razvitiia narodnogo tvorchestva v Kirgizii [Proceedings of the Pan-Republic Research Conference and Workshop on the Development of the Folk Art in Kirghizia]*. Frunze: Kirghiz SSR, 1975.

———. "Kirgizskoe prikladnoe iskusstvo [The Kirghiz Applied Arts]." *Literaturnyi Kirgizstan [Literary Kirghizstan]*, 4 (1959): 89–93.

———. "Klady pod spudom: Ob otvetstvennosti za razvitie prikladnogo iskusstva v respublike [Hidden Treasures: On Being Responsible for the Development of the Applied Arts in the Republic]." *Sovetskaia Kirgiziia [The Soviet Kirghizia]*, (14 February 1973.)

———. "Konkurs narodnykh umeltsev: Beseda s chlenami zhiuri smotrakonkursa izdelii narodnykh masterov I umeltsev, posviashchennogo 60-letiu Kirgizskoi SSR [A Competition of Folk Craftsmen: A Conversation with the Judges of the Competition and Show of Folk Masters and Craftsmen in Honor of the Sixtieth Anniversary of the Founding of the Kyrgyz SSR]." *Vechernii Frunze [The Frunze Evening Edition]*, (15 March 1984).

———. "Iurta tsennyi pamiatnik kultury kirgizskogo naroda. [The Yurt, a valuable cultural monument of the Kirghiz people]." In *Pamiatniki Kirgizstana [The Monuments of the Kirghiz SSR]* (Frunze, 1970): 65–72.

———. "Narodnoe iskusstvo kirgizov [The Folk Art of the Kirghiz]." Vol.1: *Izdeliia is voiloka, tkani; vyshivka. [Felt and fabric products; embroidery]* Frunze: Kirghiz SSR, 1971. Vol 2, 144. Frunze: Kirghiz SSR, 1977.

———. "O sostoianii naradnogo iskusstva v respublike [On the State of the Folk Art in the Republic]." In *Materialy Respublikanskoi nauchno-prakticheskoi konverentsii na temu: Kulturno-prosvetitalskaia rabota v Kirgizii za 50 leti I ee zadachi v kommunisticheskom vospitanii trudiashchiksia [Proceedings of the Pan-Republic research Conference and Workshop on the Cultural Enlightenment Efforts in Kirgizia over the Past Fifty Years and Their Place in the Communist Upbringing of the Workers]*. Frunze, 1975.

———. *Osobennosti Materialnoi Kultury I Prikladnogo Iskusstva Iuzhnykh Kirgizov. Po Materialam, Sobrannym v Iuzhnoi Chasti Oshskoi Oblasti Kirgizskoi SSR [Distinctive Features of the Material Culture and Applied Art of the Southern Kirghiz; Data Collected in the Southern Part of the Osh Region of the Kirghiz SSR]*. Frunze, 1962.

———. "Pomnia drevnego mastera. O razvitii kirgizskogo prikladnogo iskusstva [An Homage to an Ancient Master: On the Development of the Kirghiz Applied Arts]." *Vechernii Frunze [The Frunze Evening Edition]*, (15 April 1986).

———. "Traditsionnaia materialnaia kultura [Tradition Material Culture]." In *Kirgizskaia Sovetskaia Sotsialisticheskaia Respublika. Entsiklopedia [The Kirghiz Soviet Socialist Republic; An Encyclopedia]*, 380–384. Frunze, 1982.

Antipina, K. I., and E. Orlovskaia. "Na pamiat o Kirgizii [Souvenirs of Kirghizia]." *Sovetskaia Kirghizia [The Soviet Kirghizia]*, no. 4 (12 February1965)

Antipina, K. I., et al. "Narodnye traditsii v sovremennoi materialnoi kulture I prikladnom iskusstve Kirgizii [Folk Traditions in the Contemporary Culture and the Applied Arts of Kirghizia]." In *VII mezhdunarodnyi kongress antropologicheskikh I etnograficheskeikh nauk [The Seventh International Congress of the Anthropological and Ethnographic Sciences]*, edited by K. I. Antipina, A. Dzhumagulov, and K. Mambetalieva. Moscow: Nauka, 1964.

Antipina, K. I., et al. "*Sovetskii Soiuz: Geograficheskoe opisanie v 22-kh chastiakh [The Soviet Union; A Geographical Description in Twenty-Two Parts]*", S. V. Kolesnik, editor-in-chief. Moscow: Mysl, 1970.

Galitskii, V. Ia., V. M. Ploskikh, and K. I. Antipina. "Istoricheskii ocherk: Ketmen-Tiube XIX-nachala XX vekov [A Historical Sketch of Ketmen-Tubeh in the 19th–early 20th Centuries]." In *Ketmen-Tiube [Ketmen-Tube]*, 164–191, Frunze, 1977.

Ivanov, S. V., and Antipina, K. I., editors. "Narodnoe dekorativno-prikladnoe iskusstvo kirgizov [The Popular Applied Ornamental Art Of The Kirghiz People]." *The Works of the Kirghiz Archaeological-Ethnographical Expedition* Volume V, edited by S.V. Ivanov and K. I. Antipina. Moscow: Nauka Publishers, 1968.

"O prisvoenii tovarishchu Antipinoi K. I. pochetnogo zvania 'Zasluzhennyi rabotnik kultury Kirgizskoi SSR' [On Awarding Comrade Antipina K. I. the Honorary Title of Distinguished Cultural Activist of the Kyrgyz SSR]." *Vedomosti Verkhovnogo Soveta Kirgizskoi SSR [The Legislative Journal of the Supreme Soviet of the Kirghiz SSR]* 11 (10 June 1974): 200.

Pisarskoi, E. G., V. V. Kurbatov, K. I. Antipina, and B. D. Budaichiev. "Arkhitektura, dekorativno-prikladnoe I izobrazitelnoe iskusstvo KSSR [The Architecture, the Applied Ornamental and Visual Art of the KSSR]." In *Kirgizskaia Sovetskaia Sotsialisticheskaia Respublika. Entsiklopedia [The Kirghiz Soviet Socialist Republic; An Encylclopedia]*, 385–395. Frunze, 1982.

For Further Reading

Aitmatov, Chingiz. 1972. "Notes About Myself." in *Time to Speak. New York:* International Publishers, 1989.

Andrews, Peter Alford, 1986. "From Kuhrasan to Anatolia," presented at the *Fifth International Conference on Oriental Carpets* in Vienna, in *Oriental Carpet and Textile Studies,* Volume 3, Number 2: 40–50. *The Islamic Department of Sotheby's and Oriental Carpet and Textile Studies, Ltd.* London: OCTS and Sotheby's.

———. *Nomad Tent Types In The Middle East, Part I Framed Tents,* Volume I Text, Volume II Illustrations. Dr. Ludwig Reichert Verlag, Wiesbaden, 1997.

———. "Tent Screens to Kilims." Discussion of "An Argument for the Origins of Anatolian Kilim Designs" by Josephine Powell, in *Oriental Carpet and Textile Studies,* vol 3, no. 2: 40–50. *The Islamic Department of Sotheby's and Oriental Carpet and Textile Studies, Ltd.* London: OCTS and Sotheby's.

Balpinar, Belkis, 1986. "A Discussion On Central Asian Türkmen Influence on Anatolian Kilims," presented at the *Fifth International Conference on Oriental Carpets* in *Oriental Carpet and Textile Studies,* vol 3, no. 2: 7–16. *The Islamic Department of Sotheby's and Oriental Carpet and Textile Studies, Ltd.* London: OCTS and Sotheby's.

Barfield, Thomas J. *The Nomadic Alternative*, Prentice Hall, Inc., 1993.

Basilov, Vladimir N., editor. "Nomads of Eurasia." *Natural History Museum of Los Angeles and the Academy of Sciences of the U. S. S. R.* Seattle: The Natural History Museum of Los Angeles County in association with The University of Washington Press, 1989.

Bendavid-Val, Lea. *Propaganda & Dreams, Photographing the 1930s in the USSR and the US*. Edition Stemmle, Zurich and New York, 1999.

Bidder, Hans. *Carpets from Eastern Turkestan*. Tübingen: Verlag Ernst Wasmuth, 1964.

Bogolyubov, Andrei Andreyevich. *Carpets of Central Asia*, edited by Jon M. A. Thompson. The Crosby Press, 1973.

Breeden, Robert L., et al. *Nomads of the World,* Washington D.C.: The National Geographic Society, 1971.

Chirot, Danel. *Modern Tyrants, The Power and Prevalence of Evil in Our Age*. Princeton, New Jersey: Princeton University Press, 1994.

Dor, Remy and Naumann, Clas M. *Die Kirghisen Des Afghanischen Pamir, Graz,* Austria: Akademische Druk—u. Verlagsanstadt, 1978.

Eiland, Emmett.. *Tent Bands of the Steppes*. Albany, California: Albany Press, 1976.

Eiland, Murray L., Jr., and Eiland, Murray, III. *Oriental Carpets, A Complete Guide*. Little, Brown and Company, 1998.

Faegre, Torvald. *Tents: Architecture of the Nomads*, Garden City, New York: Anchor Press/Doubleday, 1979.

Harvey, Janet. *Traditional Textiles of Central Asia,* London: Thames & Hudson, Ltd., 1996.

Kalter, Johannes. *The Arts and Crafts of Turkestan*, London: Thames & Hudson, Ltd., 1984.

Kotkin, Stephen. *Steeltown, USSR: Glastnost, Destalinization, and Perestroika in the Provinces.* The Center for Slavic and East European Studies, University of California at Berkeley, Berkeley, California, 1989.

Lefevre, Jean, et al. *Central Asian Carpets*, London: Lefevre & Partners, 1976.

Longenecker, Martha, Editor. *Folk Art Of The Soviet Union, Reflections of a Rich Cultural Diversity of the Fifteen Republics.* San Diego: The Mingei International Museum, 1989.

Mackie, Louise W. and Thompson, Jon, editors. *Turkmen, Tribal Carpets and Traditions*. Washington, D.C.: The Textile Museum, 1980.

Mateeva, Stella and Thompson, Jon. *Patterned Reed Screens of the Kirghiz in the State Historical Museum, Frunze.* Part I: *Oriental Rug Review*, vol XI, no. 6; Part II: *Oriental Rug Review*, vol XII, no. 1. Meredith, New Hampshire: Oriental Rug Review, 1991.

Maximov, B., et al. *The Kirghiz Pattern*. Frunze, Kirghistan, 1986. (Revised and reprinted as *The Kyrgyz Pattern*, with a Foreword by President Askar Akiev, Bishkek, Kyrgyzstan, "AKIL", 1998.)

"Music for the Eyes: Textile[s] from the Peoples of Central Asia." Catalog of an exhibition from The Russian Ethnographic Museum St. Petersburg, held at Hessehuis, Luc Denys, Antwerp, 1997.

O'Bannon, George W. *The Kyrgyz Carpet I: K. I. Antipina*. O'Bannon, G. W. and Amanova, O. K., editors. Tucson, Arizona: George W. O'Bannon, 2000.

———. *The Kyrgyz Carpet II: L. G. Beresneva (The Kyrgyz Carpet Collection of the State Museum of Oriental Art, Moscow)*. O'Bannon, George W. and Amanova, O. K., editors. George W. O'Bannon, 2000.

Ostashev, A. S. *Soviet Kirghizstan (A Photo Album),* Frunze (Bishkek), Kirghizstan, 1983.

Parsons, Richard D. *Oriental Rugs Volume 3: The Carpets of Afghanistan*. Oriental Textile Press, Ltd. and The Antique Collectors Clug Ltd., 1983.

Powell, Josephine. "An Argument For The Origins Of Anatolian Kilim Designs," presented at the Fifth International Conference on Oriental Carpets in Vienna, 1986, in *Oriental Carpet and Textile Studies,* vol 3, no. 2: 51–60. The Islamic Department of Sotheby's and Oriental Carpet and Textile Studies, Ltd. ©OCTS and Sotheby's, London.

———. "A Reply to Dr. Andrews' Counter-Argument*,"* in *Oriental Carpet and Textile Studies,* vol 3, no. 2: 65–70. The Islamic Department of Sotheby's and Oriental Carpet and Textile Studies, Ltd. ©OCTS and Sotheby's, London.

Prior. Daniel. *Bishkek Handbook. Inside and Out.* Literary Kyrgyzstan, Bishkek, 1994.

Rodgers, Mary M., et al., *Then and Now* series editors. *Kyrgyzstan, Then and Now*, Minneapolis: Lerner Publications Company, 1993.

Rubenstein, Joshua and Naumov, Vladimir P. *Stalin's Secret Pogrom, The Postwar Inquisition of the Jewish Anti-Fascist Committee.* New Haven and London: Yale University Press, 2001.

Schürmann, Ulrich. *Central-Asian Rugs*. London: Verlag Osterrieth, Frankfurt Am Main, Distributors for Great Britain and the Commonwealth, George Allen & Unwin, Ltd., 1969.

Sommer, John L. *The Kyrgyz And Their Reed Screens*. Fremont, California: John L. Sommer, 1996.

———. *The Kyrgyz And Their Reed Screens*, in *Oriental Carpet and Textile Studies,* vol 5, part 1: 95–102. Presented at the Eighth International Conference on Oriental Carpets, Philadelphia, 1996. The International Conference on Oriental Carpets, Danville, California, 1999.

Szabo, Albert and Barfield, Thomas J. *Afghanistan, An Atlas Of Indigenous Architecture*, Austin: University of Texas Press, 1991.

Thompson, Jon. *Oriental Carpets from the Tents, Cottages, and Workshops of Asia*. New York: Penguin Books USA, 1993.

Tsareva, Elena. *Carpets of Central Asian Nomads*, Catalogue of the Exhibition, Palazzo Ducale, Genova, Sept/Oct 1993. Genova: Sagep Editrice, 1993.

———. *Rugs & Carpets From Central Asia, The Russian Collections*. Leningrad: Aurora Art Publishers, and New York: Allen Lane/Penguin Books, 1984.

Usubalieva, K. N., et al. *The Kirghiz State Art Museum*. Frunze, Kirghizstan, 1985.